The Best of Soccer Journal

Techniques and Tactics

Jay Martin, Ed.

Meyer & Meyer Sport

British Library Cataloguing in Publication Data
A catalogue record for this book is available from the British Library

The Best of Soccer Journal – Techniques and Tactics
Maidenhead: Meyer & Meyer Sport (UK) Ltd., 2012
ISBN 978-1-84126-347-2

© 2012 by Meyer & Meyer Sport (UK) Ltd.
Auckland, Beirut, Budapest, Cairo, Cape Town, Dubai, Hägendorf, Indianapolis,
Maidenhead, Singapore, Sydney, Tehran, Wien
Member of the World
Sport Publishers' Association (WSPA)
www.w-s-p-a.org
Printed by: B.O.S.S Druck und Medien GmbH, Germany
ISBN 978-1-84126-347-2
E-Mail: info@m-m-sports.com
www.m-m-sports.com

TABLE OF CONTENTS

CREDITS:

Illustrations: www.sports-graphics.com

Photography: © iStockphoto/Thinkstock

Cover Photos: © dpa Picture-Alliance

Cover Design: Cornelia Knorr

Book Design: Claudia Lo Cicero

Editing: Sabine Carduck, Manuel Morschel

Proofreading: Michelle Demeter

Chapter 1: Techniques

Critical Teaching Points in Technical Training

NSCAA Academy Staff

The following lists critical teaching points for basic soccer technique as developed by the NSCAA Staff. Go to www.nscaa.com for an update on all Academy programs.

Passing – Ground

- Look at target as player approaches the ball; identify target as you approach the ball; approach the ball while looking at target; eyes on the ball
- Support foot placement – slight hop to ball, foot is planted along side of ball pointing the foot in direction of the target
- Contact-surface head down to strike head up to see target
- Instep pass: striking foot in L-shape and toe pointed up, strike ball with ankle bone; ankle locked; contact ball with inside of ankle bone; contact ball with inside of foot
- Top of foot: strike ball with the top of the foot
- Outside of foot: toes are pointed down, support foot is slightly behind the ball, strike the ball with the outside of the foot
- Follow through the ball toward the target – transfer the weight forward; speed of foot through the ball; follow through quickly; follow through with the hips toward the target

Key Coaching Cues
- **Approach:** Look at target while approaching the ball off a slight hop, place the support foot alongside the ball
- **Contact:** Ankle is locked
    ### Action:
    - *Instep pass:*
        - Foot – L-shape and toe pointed up, strike ball with the inside of the ankle bone

- Ball – Middle, around halfway up
- *Top of foot pass:*
    - Foot – Toes pointed down; strike ball with the top of the foot/laces of the shoe
    - Ball – Middle, around halfway up
- *Outside of foot pass:*
    - Foot: Toes are pointed down, support foot is slightly behind the ball, strike the ball with the outside of the foot
    - Ball: Side of ball (left side for a right-footed pass), around halfway up
- **Follow Through:** Weight moves forward through the ball as the leg follows through low

Other Coaching Cues
- Qualities of a good pass
    - Pace / speed
    - Direction / accuracy
    - Timing: to feet or into space
    - Deception: threaten, be creative
- Head down to strike; head up to see target

Lifting Ball Over Distance: Long Driven Passes

- Ball out of feet; look at/recognize target; preparatory touch out of feet; identify the target as you approach the ball; second-to-last step, peek at the target
- Approach – power step at an angle; power step onto support foot; power step is longer than usual stride; place non-kicking foot pointed forward and alongside of the ball (actual distance will vary from player to player); hips square toward the target
- Toes pointed down & ankle locked; toes curled into shoe; push toes through the bottom of the shoe

- Contact – With big toe; longer back swing; strike through the lower half and left of center (for right-footed strike)
- Action – Strike through the ball; look at foot striking the ball; opposite hand points at the target
- Follow through – Weight moves forward through the ball; follow through high and toward the target; accelerate through the ball – positive body weight through the ball

Key Coaching Cues

- **Approach:** At sharper angle while looking at target; off a power (longer stride) step placement of the non-kicking foot varies for each player
- **Contact:**
  - Foot – Toes pointed down and ankle is locked
    - Straight drive – With big toe
    - "Outswinger" – With outside of foot
    - "Inswinger" – With big toe
- **Action:** Head is steady, player leans back, lower leg extends from a flexed position
- **Follow Through:** Weight moves forward through the ball as the leg follows through high

Other Coaching Cues

- Ball out from feet
- Identify the target as you approach the ball
- Approach ball at an angle
- Power step onto support foot, which is longer than a normal stride
- Place the non-kicking foot slightly behind the ball (varies for each player)
- Curl the toes into the bottom of the shoe
- Follow through should involve a hop on the non-kicking foot or a transfer of weight onto kicking foot
- Qualities of a good pass
  - Pace / speed
  - Direction / accuracy
  - Timing: to feet or into space

Striking Ball: Driving/Shooting

- Ball out of feet; look at/recognize target; preparatory touch out of feet; identify the target as you approach the ball; second-to-last step, peek at the target
- Approach – Power step at an angle; power step onto support foot; power step is longer than usual stride; place non-kicking foot pointed forward and alongside the ball (actual distance will vary from player to player); hips square toward the target
- Toes pointed down & ankle locked; toes curled into shoe; push toes through the bottom of the shoe
- Contact – With laces; compact back swing; strike through the lower half and left of center (for right-footed strike)
- Action – Strike through the ball; look at foot striking the ball; opposite hand points toward the target
- Follow through – Weight moves forward through the ball; Follow through low and toward the target; Accelerate through the ball – positive body weight through the ball

Key Coaching Cues

- **Approach:** At an angle while looking at target, off a power (long stride) step placement of the non-kicking foot (varies for each player)
- **Contact:**
  - Foot – Toes pointed down and the ankle is locked
    - Straight drive – With laces
    - "Outswinger" – With outside of foot
    - "Inswinger" – With inside/big toe of foot
  - Ball – Lower half and left of center for a right-footed strike
- **Action:** Head is steady; player stays low, lower leg extends powerfully from as fully flexed knee as possible
- **Follow Through:** Weight moves forward through the ball as the leg follows through low

Other Coaching Cues

- Ball out from feet
- Identify the target as you approach the ball
- Approach ball at an angle
- Power step onto support foot, which is longer than a normal stride
- Place the non-kicking foot next to the ball (varies from player to player)
- Curl the toes into the bottom of the shoe
- Compact back swing with kicking leg
- Follow through should involve a hop on the non-kicking foot or a transfer of weight onto the kicking foot
- *Aggressive attitude*
  - Shoot at any opportunity
  - Positive attitude about the success of the shot
- *Power shooting*
  - Round and compact over the ball
  - Horizontal body movement and speed through the ball
  - Stay down on the ball with head steady
  - Last stride is longer onto the non-kicking foot
  - The non-kicking knee is slightly flexed
  - Non-kicking foot and knee are pointed in the direction of the shot
  - Ankle of the kicking foot is locked
  - Strike through the center of the ball
  - Hip and knee of the kicking leg are pointed in the direction of the shot
  - Follow through toward the goal with the weight going forward
  - Land on the shooting foot
- *Placement of shot*
  - Make an early decision on the target
  - Attempt to get into position to shoot prior to receiving the ball
  - Support foot, hips, and shooting knee; aim at the target when kicking through the ball
  - Shoot the ball before the advancing goalkeeper sets their feet
- *Volleying*
  - Side foot
    - Toe raised
    - Ankle locked
    - Lift outer border of foot

- *Instep*
  - Coil shoulders
  - Toe pointed down
  - Ankle locked
  - Upper leg parallel with ground
  - Kicking of kicking leg points at target
  - Power from knee extension

Heading

- Get into the line of flight of the ball; sight the ball (includes depth); read the flight of the ball
- Elbows up at chest height – arch back; hyperextend the hips; slingshot/bow-and-arrow position; arms out for balance; balanced start position – feet apart, knees slightly flexed
- Move the head forward, versus up and down, through the ball – no backspin; hands apart and elbows thrust backwards as back and neck snap forward; chin in; snap through ball; head, neck, trunk into ball; move eyes forward through the ball; throw eyes at ball
- Point of contact: Head ball between eyebrow and hairline; on forehead between eyebrows and hairline
- Air-Heading – Time jump to head at top of jump; jump first using arms to gain lift; use arms to make a cone of space and to ward off opponents; judge ball and attack space first; Note the difference between power heading and redirection heading

Key Coaching Cues

- **Approach:** Read the flight of the ball – eyes on ball with the hips hyperextended and the elbows out at chest height with arms apart
- **Contact:** Head ball between eyebrows and hairline
- **Action:** Move the head forward, versus up and down, through the ball thrusting the arms backwards
- **Follow Through:** Chin up and looking toward the target

© Thinkstock/iStockphoto/Fluid Illusion

Other Coaching Cues
- **Preparation**
  - Judge the direction and depth of the ball
  - Keep the eyes open and on the ball
- **Ready Position**
  - Mouth closed
  - Chin up
- **Action**
  - Eyes on ball
  - When heading while on the ground, use the legs to increase power into the header
- **Contact**
  - Neck should be firm
- **Follow Through**
  - No back spin on ball

Heading Out – Clearances – Objectives are height, distance, width, and accuracy if possible
- Leave late to attack the ball
- Use a one-foot take-off from the run
- Jump first
- Be side-on when jumping to head the ball
- Contact the ball below its mid-line (bottom half)

Heading Down – To Goal – Objective is to hit the goal line
- Bend run to side of field opposite ball
- Leave late to attack the ball
- Use a one-foot take-off from the run
- Jump first
- Contact the ball above its mid-line (top half)

Changing Direction of the Ball
- Side on – foot farther from the ball is farther forward
- Open hips toward the target as ball is headed
- Follow through with the chin up and looking toward the target

Receiving

- Move into the line of flight; sight the ball; read the flight of the ball
- Calculate part of body to be used; prepare the surface
- Present body part to ball to the flight of the ball – generally 90 degrees to the line of flight of the ball
- Relax and give (maybe a slight hop) as ball arrives; absorb the ball
- Touch ball out of the feet and explode (or accelerate) in desired direction; use controlling touch to move the ball in desired direction; respond to your touch; prepare the ball into the new space; be aware of defenders and touch ball away from pressure

Key Coaching Cues
- **Approach:** Read flight of ball – eyes on ball and decide which part of body to use
- **Contact:** Absorb ball as it arrives
- **Action:** Touch ball out of the feet
- **Follow Through:** Accelerate away from pressure in the desired direction

Other Coaching Cues
- Look at the next target as the ball is being played to you
- Feint before and/or as ball arrives

© Thinkstock/iStockphoto/Fluid Illusion

- Ball is on the ground
  - Keep hips open
  - Receive the ball across the body on the farthest foot if unmarked
  - Receive the ball with the toe pointed up and the ankle locked
- Relax and give (maybe a slight hop) as ball arrives
- Do not stop the ball – prepare ball for the next action: shot, dribble, pass
- First touch alters angle of the ball to:
  - Relieve pressure – angle of touch
  - Attack defender who has laid off – distance of touch
  - Trick the defender
  - Players can "buy" time by gesturing or feinting toward the ball and letting it run, or playing the ball in another direction

Dribbling

Running with Ball
- Running into space with ball; run with ball; head raised – look through the eyebrows – to see options
- Approach ball at speed – straight on with the head up; make up ground quickly
- Take ball with forward stride on top (with instep) or outside of foot with the toe down; contact ball with laces or outside surface of foot
- First touch is long
- Shorten touches as player approaches defender

Key Coaching Cues
- **Approach:** At speed – straight on with head up
- **Contact:** Take ball with forward stride with a quick short extension of the lower leg with the toe down contacting the ball with the instep or outside of the foot
- **Action:** First touch is long; touches shorten as player approaches defender
- **Follow Through:** Leg follows through low

To Beat a Defender
- Head up
- Attack defender's lead/front/inside foot with

smaller steps as you approach defender; 1st touch forward as large as possible based on the distance to the defender; smaller steps as player approaches defender; attack on a straight path to goal or space; decide early which side to attack

- Beat the defender by
  - Change of speed
  - Change of direction
  - Use deception – a feint or trick
- Explode past defender
- Cut ball behind defender toward goal (cut off recovery run)

Key Coaching Cues

- **Approach:** Head up, smaller steps as player approaches defender
- **Contact:** With the inside, outside, top or bottom of shoe
- **Action:** Beat the defender using deception by changing speed, direction
- **Follow Through:** Explode past defender and cut ball behind defender toward goal (cut off recovery run)

Shielding from Opponents

- Side on
- Lower center of gravity – "sit down" at a right angle with hip and shoulder to and into opponent
- Elbow out and bent to make bigger; elbow out to make and keep space
- Ball on outside of foot; ball on foot away from defender
- Dribble away from the goal or move laterally; keep the ball moving

Key Coaching Cues

- **Approach:** Side on and lower center of gravity with elbows out and bent
- **Contact:** On the outside of the foot
- **Action:** Body between the defender and the ball, ball is on the foot away from the defender
- **Follow Through:** Dribble away from the goal or move laterally

Turning with Outside of Foot:

- Approach ball at an angle with knees bent; forward foot steps to meet the ball
- Lower center of gravity; lean into opponent; drop shoulder and lean into turn and receive the ball as the player turns
- Support foot planted beyond the ball
- Turning foot over ball, pronate out and plant beyond ball
- Outside anklebone and foot contact ball and takes full weight; wrap outside of foot around ball; turn body after touch to shield opponent from the ball; outside edge of front foot contacts the ball
- Player moves in opposite direction and head up; turn to follow ball and accelerate away from pressure

Key Coaching Cues

- **Approach:** At an angle, lower center of gravity and place the support foot beyond the ball
- **Contact:** Outside edge of front foot
- **Action:** Turn to follow ball
- **Follow Through:** Accelerate away from pressure with the head up

Other Coaching Cues

- Look at ball as you approach
- Feint in the opposite direction prior to turning with the ball
- Turn into defender by dropping a shoulder and leaning into the defender
- Turn ball as you receive a pass

The attacker should consider the following choices *before* receiving the ball:

- Can I penetrate by:
  - Shooting
  - Beating a player and shooting
  - Passing to a teammate
  - Possessing the ball

Individual Defending – Tackling

- Becoming the first defender; angle and speed of approach
- Purpose is to delay the attacker
- Close down quickly – long steps
- At approximately 5 yards away, slow down (short steps)
- Lower center of gravity; Body mechanics at arrival – lower base
- Angle to right or left
- Begin to move backwards (shuffle feet) with eyes on ball
- Distance from attacker
- Single leg tackle – with solid block on the ball with tackling foot; knee flexed; non-blocking foot close to the ball

Key Coaching Cues

- **Approach:**
  - Speed – Close space to attacker quickly, lowering center of gravity
  - Angle – Bend run as defender approaches the attacker to the right or the left so that the body is positioned side on (one foot in front of the other foot)
- **Action:** Eyes on ball and shuffle feet backwards at an angle forcing attacker to a covering defender, the touch line or the goal line
- **Contact:**
  - Decision on When to Tackle
  - Instant the ball arrives/just after the attacker touches the ball
  - When ball is misplayed
  - When defender is within one step of reaching the ball
  - Defender has cover, has the attacker against the touch line, or the attacker is within shooting distance
- **Action:**
  Poke Tackle – With the Front Foot
  - Keep weight low over the back foot (be able to recover if the poke is missed), poke at an angle
  - With back to goal – moving backwards with shuffle steps, use feints
  - Side to Side with Attacker – run level with attacker and poke the ball when it is in the middle of the attacker or closer to the defender
  Block Tackle – With the Back Foot
  - Step forward with the weight low next to the ball with the back foot, tackle with other foot – ankle locked, toe up – across the ball, move forward to gain possession
  Slide Tackle – Closest Foot to Attacker
  - Slide on the outside of the lower leg and hip with knee flexed, ankle locked, toe up

Follow Through:

- Move forward on the diagonal to gain possession

Other Coaching Cues

- Close space with long steps, shorten steps as defender approaches attacker – around 5 yards
- Distance from attacker depends on the relative speed and ability of both attacker and defender, but it is generally around 2 yards with the lead shoulder the defender aligned with the shoulder of the attacker

Good Technique Is Not Enough

Lang Wedemeyer
NSCAA Academy Staff

On several occasions, I have heard former U.S. National Team coaches Bruce Arena and April Heinrichs mention that one of the biggest problems with our rising youth players, boys and girls alike, is that they do not have the ability to play effectively under pressure. The players' technique breaks down when under pressure and their speed of play is not fast nor accurate enough to create a flow in high-level games. This raises a question: "What is the youth coach's role and responsibility in teaching technique that leads to better speed of play and the development of more creative and skillful players?"

We constantly preach "technique, technique, technique" to our younger players, but are coaches truly helping them develop efficient technique under pressure? Or are we constantly setting up unrealistic situations for them?

Take for example the "Coerver Craze." Fast footwork is wonderful; I do it with my players all the time. But what are the situations in which coaches are training their players to use these technical skills? Are we having them make moves against phantom defenders? What happens when they are faced with a real live defender coming at them at different speeds or different angles or in different parts of the field? Are we doing enough to help prepare and develop our players to deal with these types of situations? Often, we are left with technical repetition without tactical context.

What is the coach's responsibility in relation to training technique? The responsibility is three-pronged:

- Giving the players tools with which to practice on their own
- Repetitively putting players in a pressured environment in training sessions, and
- Emphasizing the important coaching points during the games.

Defining technique and skill

Technique is the mechanism with which the body maneuvers itself to be able to complete an objective. If the objective is to pass the ball 15 yards to a teammate, the brain informs the body to maneuver itself in order to kick the ball in that direction. How well the body adjusts to the demand determines how good the technique is, while how quickly the brain interprets the cues and the message sent to the muscles determines the speed of play. The better the technique, the greater the likelihood that the ball will go where we want it and how we want it played.

Then what is the difference between technique and skill? As taught to me by the late Mike Berticelli (former Director of Coaching on the NSCAA) in my first NSCAA National Course, technique is the mechanics behind solving a problem, and skill is being able to solve the problem regardless of the mechanics. Skill is basically getting the job done no matter how it looks. But with better technique, the player's success rate is heightened.

In the early stages of the coaching schools, we teach youth coaches about progression in their training sessions. The first progression in a technical session is referred to as fundamental. This is placing players in an environment in which they are receiving lots of repetitions without initial pressure. Then pressure is added progressively, judging by the success rate of the players. Most coaches still organize technical training based on this format. What I am proposing is using these ideas to help players start to practice on their own outside of the team training sessions. Youth coaches need to instruct players on how to effectively self-train. Most coaches give our youth players "homework" to practice between training sessions, and that is a good start. The problem is how to get these players to really self-train when there are so many other things that they want to be doing. Coaches have to compete with Nintendo, birthday parties, other sports, watching TV – the list goes on and on. The only real way that I see is to continually stress the importance of ball work to the players and their parents. The ones who are practicing on their own will naturally be the more motivated and usually emerge as the best players as they develop at a faster rate.

The rest are the players whom coaches have to motivate in terms of self-development. There is an unlimited number of exercises that coaches can give their players to practice on their own – everything from the Coerver techniques to passing against a wall to juggling, etc. But there is still a problem. Tom Turner, Region II DOC, talks about a girl at one of the regional camps who had unbelievable technical ability. This youth player could juggle forever and do Coerver moves faster than anyone in camp, but was lost and ineffectual on the field. Here is where the role of the coach must emerge to place these players in environments where their technical ability is under pressure. If they are successful in a more challenging environment, they will turn each technique into skillful play.

Evaluating technical progress

How do coaches evaluate players' technical progress? The coach could test them with how many Coerver moves they execute in a minute, how many juggles in two minutes, how many correct receptions out of 10 tosses, etc. But that all takes too much practice time, though such testing might be a worthy self-testing mechanism for off-field work. Such testing is quantitative as opposed to qualitative.

The coach's responsibility is to create the environment in which players are placed under immediate pressure. The role of the coach is to help players understand the cues that allow them to apply proper technique in game-like situations. We always hear there are no tactics without technique. Well, there is no technique without tactics. The use of the proper technique comes from decision-making ability in pressure situations. This will help the speed of play while also enforcing a higher level of technical ability, but all within the context of the game.

A sample practice

An example of this would be if a coach has a group of U-10s and wants to improve their passing ability. If the coach teaches them early on in the season how to practice passing on their own, then come practice time they shouldn't have to be lined up to practice that technique. Perhaps the warm-up might have some small group line drills (passing back and forth and exchanging line positions, etc.) but the session could move right into a 5 v. 2 game for warm-up where they are passing under some type of initial pressure.

In this situation the coach can now help players with understanding, of the technical nuances of the weight of pass, deception, etc., which are all decisions that lead to the success of the technique of passing.

This must progress into a more game-like situation in which there is free movement and free decision-making on the part of the players. The technical aspects of passing along with the cues that lead to the use of those techniques would then be continually emphasized throughout the session.

A key point here is to still keep the numbers small, especially with younger players. In situations where they are placed in two goal games of 4v4, players can't hide and are forced into pressure situations more often. So now we are getting the repetition of using the different techniques over and over. The players are also in an environment in which they are constantly making the choices based on cues from the game. This must be progressed into a bigger game, depending on the age group, so that more technical abilities come into play, such as long passes, crosses, etc.

Playing the game

But what do coaches do when it's game time? For younger players, U-12 and down, it is a good idea to set different goals for their games instead of winning and scoring. Set goals of completed passes in a row or everyone using the outside of the foot to pass the ball at least once or everyone chipping the ball at least once during the course of the game, etc. In setting these goals, coaches can emphasize the use of techniques in the game atmosphere. When the technique breaks down for a player, the coach can then make the decision whether it was a simple mechanical mistake or the decision to use that technique was not the right one for that situation. Hopefully the player has already determined what the problem was.

It is in the game environment, where players are under the most pressure to perform, that coaches can evaluate how well their training regimen. has prepared them. When evaluating their performance, the coach should make some notes on different situations that can be recreated in a training environment to help prepare the players to understand the technical cues. An example would be if the coach has been emphasizing passing in the team's training sessions for a period of time, but realizes that the team is weak on shooting the ball, then shooting might be the focus of subsequent training sessions.

Problem solving

Having reviewed technical training methodology, we are still faced with two real problems:

- How do we get our players to practice and improve their technical ability so they are proficient enough to place them into games?
- How do we as coaches learn and understand how to give our players the proper combination of technique with tactics?

There are different ways of answering both these questions. The first one is up to the individual coach. Only you as the coach can determine what will inspire your players to go out and practice on their own. Maybe you have them keep a juggling record or rewards system for younger players or give homework sheets to the parents. But all in all, it will be the more inspired and dedicated players (even at that age) who want to practice on their own, who want to become better. The ultimate test is how they perform in the game under pressure. As these players progress, it will more than likely be the motivated players who will develop the fastest and go on to higher levels of soccer. Your job with these youth players is to try and inspire all of them, but also to nurture the ones who really have the desire.

As for the second question, if you are reading this article, then you are the kind of coach who will also learn on his/her own. You have taken a big step by just being a member of the NSCAA and reading the magazine. Another way is by attending coaching courses.

Also watching and evaluating games at every level as often as possible is a great way to enhance your knowledge. By watching an MLS or WUSA game on television, one can learn how and why players succeed by using their technical abilities. The coach must also watch other games at or just above his/her own coaching level to see how other players handle speed of play issues. This is not only for the coach. The players can also learn a lot by watching other players or by trying to emulate them.

Conclusion

The teaching of technique is very important. But technique without game application is worthless. Players must have the ability to match technique with tactics to be more successful in the game. A player who can juggle 3,000 times is not effective if the individual doesn't have an impact on the game. It is up to the youth coaches to help inspire players to work on the fundamentals of soccer outside of regular team training sessions. It is also important for the coach to create a training environment where the repetition of application of technique is taught within the context of game-like situations. Having said all of this, players should always be encouraged to collectively play on their own. It is within the game that they learn the most.

"Creative, skillful players will develop in response to an environment where techniques and tactical awareness develop together," Tom Turner says. Wouldn't it be much nicer to coach players in the game as opposed to constantly setting up stagnant drills, not to mention more fun for the players? By expanding time spent by the players training technique on their own, coaches have a better chance to achieve this ideal.

Teaching Technique Tactically

Mark Nicole

Most would agree the modern game continues to evolve into one of increased speed of play in attack, immediate transition both ways, and the pressure of playing efficiently in decreased space with less time. As a consequence, much higher levels of competence are being expected of players as individuals and as a collective unit. These levels are of course technical and tactical in nature as well as extremely demanding psychologically and physically. Youth training sessions must now incorporate less exclusive teaching of technique in preparation for this phenomenon. The "drilling" of technique without adding difficulty and pressure is myopic. What is taught must be match related to effect a more complete personnel development of the young player. This is not to profess that practicing a specific technique in isolation outside of the moving game is counterproductive. This type of training is of course necessary but should be made more realistic as soon as possible

The Challenge

The challenge now becomes how to effectively present, demonstrate, and teach "advanced technical training" topics within a format that incorporates other facets of the game. To succeed, training must be stimulating for the players, manageable for the coach and relevant to the match. For example, basic concepts, such as looking up field to play an early pass forward to feet and striking the ball with the instep, must be taught simultaneously. The technical ability becomes an acquired skill enabling the player to solve tactical soccer problems more efficiently which in turn will ease to some degree the psychological burden developing players are confronted with. Individual

confidence and composure on the ball will manifest into collective cohesiveness of the group. Through this cycle, players will continue to influence one another in a self-directed, player-coaching-player environment. This facilitates personnel growth within the team structure increasing the probability of the individual reaching their full potential as a soccer player. Over time, this culture becomes the accepted norm and each player benefits immensely from the combined experience. The message here is training must incorporate both technical and tactical areas of focus in concert with one another. If structured correctly, this vision can be offered to players at an early age.

Small-Sided Tactical Games

To institute this type of mindset, it is important to illustrate the differential between two commonly used terms and approaches, these being "tactics" and "small sided games." Team tactics are the framework by which the collective group attack and defend in specific situations and locations on the field. Playing direct versus the patience of the counterattacking team is a pertinent example. This type of knowledge at this level should be discussed and demonstrated as briefly as possible to orientate the group to operate within a few general guidelines setting the stage for the more important matter of teaching individual tactics. Learning to understand the problems and solutions of playing out of pressure near the touchline against even numbers is vastly more important at this stage than to understand that the game plan is to stroke a long flighted ball from defending third to attacking third and chase. There must be a separation of learning how to win games versus how to play the game correctly from an early age.

A small sided game played without a specific technical and tactical focus becomes an exercise in playing a game to justify its own title. Without specified and understandable teaching topics, what is there to be learned? A more directed methodology would be the utilization of training games to elicit the desired behavior from the players, again as individuals and collectively. Various tactical elements can be identified and presented in a forum that provides the trainer with a plethora of teaching opportunities. The proximity and small numbers assure that all will see and hear. There are also ample chances to repeat positive and correct match-related solutions in the correct sized area of the field where the training topic occurs. It then becomes important to relate the issues learned back to the general team-playing guidelines. Within this framework, the players become stimulated and in turn have the confidence to experiment and partake in alternative solutions to the problem to be solved. The willingness to fearlessly take risk in the attack is a prime and desirable example of a player who has the confidence to deal with the challenges of the situation. The individuals grow self-assured and more mature, freeing themselves to experiment with new self-taught solutions.

purpose of this series of articles, it has been assumed that the players are somewhat "free of the ball" and have acquired a level of skill that allows them to perform technically while moving.

TOPIC: Attacking 1v1 with the Dribble

Objectives:

Technical: Change dribbling direction.
Tactical: Change of pace during move.

Teaching Points:

- Sharp cuts with the ball.
- Drive defender one direction, attack opposite.
- Once past, cut into the defenders running path.

Organization:

Players: 12 players
Gear: 16 cones, spare balls
Field: 10 yards x 20 yards with a four-yard middle zone (two fields)
Time: 40 minutes

Practice Design

The crux of all this lies hidden within the ability of the trainer to design sessions that continually teach and recreate an identifiable technical and tactical topic utilizing small player numbers. Building to a team versus team training game on full goals is the objective. This should be considered a worthy endeavor that will indeed take considerable time and patience from all participants involved. Over time, a multitude of rewards will become apparent to the teacher and the tasks required to enjoy them will be vastly outweighed by the pleasure of the experience. The following example of teaching dribbling with a tactical twist is but one example of the aforementioned training concept. For the

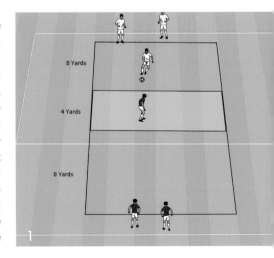

8 Yards

4 Yards

8 Yards

1

Instructions:

There are six players on each field. A defender is positioned in the middle zone and may not chase attackers out of it. The other five attacking players are split at each end of the field. To begin, defenders must hold their hands behind their back. Upon winning a ball, the defender dribbles out of the zone and passes to a player on the end. The ball loser becomes the defender. If the attacker beats the defender, a pass is made to the end and that player attacks the defender. The game should be high tempo.

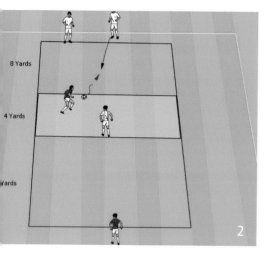

8 Yards

4 Yards

Yards

2

Progression:

Next, the middle defender then plays completely live. Players score one point for each defender beaten. The games are five minutes long. The player on each field with the most points at time wins.

Progression:

Thirdly, when the middle defender is beaten, a second defender steps onto the field from the opposite end line. The attacker attempts to beat the second defender over the end line. If the second defender wins the ball, the middle zone is

attacked. The original attacker may chase until the player reaches the middle zone. If the player gets past the middle defender, a third defender will step onto the field on the opposite end. The scoring is the same.

Organization:

Players: 6v6 with two goalkeepers
Gear: 6 vests, 8 cones, 2 goals
Field: 60 yards, two goal areas and a middle zone, field box width (44 yards)
Time: five 10-minute games

Instructions:

There are two teams of six players. One player from each team is positioned in the defensive zone in front of their own goal. The other 10 players begin in the middle zone. The players in the middle must defend in front of their defensive line on the field and may not chase attackers in. Players, as an initial restriction, may not pass the ball forward.

The ball must be dribbled into the attacking zone, not passed. The dribbler takes the lone defender on and attempts to score then rejoins the middle group at the end of the play. If the defender wins, the ball is dribbled free back to the middle to

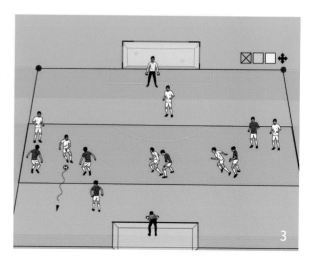

3

restart game. A teammate will then become the new single defender.

Progression:
- The individual beaten in the middle zone may chase the dribbler into the box;
- Then the teams may now chase into the attacking zone after the ball has been dribbled in, though no goal can be scored unless a defender is beaten off the dribble;
- Play full field with the restriction that no forward passes are allowed by either team. Coach looks for opportunities to reinforce both positive and negative individual dribbling decisions.

© Thinkstock/iStockphoto/Fluid Illusion

Developing Speed of Play

Gary R. Allen
U.S. Youth Soccer National Staff

In the post-2010 World Cup game between the United States and Brazil, I was struck by the fact that the Brazilians, using many young players, seemed to move at a much different pace than the presumably more experienced Americans. The Brazilian players moved the ball in and out of space with pace and fluidity, often leaving U.S. players stranded in unfortunate positions as they hopelessly chased the ball. The Brazilians were not physically faster than the U.S. players. Something much more subtle occurred.

Throughout the World Cup, and in this game with Brazil, the *speed* of the U.S. team appeared to be one-dimensional. It was a "fight back hard" unFeintingd full-speed-ahead type of effort. This embodies the American spirit and it is an attribute that has no parallel elsewhere. It served us well against mainly physical teams like England, Slovenia and Ghana. However, the limits of its effectiveness were evident against the guile and intelligent play of Brazil. While this attribute is emblematic of our culture, its predominance to our detriment also is a direct result of our youth soccer programs, which I will discuss later.

Our coaching education programs also have contributed to our lack of development of speed. They have focused primarily on general concepts of *speed of play*, broadly addressing the areas of technical, tactical and physical speed. This analysis, however, has overlooked how different kinds of speed are developed and nurtured from the earliest stages. U.S. Youth Soccer, through the work of Drs. Tom Fleck, Ron Quinn, Dave Carr and others, has begun to apply educationally grounded concepts of learning by focusing on how players at different ages develop cognitively, socially and physically.

These concepts concern the *process* of learning, an indispensible ingredient to developing speed of play. Unfortunately, many involved with youth soccer in the United States only pay lip service to these new considerations. A disconnect still exists in our recognition of how the nature of the game and the process of learning work together in the development of *speed of play*.

The Game Defines Speed

Soccer truly is the only team sport that reflects the culture of its players. The game is free flowing, presents myriads of situations and involves constant changes that require the players themselves to individually and collectively solve problems in spontaneous and natural ways. The problem-solving nature of the game makes the concept of "speed of play" much more multi-dimensional than our current coaching schemes allow. Sports trainer and author Vern Gambetta has defined different types of speed in sport. These concepts have been applied to soccer by Drs. Don Kirkendall and Joe Luxbacher. (See Dr. Kirkendall's March 8, 2002, article in Active.com.) In addition to physical speed, they have described such aspects as speed of perception, anticipation, reaction, decision-making, and speed on and away from the ball.

These aspects of speed make perfect sense when we consider discussions about Pelé or other great players. In addition to recognizing their superior technical ability, descriptions of them often focus on their ability to see two plays ahead or having eyes in the back of their heads. They always appear to think and act more quickly than those around them. These descriptions concern their perceptual, anticipatory and decision-making speed, as well as speed away from the ball. There also is another component to speed of play that few have recognized: that of slowing down opponents' perception, anticipation, reaction and other speeds. The way players use the ball, the runs they make, as well as body and head fakes, all play a part in speeding up play by slowing opponents down. And slowing opponents down is a crucial part of speed at the highest levels of play.

In the youth game, our quest to produce more efficient play from an adult's perspective has focused on physical speed, stifling the development of other types of speed. We have paid little attention to the fact that it is only through play and the seemingly inefficient process of experimentation that players can develop these other areas of speed. Currently, we try to fit our young players into our adult perception of what soccer should look like to win particular games rather than provide training and game environments that *require, encourage and allow* the young players to think, act – and yes, make mistakes – for themselves, as the "culture" of their particular age group dictates.

Most youth soccer programs, from early ages, are driven by adults who measure success by the creation and development of teams that will accumulate trophies and achieve results at each age group level. Our young players never really are given opportunities to think, act and experiment for themselves. We have subordinated the *process* of learning to results that can be measured by objective adult standards.

Our Concept of Speed Is Too Confined

The development of the organized youth soccer programs in the United States has no parallel anywhere else in the world. Although the British and Europeans have begun their Academy and other youth programs, they are all extensions of their professional leagues. At their core are financial considerations. Although some of the latest iterations of the Academy programs in the United States are based in MLS clubs for the same reason, the structures for organized youth development here commenced in the 1970s outside the professional leagues and school-based programs and have grown tremendously over the past 40 years.

Currently, because of our concern for results, our developmental programs focus on athletic prowess and physical speed. This has led us to search for elite players to create elite teams from eight years old on. We have mistakenly considered physical precociousness to be an accurate indicator of future success. We have compounded the problem by segregating these players from those less precocious to form elite teams. The team is the focal point, rather than the players. The success of the team governs, and because games are won mainly through athleticism, *speed of play* is almost exclusively defined in physical terms. Furthermore, players at these ages generally lack the ability to think abstractly; therefore, the central tactic is direct play, i.e., playing a ball into empty areas of the field for players of both sides to engage in a footrace.

Because we select the biggest, fastest and strongest youth for our *elite* youth teams, this tactic (read problem-solving) predominates throughout our youth players' formative and teenage years.

This stress on physical speed has had extremely detrimental effects on the development of technical speed in our young players. We have selected younger and younger players based upon their physical development; we have cast them in specific roles that reward speed at the expense of tight technical play. This system has deprived our young players of many opportunities to experience the *process* of using multi-faceted technical skills in different situations and areas of the field. To compensate technically, we have tried many programs (such as the Coerver Method) that seek to isolate the development of technical speed outside the game itself. Unfortunately, these programs treat technique outside the crucible of the game. But technical speed involves types of speed that can occur only in the game (such as perceptual speed, anticipatory speed, reaction speed, decision-making speed and speed without the ball).

These can be nurtured and developed only through the process of being in situations presented by the game itself. Furthermore, players must be allowed to solve problems for themselves through experimentation and failure, concepts that are anathema to result-oriented adults.

Our primary focus on discovering and developing the *elite* player at younger and younger ages also ignores all of the prevailing educational expertise concerning how people learn and develop mentally, physically and socially. Instead of allowing the natural process of development to occur, we have all but extinguished it. There are numerous articles on this topic, so I will not repeat those points here, but here is one example of our skewed focus: the glaring contrast between initiating programs for discovering *elite* players versus our attempts to have small-sided youth games.

Despite the strong evidence that early identification is not reliable, in the space of 30 years we routinely have developed local, state and national programs for Olympic Development, the Super-Y Leagues, U.S. Club Leagues, USYSA Regional Leagues and now Academy teams and leagues for younger and younger *elite* players. In contrast, it took 15 years of debate to even begin small-sided play for younger players, then only sporadically and on a graduated basis over a number of years throughout the country. Yet the tremendous benefits of small-sided play were made obvious by the dramatic increase in our level of play in the 1994 World Cup. For the four years preceding that Cup, the U.S. team trained almost exclusively using small-sided play.

We Have the Framework, but Not the Art

In all earnestness, we have perceived a problem, sought to define it in terms we understand and overcome it through planning. In so doing with our youth programs, we have created an intricate framework for youth play. Unfortunately, we have tried to fit the players into the framework rather than adjust the framework to fit the evolving needs of the players.

Similarly, our coaching education system has focused on the structures of activities and tools for imparting information to players. Like our youth programs, we have created a skeleton that does little more than state that "the game is the best teacher" and only generally defines principles of play. The system does not provide much substance as to what to see in the run of play or how to use the structure of activities to develop the game's principles in a cohesive fashion. The system sporadically addresses some of the aspects of speed in isolated technical and tactical areas, but there has been no concerted nor cohesive effort to teach coaches how to incorporate them in every facet of play.

Over the years, many have opined that if we could just be like Brazil, we would succeed. Unfortunately, these critics do little more than cite Brazil's "creativity" as the answer. Beyond describing the cultural influences that cause these traits, few have analyzed how Brazilians use each of the aspects of speed of play, individually and collectively. When they compare the United States with Brazil, they liken the U.S. status as the framing studs of a building, stating that it needs windows, walls, doors and architectural design, but provide no guidance as to how to obtain these things.

Despite the limited scope of the criticism, it does have some value. It recognizes that the United States is stuck at the framework stage. We need to take the next step and focus on how our coaching

© Thinkstock/Stockphoto/Fluid Illusion

first touch can speed up our play and slow down opponents, different ways to use the ball (the fastest thing on the field) as a decoy and to slow opponents down, how and when to use width and depth to create spaces between opponents, how and when to run to see more of the field more quickly, how and when to use different combinations between players. These are just a few examples that I will address in the second part of this article.

Soccer Speed, Like Art, Requires Developing Its Many Aspects Together

The aspects of *speed of play* are not isolated concepts. They define and are defined by the environment in which our young players play. They also are achieved only through the *process* of play and experimentation. In essence, the *process* is the *end*. For us to develop players who can play with multi-dimensional quickness, we must focus more on the process for each player rather than on creating tiers of result-seeking teams at younger and younger ages.

It is like creating a painting in black and white without using any other colors. Although it may be art, it has certain limitations. The different kinds of *speed* listed above are like different colors of paint that an artist can use to create a more vivid work of art. By themselves on the palette, they are mere globs of paint, but when they are mixed and used in various ways by a skillful artist, they can become inspiring images. It is *only* through the mixing *and experimentation* by an inspired artist that true art is produced. We, the coaches, are not the artists! The players are the artists, and it is they who must learn the craft of playing. Our role should be to provide the problems to solve with playing and training environments (the canvas) that foster the process of learning – *the mixing, experimentation and inspiration* of the players themselves. Thus our aim, especially before the age of 14, should be to provide as many of these opportunities for as many

education program can positively affect our speed of play. We can use the framework of activities and "toolkits" the coaching school curriculum currently provides to teach coaches how to recognize opportunities for developing speed. We can put flesh onto the bones of the framework of training sessions by seeking to provide coaches with a better understanding of the various components of speed and how to recognize and nurture them within training activities. For example, how and where a

players as possible, not artificially create more elite teams for fewer and fewer with an immediate focus on winning.

The Game of and by the Players Themselves Is the Best Teacher

Most of the different aspects to speed listed above relate to speed of vision, thought and decision-making. These are concepts that require much more than mere repetition in controlled environments. Furthermore, they do not concern only individual speed, but that of the collective group. Since high-level play requires the development of all of these types of speed together, our training environments must incorporate all of them in less contrived and dictatorial ways. The players' perceptions, decisions, anticipation, reactions, etc., must be in response to the problems the game itself presents. We are seeking "game speed," not just the ability to succeed in an exercise. Furthermore, while we create problem-solving environments in our training sessions, we must allow players to solve the problems presented.

Players also must be given time and opportunities to play in small-sided situations with and against players of different abilities. These types of games provide increased numbers of touches, increased opportunities for decisions on both sides of the ball and do not reward physical speed as much as larger-sided games. Furthermore, playing with and against many different caliber and types of players requires each player to adjust and make differing decisions as to how to compete individually and in groups. It is the process of making these differing decisions that *is the process* of developing speed.

Emphasis on Speed of Play

Speed of play should be a continuous touchstone for all youth coaches, yet it is often overlooked. One reason is that many youth coaches focus primarily on the exercise itself, rather than on the elements of speed within it. As a result, they create

"coach-directed" activities, rather than activities that encourage both problem-solving and other types of speed by the players themselves.

As an example of this, consider an exercise involving dribbling where every player has a ball and is dribbling freely in a defined area. Some youth coaches condition the game by saying, "When I say 'change' then change direction." They aim to train players to react quickly to direction changes but miss seeing that the decision to change directions is dictated arbitrarily by the coach, rather than what the players themselves see happening around them. Such exercises might help develop technical speed, but they are divorced from other important components of speed, such as visual speed (what the player sees and when he sees it), anticipatory speed (anticipating when, where and how fast to move), and reactive speed (movement of others around him create new openings and block others). Only game-like environments nurture these types of speed. Therefore, coaches would do much better if they provided problems for the players to solve and aims for them to reach, rather than directing how players should react to each situation.

For example, in the same type of exercise described above, the coach might pose a problem for players to solve: "See how many times you can move the ball between two other players without touching anyone or their ball." The game itself, which creates the environment around the players, will dictate where and when openings occur for dribbling or passing. Success will be dependent upon each player's ability to recognize, react and technically move into those openings.

From Simple to Complex

The exercise described above is a very simple environment because there are no opponents and there is no prescribed direction to move or goals to attack or defend. The size of the space and the other players provide the complexity. The following progression of activities provides a canvas for discussing the development of different aspects of speed. This is just one example, limiting the concentration to the development of speed for one type of decision-making. As a coach, you should seek to find ways to help players develop different components of speed in every activity they perform. For continuity, the technical aspect in the following activities will be passing and receiving ground balls. The activities will gradually become more complex, moving from a warm-up phase, then a 4v4+4 (windows) non-directional activity, then 6v6+2 to three goals, and finally 6v6 to goals.

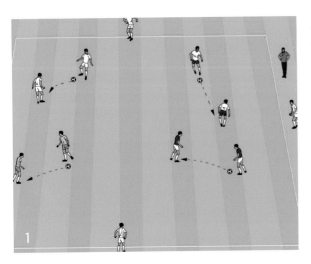

Warm-Up: Windows with four pairs passing inside and four (window) players outside

Technical Speed

Technical speed depends on players' first touch. Players should be encouraged to never stop the ball dead. They should always move the ball somewhere with their first touch. This general concept provides a technical foundation for speed because it immediately puts opponents in the posture of chasing, rather than dictating, the direction of play. In the "Windows" format, the movement of the other players in the area creates the spaces that open for moving the ball with the first touch. Players can be encouraged to find these spaces *before* they receive the ball to determine how they should approach the ball, as well as the speed, direction, and distance of their first touch. Furthermore, communication among the players can be encouraged as part of technical speed. This is especially crucial for young players who may be self-conscious about talking.

Decision-Making Speed

The warm-up phase also provides a simple decision-making environment for tactically applying the technical movements. Since there are no opponents, the technical and tactical aspects are readily recognizable, and only where spaces open and close and not the pressure of opponents trying to gain possession of the ball affect the decisions of where, when, how to react and make or receive passes.

Decision-making includes how players run to receive passes. Do they open their bodies before receiving the ball to increase their vision of the field? Do they come back toward the passer at an angle? Do they go away? Do they run diagonally? Do they burst into short sprints? Do they fake one way before going another? Similarly, issues for the passers include how hard they play the ball, whether they play it to feet or to space and to which foot. All of these actions involve technical development, but all are dictated by tactical decisions about their immediate environment.

Windows: 4v4+4 (neutral window players)

Technical speed becomes more complex when opponents are trying to take the ball away. Outside targets create a numbers-up situation for the team with the ball. The lack of directional play makes all of the real estate inside the playing area worth the same. Players can find space wherever it appears without worrying about where they are on the field, which helps to develop speed because it introduces

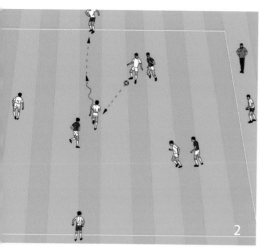

2

anticipatory and reactive speed based upon where opponents are located. Players should understand the field in a 360-degree dimension. Not having directional play encourages players to seek out the spaces not occupied by opponents, regardless of where they are on the field. Its importance lies in the truth that the ball can move faster than the player. Therefore, when there is no particular direction to play, the possessing team will freely move *wherever* space is open, freezing opponents in certain places, or drawing them into those spaces when the ball is played.

In this environment, different aspects of technical speed become important – the direction of the first touch is still paramount, but fakes before receiving the ball and the distance the ball is played become more important because opponents are reacting to the passes. "Slowing down" opponents is another aspect of speed. Coaches can help players develop the ability to make opponents go or lean the wrong way by focusing on what players do *before* they receive the ball, e.g., calling for the ball to draw opponents toward them or checking for a pass in one direction and then playing the first touch in a different direction. In each case, the focus helps players recognize how to "wrong foot" opponents. With the introduction of opponents, the technical and tactical aspects of speed converge. Speed is recognizing how to use space and the ball to make opponents move where we want them to move. Using neutral players outside gives coaches the opportunity to help the inside players create and recognize spaces in the middle of the playing area. Ever moving outside target players also help inside players recognize the importance of body position for increasing field vision, and, thus, visual speed, when receiving passes from outside players.

Here, we want players to learn to immediately recognize and exploit spaces away from opponents. There are many different concepts for developing speed of play: some coaches focus on combination play, others on space in certain parts of the field. My method here is to provide a general foundation, based upon attacking principles, before defining particular methods of applying those principles. I usually begin by teaching players to look for "meadows" on the field, in which to run or play the ball as soon as they gain possession. A "meadow" is any space where there are no opponents or other teammates. The "meadow" concept can be contrasted with a "forest" (where players of both teams are defined as the trees). We encourage players as soon as they gain possession to find "meadows" for playing and receiving the ball. Once they do so continuously, then we can show them that the tendency of opponents is to follow the ball into the "meadows."

Once players understand this concept, we can shift the focus to help players recognize the spaces they have created between opponents. Using the "meadows" and "forest" picture, we can show players how their movement and the movement of the ball into "meadows" cause opponents to move, thereby increasing the amount of space between the "trees" in the forest (we can call these spaces "doorways"). Now players can look to leave the "meadows," run into those "doorways," and to play the ball (which is faster than the opponents) through those "doorways." It may sound simplistic, but it is all about players continually recognizing and reacting to the spaces that exist around them, regardless of where they are on the field.

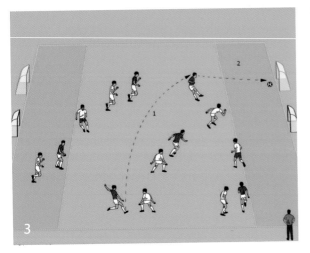

When we add direction, the environment becomes much more complex. Players have objective areas to attack and defend, and these areas take on different values for both teams. Attacking teams want to score points, so they often "rush" into the opponents' crowded goal spaces (forests) without creating the spaces between the "trees." Defending teams protect the goal areas more intensely by increasing the number of "trees" in these areas. Focus shifts to using the ball to speed up our own play and understanding how to use the ball as a decoy to slow opponents down. Where players before considered all "meadows" equal, coaches now can help them see how to play the ball into and out of more and less important areas to draw opponents away from their own goals and thereby increase the size of the "doorways" between them. The three goals at either end encourage attacking teams to find "meadows" in other areas of the field when the "forest" gets to thick near a particular goal.

6v6 to Two Goals

We can play 6v6 or 7v7 to two goals, building upon the same space concepts. More complexity is created both by having teams of equal numbers and only one goal each to attack and defend. Many coaches will try to choreograph play to show players "how" to find space. "Guidance" and "choreography" are two different things, and coaches must resist the latter. Players' decision-making and the development of speed are all about adaptation. Within this more difficult environment, the coach helps players develop the ability to recognize for themselves where the "meadows" exist and how to use them to create "doorways" to penetrate to an opponent's goal.

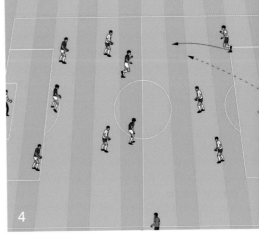

Speed: It Is Player-Centered

Using progressively more complex environments provides opportunities for players to develop their own eyes and ways to solve the problems presented. Speed of play is tied to each player's recognition of, and adaptability to, what the game presents. Rather than focusing strictly on defining ways to move the ball to goal, "guided discovery" enables coaches to help players recognize for themselves where spaces exist and how to play the ball to open spaces where they want to go. These are the types of environments that will truly develop the different aspects of speed of play.

Keeping the Ball in Play

Lou Pantuosco, Ph.D.
NSCAA Associate Staff Member

How many hours have you spent in practice waiting for players to come back in-bounds after launching a pass or shot? How many times have you seen a defender toe poke a ball 30 yards away from the offensive opponent?

My guess is that most of the readers see these every practice session. If you are like me, you must say over and over, "Keep the ball in play." As coaches, how can we teach and how can they become better players if the ball is out of bounds? If the game is indeed the best teacher, we should footnote this common statement by saying, "this is true only if the ball is in play."

On the surface, this sounds like a simple problem to address, one that can easily be solved by yelling, "Stop kicking the ball out of bounds." But we know that's like saying, "Just put the ball in the back of the net."

We as coaches have recognized the problem; now we have to implement solutions. In order to implement solutions, we have to find the core of the problem. I think there are two simple roots that can be addressed: offensively, players must focus on their first touch being soft and away from the closest defender; defensively, players must win the ball, as opposed to kicking it away from the opponent.

Focusing on these two concepts has many benefits. Practices become more competitive, players are more confident on the ball in tight spaces, players are placed into a game-like environment and the conditioning of the players improves. Like any specific training, there are limitations, but I won't mention those.

Approaches to teach ball winning

Starting with the defensive perspective, it is not complex to set up a session that emphasizes ball winning. Put four players in a 10x10 grid. The player with the ball is on offense, the other three on defense. When the ball goes out of bounds by a little, let play continue. If the ball goes far out of bounds, one player chases the ball while the other three players get on the ground and do push-ups, sit-ups, whatever. Just make sure it is something they do not enjoy doing and it is something they can start and stop quickly. For groups of nine, make three grids. After two minutes, take the players you believe performed the best in each grid and put them in grid 1. Take the players you thought were the second strongest in each of the three grids and put them in grid 2. Put the weakest three in grid 3. Now play again for two minutes, continuing the process. Now let's look at the coaching points.

Technical aspect of ball winning

For a great example, watch the Italian defense. The one-on-one lesson begins after the defense is organized behind the first defender.

Step 1: The first defender shows the offensive player a side. Let's say the first defender pushed the attacker to the attacker's right. Now the defender is standing right foot forward.

Step 2: At the appropriate time, when the attacker exposes the ball, the defender wants to get the right foot as far in front of the attacker as he can. Ideally, the defender should get his foot to the other side of the attacker's right foot. The next

step for the defender is to turn the shoulders in the direction the ball is traveling and drop his/her left foot back. The next step is to take one touch away from the attacker with the right foot. Now the defender has the ball. A key phrase to stress to the defender is to not worry about the ball when initiating the tackle – worry about the attacker.

What if the attacker is quick and skilled enough to avoid the initial tackle (step 2 in the process above)? This is not a problem because the appropriate way to tackle is to use the front foot for balance, getting it as close to the ball as possible (the right foot in this example) and the back foot wins the ball. Stressing this technique to win the ball will pay dividends, but be patient. Players will have a tendency to lunge, and a lot of times the lunge works. But that doesn't mean it is correct or that we should encourage the lunge technique.

How to receive under pressure

Again, the setup doesn't need to be complex. Put players in groups of three. One player serves the ball, the other two fight to receive and pass the ball back to the server. Let's call one of the non-servers the offensive player and the other non-server the defensive player. As the ball is served in, the first step of the offensive player is into the defensive player's path toward the ball. So if the defender is on the offensive player's right side, the offensive player first steps with his right foot into the defensive player's path. Absorbing the pressure, the offensive player then wants his first touch to be with his left foot, and the ball should be pushed away from the defender, to the left. Players must remember that they cannot receive a ball while running at top speed. Even the best players slow down their bodies when they receive. This is a common high school problem. As players mature in skill level, the speed at which they can receive and control their first touch will increase.

The difficult part again is for the offensive player to forget about the ball for a split second and think about who may take the ball – the defender. The ball has never stolen the ball from anyone, so why worry about the ball?

Turning without moving the ball

This is something every coach should emphasize during sessions on shielding. The offensive player, A, has the ball on his right foot with his left foot forward. The defensive player, B, is playing with his right foot forward, allowing player A to go right. Player B lunges in with his right foot. What should player A do? The obvious answer is to move the ball either forward or backward with his right foot. Neither is necessarily correct. If you watch good players, what do they do in this situation? As B lunges with his right, A steps over B's foot with his left, shielding B from the ball. At the same time, A turns his back as he shields. A then takes his right leg and drops it back into the path of B. Next, A pushes the ball with the inside of the left foot in the direction he originally wanted to go. The whole process takes about one second, because the feet are working together to keep the defender away from the ball. In summary, as B steps with his right, A steps with his left, then steps backward with his right and pushes the ball with his left. The offensive player has to forget about the ball for a split second and worry about the defender.

What about obstruction? Obstruction is nearly impossible to call in this example. A is always playing the ball. I have not mentioned anything about how the offensive player uses his arms (that is for another article).

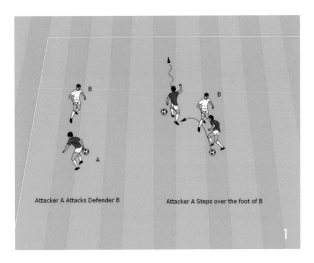

Attacker A Attacks Defender B   Attacker A Steps over the foot of B

Any small-sided game in tight space can be used to emphasize this ball winning and possession oriented first-touch technique. The results are that players will be less likely to turn into the defender and expose the ball, players will learn to use their bodies, defenders will be forced to play offense, practices become more intense, and the ball stays in bounds.

© Thinkstock/iStockphoto/Fluid Illusion

Learning to Be Creative

Ron Quinn, Ph.D.
Xavier University
US Soccer Staff Coach

The game of soccer has been described as a simple game, a beautiful game, a game of strength, speed and finesse. A game of creativity and problem solving. Much effort has been spent on developing players' technique, strength and speed; however, creativity and problem solving receive the least amount of attention.

Creativity in soccer is the ability to solve technical and tactical problems in the most efficient manner. A creative player is able to do the unexpected at the most opportune time. Problem solving is the ability to interpret multiple incoming stimuli and select the most appropriate solution. When it comes to playing the game, coaches instruct young players when and where to pass, dribble, shoot or position themselves on the field, consequently not providing much chance to solve problems.

Even though small-sided games have gained acceptance as an appropriate component of a youth soccer practice, we still see strong evidence of the drill mentality.

How an individual acquires these skills is a combination of individual characteristics and environmental conditioning and development. It is believed in most sports, soccer included, that our best players may come out of an urban environment and may be underprivileged. Perhaps these individuals at a very early age learn how to solve problems and develop creative solutions just to survive, and as a result, their ability to survive through problem solving is transferred onto the soccer field. Although this certainly has merit, it also ignores a majority of the present soccer-playing population.

The real issue is not so much the childhood environment but the playing environment to which young players are exposed. Just as we improve ball handling ability through dynamic practice repetition, we can improve problem-solving ability through a training setting in which players have multiple opportunities to scheme, create and figure out activity solutions. As an example, if young players aged 5-9 play 4v4 without goalkeepers, the player who recognizes an opportunity to shoot from 20 yards out has just extended his or her field of vision and was able to quickly respond to a penetrating channel on the field (Diagram # 1).

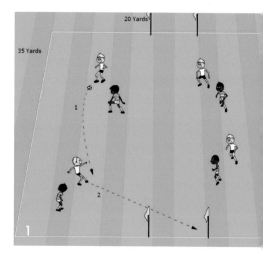

If we played with goalkeepers, the opportunity and therefore ability to recognize the particular shot or field of vision are not created. We also use games/activities, such as a variety of ball-chasing and freeze tag type of games with young children so that they develop a certain way of thinking that has implications for the game.

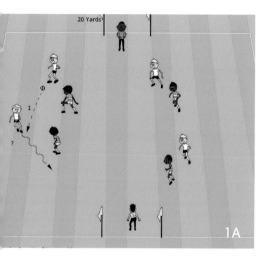

20 Yards

1A

The development of a young soccer player takes time. All aspects of the game are at work all the time; nothing happens in isolation. The physical, psychological and emotional domains continuously interact in every practice activity. The difficulty we have seen with youth soccer practices is that they are too scripted and comprised of static, mindless types of drill. Slalom dribbling through a series of cones in a straight line is a prime example. What game problems are solved and what psychological/motivational aspects of the game are addressed?

When we examine the thought process in motor skill development, action is always preceded by thought or some process of interpreting stimuli. In soccer, players receive countless amounts of environmental information. Individual movement, teammate movements, opponent movements, ball movement, coach instructions, parent/fan instructions, etc., are received by every player.

How players handle and process this information, which at times could be called information overload, plays a critical role in the decision-making process. Information is first received via a stimulus identification stage, followed by a response selection stage in which relevant information is selected and sent to a response programming stage. The response programming stage organizes this information into a specific plan of action, which is then sent onto the motor program stage for execution. What coaches need to understand is that all of this information is received simultaneously, but the resulting actions are serial in nature, meaning that in the early stages of skill development, performing multiple tasks at the same time is very difficult. In addition, the age and maturity level of players affect their information processing ability, as well as their comfort level and sense of maturity within the training session.

Younger players, age 5-9, for example, have a more limited field of vision, motor control, spatial awareness, knowledge of rules, etc., than players age 10 or older. Therefore, we need to provide a game structure that is appropriate for the age in terms of matching the players' ability to process relevant information better. In short, the need for small-sided games and a variety of game/activities is critical for the beginning player. Additionally, we need to realize that it is difficult for a child, or any player for that matter, to be creative when being yelled at.

Memory is another component. When someone has to think about doing something – making a decision – a great deal of time is needed. Time in soccer is a precious commodity. Thus the task of the coach and player is to develop skills and decision-making abilities that are more or less automatic, without a high degree of conscious thought.

Essentially, we need to develop positive tendencies that are automatic. To arrive at the level of "automatic pilot," a player needs to move through three distinct stages: a) verbal cognitive stage, in which a player has a basic understanding of what he or she is trying to accomplish; b) the motor stage, where the various motor programs and abilities are developed; and c) the autonomous stage, in which we perform certain movements without thought. The soccer coach needs to be familiar with this motor program concept from the standpoint that each movement in soccer is singular, yet never completely new. What this means is that every movement produced is, to some degree, a variation of previous movements. In soccer, there are an unlimited number of movements, responses and decisions. However, when practice exercises are presented in which the player repeats a movement at the same distance and speed, through several repetitions, the effectiveness of learning is questionable.

Therefore, the effectiveness of "passing drills" that are at a fixed distance or slalom dribbling through cones should be seriously questioned. If we want to improve a player's passing ability to a target, then each passing trial should be different from the previous one. An example is using what is called variable practice. With variable practice, each trial is conducted within a range of predetermined distance. Instead of two players passing back and forth from a distance of 15 yards, they should pass and move within this distance, making one pass at a five-yard distance, then another at 10, then three, followed by 12 or 15 yards, etc. In this way, although it may not look as structured and effective as the common one- or two-touch passing at a fixed distance, the ability of a player to reconstruct the needed motor program during match play would be stronger. Essentially, rote memory (rehearsal) does not provide the player a better opportunity to understand and execute match demands. Variable practice does.

In Diagram # 2 we see an exercise in which the coach has established a variable passing sequence through a cone-defined target. By varying the distance and/or the size of the target, the players are required to make technical adjustments from pass to pass. In the first exercise, they must pass the ball accurately so it can be handled by the receiver from a distance of five yards within 2-3 touches. As the pass is released, the player moves back to the next line (7.5 yards), ready to receive and re-pass the ball to the other player who repeats the sequence. Finally, following the second pass, the players move back 10 yards from the goal

and repeat the process, eventually moving back to the five-yard distance with the next two passes.

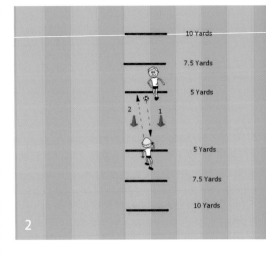

By establishing as many of these passing gates as needed to accommodate the squad, the coach can have the team achieve a great many passing and receiving touches at varying distances.

A second variation would include passing from constantly varying distances but having one player return the ball outside a widened, cone-defined target to the originating passer. This assures movement by his or her teammate in receiving the ball (Diagram # 3).

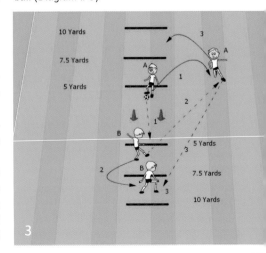

Further, the exercises, after practice and technique correction have taken place, can be made competitive. How long to make 10 passes between teammates? Establish a time limit and count passes. The size of the target can be widened or shortened. While this is a reasonable exercise for 5-9 age group players, adding footedness or surface of the feet or number of touches, can elevate its degree of difficulty for older youth players as well.

The purpose of practice is to create an environment so that what is "practiced" transfers into the game. We measure learning from what we see in the game performance. However, how many times has a coach watched a game only to say to an assistant or players on the bench, "When did we practice that?" obviously referring to a play that was not, in his or her mind, practiced. The problem may arise from a common notion that if we repeat a movement continuously until it meets a certain level of performance, also known as blocked practice, it then appears as if the player has learned the movement. The coach and players leave practice happy, only to find that the transfer of the movement into the game may be minimal. Research has demonstrated that practicing a criterion skill in a blocked or an unvarying practice format does not enhance the learning process.

A random practice format in which the player performs different movements in a random fashion is more effective in the actual retention, learning and transfer of that movement task. Earlier, we discussed the aspect of the production of motor programs. Each time an individual presented the opportunity to reconstruct a particular motor program, it is strengthened. The player is presented a situation in which he or she must perform a technical movement from a range of alternatives. This process is effective because it more actively engages the player. Repeating a movement without variation of change does not provide the depth of learning as with random practice. Although "functional training" is not recommended for young players, game activities and small-sided games are strongly encouraged.

Game activities and small-sided games have been increasingly used (but not enough) in youth practices for their fun, social interaction, increased ball touches and decision-making opportunities. However, the motor learning research on the effectiveness of random practice on skill acquisition clearly reinforces the need for young players to learn the game through game activities and small-sided games. Organized drills may look good and give the coach a sense of control, but they are truly not an effective practice activity. Drills in this sense are a practice structure in which players are repeating the same movement over and over without variation, usually in some form of line that involves players waiting for their turn. Game activities, on the other hand, engage all players, allow for a wide range of ability levels, allow for the opportunity to practice a variety of movement tasks and engage the body and mind more completely.

In Diagram # 4, we see a 4v4 game with each team defending two goals and attacking two goals. Player O1 with the ball must make a decision to

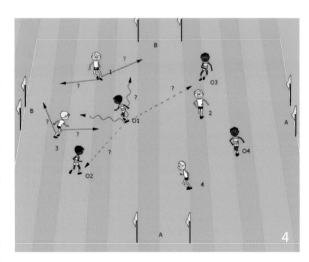

dribble and attack either of the two B goals or possibly pass to a teammate while the players without the ball must also make decisions whether

© Thinkstock/iStockphoto/Fluid Illusion

to attack the ball or defend spaces. The transition in play is readymade to elevate the decision making ability of all eight players. Again, depending on the maturity of the age group, the demands can be lessened (3 v. 3, larger or smaller spaces, etc.) or increased (two balls in play, regulation goals with keepers, etc.) in order to make the game work.

Coaches must realize that the mind does not disengage when the body engages. If we want players to become better decision makers, thereby improving playing performance, then decision-making and production of motor programs must not be exclusive.

From the perspective of player development, we must embrace the viewpoint that growth is a process. Players do not develop in just one season; it takes several years. Unfortunately, many young players are either selected out or drop out at too early an age, largely because playing is no longer enjoyable. Players need to play fast, think fast and act fast, but in order to develop these fast players, we need to maintain their interest in the game. Speed is relative.

In our fast-paced society, in order to develop the brilliant player, we need to slow down in order to go further.

References

Quinn, R.W., (1991). *The Peak Performance: Soccer Games for Player Development.* QSM Consultants, P.O. Box 15176, Cincinnati, OH 15176.

Torbert, M., (1982). *Secrets to Success in Sport & Play. Prentice Hall, Englewood Cliffs*, NJ.

Schmidt, R.A., (1991). *Motor Learning and Performance: From Principles to Practice.* Champaign, IL: Human Kinetics.

Coaching Long Passing

David Saward, Jeff Vennell and Doug Williamson
NSCAA Academy Staff

Long passing is a technique that is not practiced enough by many coaches. Long, accurate, penetrating passes, especially to forwards who are showing for a ball, and the ability to change the point of attack quickly and accurately are musts in the modern game. Coaches should be aware that they should focus on one central theme during a practice session using only a limited number of exercises for a specific technical practice. The exercises that follow may also be used for other techniques. Remember that the selection of practice exercises is determined by the thematic "thread" that the coach pulls throughout the fabric of the practice session.

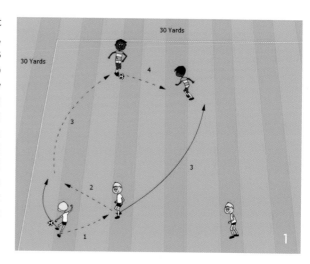

Warm-up exercises

Coaches should be careful during the warm-up phase of practices that players begin with passes that are somewhat shorter than the length of passes that will occur during the concluding warm-up activities. Be certain that your players are warmed up properly and are stretched sufficiently to prevent injury.

Exercise 1

Short, short, long passing in groups of five. Begin with players in a 30 x 30-yard space and expand as needed (Diagram # 1). Player receiving the long pass should take a controlling touch and dribble the ball a few times. Then passes begin again – short, short, long. The long pass should be made to the player farthest from the passer as other players run to support the player receiving the long pass. Keep the ball moving, using the central players as obstacles to play around or over.

- Add a wall-pass upon reception of the long pass (Diagram # 1A).
- Add a double pass upon reception of the long pass.
- Add takeover upon reception of the long pass.

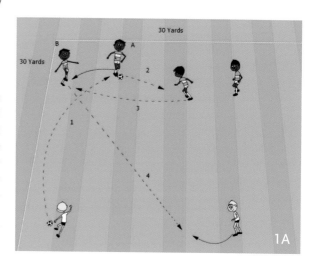

Exercise 2

This is a team knockout activity with two teams of eight or more players in a half field. One team begins inside the field each with a ball with the objective of keeping possession of the ball through dribbling. The other team begins on the outside and enters the half field at the start with the goal of dispossessing the dribblers and then clearing all the balls into the other half field. Keep time until all the balls are cleared out of the half field. Change roles. Use a reward, e.g., winning team does 15 sit-ups, losing team does 30 sit-ups.

Main lesson exercises

Long passes are struck to:

- feet of players showing for a pass or
- spaces, usually ahead of attacking players running toward goal.

There are three basic types of long passes:

- driven or line drive passes;
- lofted or air passes;
- hooked or sliced passes.

Coaching long passing or any technique should involve movement to replicate game conditions. Technical coaching points for all three types of long passing include:

- having the ball "out of feet" to enable a good strike of the ball;
- an approach to the ball from an angle;
- a hop onto the support foot, with the hop step slightly longer than the last running step;
- some coaches recommend that the support foot should be placed slightly behind the ball, others recommend the support foot be placed slightly farther away to the side of the ball;
- follow through toward target, except for the long sliced pass;
- Each type of long pass has its own individual technical coaching points: for the driven long pass, the toe is pointed down and the ball is struck through the middle of the ball; for the lofted long pass, the toe is again pointed down, but the ball is struck below the center; for the hooked long pass, the toe is pointed up at impact and the ball is struck left of center for right footed pass;
- for the sliced long pass the toe is pointed down and the ball is kicked "across" the ball following through with the leg across the body.
- Coaches are reminded that the sizes of the spaces noted for each exercise should be adjusted for ability levels. It is always better to start larger and then make the area smaller if the technical level of the players permits a smaller space.

Exercise 1

6(3+3)v3; 30 x 50-yards. Three teams of three
(Diagram # 2).

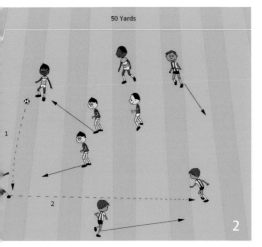

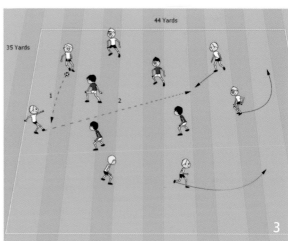

Exercise 3

3v3 plus two targets; 44 x 50-yards
(Diagram # 4)

Two teams play possession from the third team; team that loses possession becomes the defender. Note: the most effective pass most of the time is a longer accurate pass to the far end of the space.

- Play two or three touch.
- Keep the same three players on defense for a certain time frame, counting the number of touches by the defensive teams before changing the defensive team.

Exercise 2

7 v. 4; 44 x 35-yards. Seven players maintain possession from four (Diagram # 3)

Play for 2½ to 3 minutes and then change offensive and defensive players. The incentive for the four defenders is to touch the ball equal to or more than the number of long passes by the seven offensive players.

- 7's – three touches maximum, seven consecutive passes equals a goal. 4's – unlimited touches, four consecutive passes equals a goal.

Teams of three players attempt to make a penetrating pass as soon as possible to target player at the end of the grid.

- To encourage long pass, reward if ball arrives to target player in the air.
- Team that makes successful pass maintains possession and plays to target player at the other end.

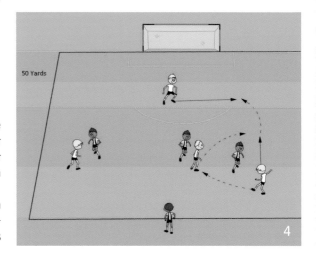

Exercise 4

8v8 ; 40 x 40 yards in equal side zones
(Diagram # 5)

One red vs. three blue/white in one zone; one
blue/white vs. three red in the next zone; one red
vs. three blue/white in the next zone; three reds vs.
one blue/white in the final zone. Complete passes
across zones for points. Two or three touches per
player. Players leave their zone.

- Two balls, unlimited touches; one defensive
  player in each half can go into another zone to
  create a 3v2.
- One ball, otherwise the same as previous
  exercise.

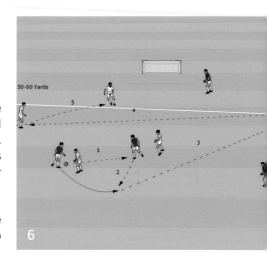

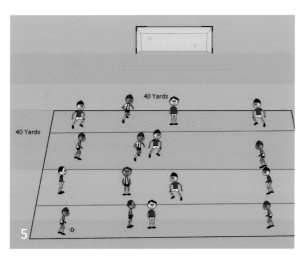

Exercise 5

4v4 with two target players; full width x 60
yards with field divided into two 30-yard
halves (Diagram # 6)

- Play to the target players but the pass must
  originate from within the half of the field most
  distant from the intended target player. The
  target player receives the ball and plays a

long pass to the other target player, who then
plays the ball to the other team. Coaches can
suggest/limit the type of pass, i.e., driven,
lofted, bent, etc.
- Alternate the target players with field players
  frequently

Exercise 6

5v5 ; half field; four full-size goals. Change
the point of attack options (Diagram # 7)

- Unlimited, three, two and one touch restrictions
  can apply
- Can progress to 7v7 with two balls
- One goal halfway along each side of the end
  line, 10 yards into the field or can establish four
  goals 10 yards from each corner of the field
- Can also make the field wider than it is long,
  i.e., 60 x 40 yards

Exercise 7

6v6; two full-size goals "facing" out; 30 yards
offset; 30 yards apart (Diagram # 8)

- Unlimited, three and two touch
- Add a second ball

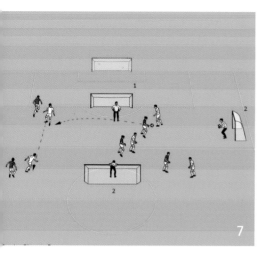

7

8

End games and concluding exercises

Field sizes:
* To practice vertical penetrating passes: 5v5; 30 yards wide and 60 yards long
* To practice change of direction longer passes; 7v7; 80- yards wide x 60 yards long

5v5 plus goalkeepers; 60 x 44 yards with a 20-yard neutral zone (Diagram # 9)

Players may not dribble ball into the neutral zone
* Play 2v3/3v2 in each end zone. Players may not leave their zone.
* Permit one player to go forward to join teammates to create a 3v3
* Players may run anywhere they wish, but have only one touch in the neutral zone
* Eliminate the neutral zone, with an emphasis on long passing

Developing the Long Game

Paul Payne
NSCAA Academy Senior Staff

As a coach, you need to recognize your players' abilities in performing a successful long pass. Once players have the leg strength, the proper technique of striking a ball over long distances needs to be addressed in your training. An example of such a training session is set up below. I have used this session with youth players as well as college age players. As with any session, the coach needs to adapt the training to the team's abilities.

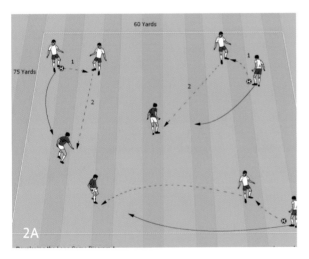

2A

Warm-up and fundamental stage (Diagram # 1)

Organization

12 players: 8 players paired (blue/ white) knocking short balls to each other while freely moving around the field; four neutral players (red) moving around the same area. When a neutral red calls for a ball from the blue pairs, the ball is served using the proper technique. The non-serving blue player moves to support the long pass and receives back

from the neutral red player. The blue pairs then continue to pass short until another neutral red player is free. It is important that the players are properly stretched, focusing on the quadriceps and hamstrings prior to beginning this phase of the session.

Progression

Begin by having players work on serving driven balls both on the ground and in the air.

Coaching points (for driven balls)

- Ball must be "out of feet."
- Approach from a slight angle.
- "Hop" onto support foot, pointed forward, slightly behind ball.
- Toe pointed down, ankle locked striking through the middle of the ball.
- Follow through to target.

After a brief stretch, demonstrate the next service of a lofted pass.

Coaching points

- Ball must be "out of feet."
- Approach from more of an angle.
- Hop onto support foot, pointed forward slightly behind ball.
- Player leans back more.
- Toe pointed down, striking ball left of middle.
- Strike through ball, extending to the target.

Stretch before introducing the proper technique of bending and hooking a long ball pass.

Coaching points

- Toe pointed up at impact when hooking with inside of foot.

- Toe pointed down at impact when slicing with outside of foot.
- Kicking "across" the ball.
- Follow through is across (slicing) or away from (hooking) the body.

Main phase: exercise 1 (Diagram # 2)

Organization

Playing in three zones across the field, divide players into three teams of four. Four reds play against two blue/whites in Zone 1, looking to play the ball safely into Zone 2, where four white players are stationed. Restrict to two touches and a maximum of three passes before the ball must be played into next zone. If the two blue/whites displace the reds of the ball in Zone 1 or if the ball is not played cleanly through the neutral zone, blue/whites play the ball into Zone 2 and the waiting white players. Two reds must then go defend against the four whites in Zone 2 while the other two reds occupy the neutral zone. Vary conditions to ensure early success, then increase demands on the players. For example, make a tighter space in which to play or allow three defenders in.

Coaching points

- Make sure players are using the proper technique when choosing to serve.
- Defensive pressure will dictate what type of service is best.
- As always, communication and vision need to be stressed.

Main phase: exercise 2 (Diagram # 2B)

Organization

Divide a rectangular playing area into four zones. Three teams of four whites, four reds vs. four blue/whites. In each zone, a 10 x 10 target is laid out with a white player in each target area. Free play, with each team looking to maintain possession until the long diagonal pass is on. In order to score, the ball must be played cleanly into a white target player from a diagonal zone.

Variations

- For a point to be scored, a supporting player from the servicing team must receive a one-touch pass from the white target player.
- The white player, upon receiving a quality long pass, plays the ball to another white target player, who then would play the ball out to the team that successfully serviced the ball.

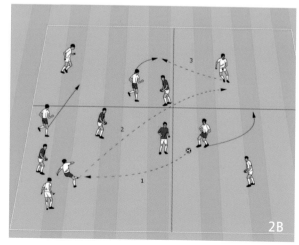

20 Yards

2A

2B

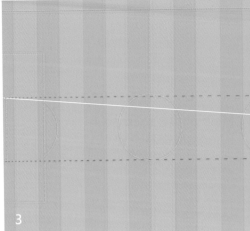

3

Coaching points

In addition to the points mentioned in exercise 1, also look at how quickly players can recognize that the long diagonal pass is on and that the proper technique is executed.

Final phase (Diagram # 3)

Organization

Playing full-sided soccer with goalies, divide the field into thirds lengthwise. Have players look to play long balls safely from one flank zone to another flank zone. You also can place the restriction that the ball must be played through all three zones to encourage opening up the field, which will lend itself to more opportunities for long ball passing. As with any training session, always end with free play with no restrictions.

The first principle of attack is penetration. Ideally you want to accomplish this by focusing on the techniques that will achieve it. A successful long ball pass is just one technique that can do just that.

© Thinkstock/iStockphoto/Fluid Illusion

Shooting Exercises

Jeff Vennell
NSCAA Senior Academy Staff

Following are shooting exercises utilized by Jeff Vennell as part of the teaching process at the NSCAA National Diploma Courses. Each involves a great many shooting opportunities for the players – with little down time!

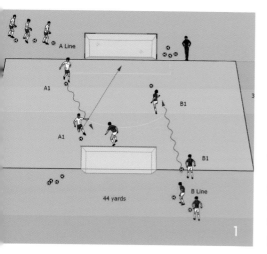

1v1 Recovery Game: Diagram # 1

A1 dribbles as close to B's goal as he/she wants and shoots. As soon as A1 shoots, he/she retreats to play in goal as B1 dribbles and shoots at A1. Repeat with A2 dribbling at B1, who is retreating to play goal. Four players by each goal, alternating in and out after each shoots once and defends their goal one time. Have plenty of balls available or arrange for the shooter who misses to be responsible for retrieving their ball.

2v1 – Both Directions: Diagram # 2

A1 and A2 attack B1 and shoot on B2 (who tends goals). If they score, they get another ball and attack B3 (B4 becoming the goalkeeper). If they miss or the shot is saved or if they lose the ball, B2 joins B1 and they attack A3 & A6 (one of whom becomes the goalkeeper). Another variation would be to have the two-person teams remain on the field for a short time (60 seconds) with rapid attack/counterattack taking place.

2v2 + Side Support: Diagram # 3

Eight players form four two-person teams. The two teams in the middle play 2v2 with goalkeepers. If a team scores, it receives another ball from its keeper and re-attacks. If a team loses the ball before shooting, they are on defense. Either team with the ball can utilize any of the four support players to maintain possession and/or to free

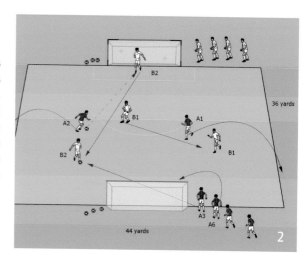

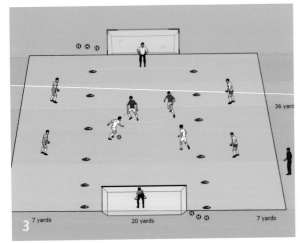

3

The manner of scoring may be restricted in that goals may be scored only via ground passes or perhaps passes in the air (volleys or headers).

Three-Sided Goal Game: Diagram # 5

Three teams of six players each play in a triangle 44 yards long on each side. Place balls by each goal. Three of the six players from each team deal with two balls being in play at the same time. When a ball crosses a team's sideline, then one of the players (a designated server) plays the ball in to a teammate (one player serves as goalkeeper,

themselves for shooting opportunities. Restrictions (time of game; number of passes before a shot must be executed, limited touches, etc.) can be placed on the game.

2v2 + End Support: Diagram # 4

This game places the supporting players at the end lines of a 36-yard x 44-yard field. One game may be staged where the attacking team may use their end line players for support in order to free themselves for a shot on goal, while another game can require the teams to use those players before they can attempt a shot on goal.

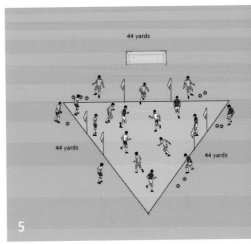

5

the other as a ball chaser). Teams score in either of the other two goals. Again, restrictions can be put on the game. Following a prescribed period of time, the teams change positions.

Services/Crosses Exercise: Diagram # 6

Two teams of four organized around the penalty area. The shooting bouts last 90 seconds, with services alternating between those from the coach and crosses from the sides. The shooters are restricted to one-touch shooting or one-touch passing to a teammate, who then must hit a first-

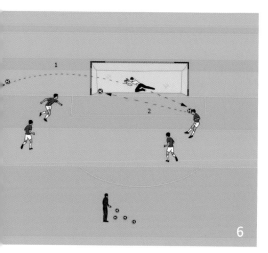

servers. There are no headers in this game. Rotate groups and keep cumulative scores for each team.

Knock Out — 4v4 + Goalkeepers: Diagram # 8

Play 4v4 for a set number of goals or for a set time. Play can start with a two-touch restriction, then go to one touch. Goalkeepers can shoot only on a back pass, not to start or restart the game. There are no corner kicks in the game. A third group can be used of four resting/retrieving. The winners stay

time shot. Have plenty of balls available. Coaches may wish to add a third four-person team on the goal line to retrieve balls.

Opposed Shooting: Diagram # 7

The game emphasizes one-time shooting or one-time passes to teammates for one-time shooting. In the Diagram #, Team A is defended by Team B. If B wins the ball, they play it out to the coach, then compete for possible shots on goal with A defending. Establish a rotational order for the

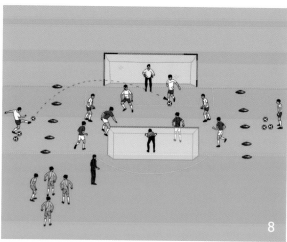

on, losers go off. If shots miss, a rotational order can be established for the X servers to play balls in to restart play.

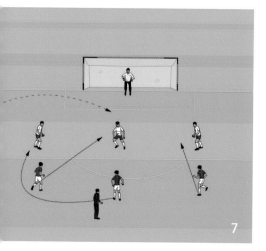

Exercise for Sharp Shooting

Mike Berticelli
Past Director of Coaching NSCAA

Modern soccer has put all kinds of new demands on players, and shooting is no exception. According to recent analysis, most successful shots come from inside the penalty box. However, shooting from outside the box can be a very effective way of stretching compact defenses. And while space is limited and defensive pressure heightened for all players, attackers are operating in minimal space and maximal opposition as they try for quality strikes on goal.

For all these reasons, it's time to rethink traditional shooting exercises and construct more practical practice games that replicate the real demands of today's soccer.

Warm-up exercises: Exercise 1

- Two goals with goalkeepers, about 40 yards apart, 20-25 yards in width.
- Two teams of three.
- Divide the field into three zones of 5, 10 and 15 yards.
- Each team starts in one of the end zones.

Combinations and shot on goal (Diagram # 1)

- The players in group A pass back and forth among themselves inside their zone until one of them is in a position to shoot.
- The shooter dribbles a short distance, then shoots out of the zone on the opposite goal.
- As soon as player A shoots, the players in group B must run around the corner cones or the goal, as shown.
- After the shot, the goalkeeper distributes to one of the players in group B. They repeat the above procedure and so on.

Focus on

- Accurate passing (right pace on the ball).
- Confident ball control (watch first touch by shooter).
- Accurate distance shooting (sight keeper first, watch ball).

Exercise 2 (Diagram # 2)

Setup is the same as in exercise 1, but with extra balls placed by each goal.
Combinations and direct shot:

- Same as above, except now the shooter shoots on the first touch, that is directly off the pass without dribbling.
- If this proves too difficult, back off and allow the shootern a second touch to control the ball before shooting.

Focus on

- Precise ball striking/accurate distance shooting; correct body position prior to the pass and examine body/leg position as strike ball as well as follow through (strike through the ball).
- Accurate passing.

Exercises with opposition pressure: Exercise 3 (Diagram # 3)

Setup is the same as before except there are four players in each zone instead of three, creating a 3v1 situation in each end zone.

- Note that as with all the exercises there are plenty of balls available by the goals so there is no shutdown of play.

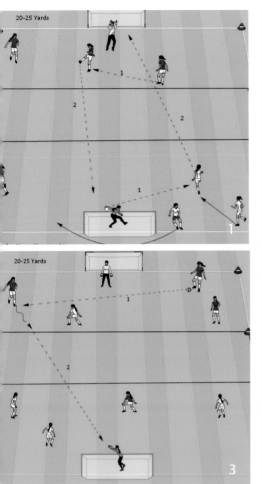

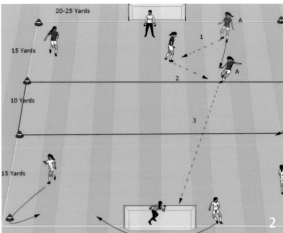

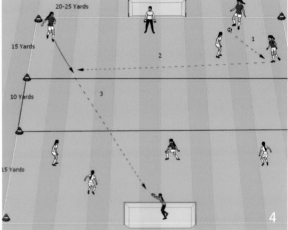

3v1 with distance shot:

- Play starts with a 3v1 in front of goal 1.
- The three attackers try to get a clear shot at the opposite goal, while the defender tries to interfere with their combinations and/or block their shots. If the defender wins the ball, he can attack on goal 1.
- After a long shot, play starts again in the opposite direction either by goalkeeper distribution off the shot or with the insertion of a new ball.

Variations

- To emphasize ball control, limit shooters to one touch prior to the shot.

- Elevate play by insisting on first-touch shooting.
- If ball control is not up to standard, evaluate whether to lengthen and widen the grid (i.e., 50 x 30 yards).

Exercise 4 (Diagram # 4)

Setup is the same as in exercise 3.

3v1 with direct distance shot:

- As above, play starts with a 3v1.
- Now, however, the shooter can play the ball ahead into the middle zone before shooting.
- The shooter runs onto the ball in the middle zone then must shoot directly.

Variation

- The shooter is limited to two touches (he or she may control the ball in the middle zone with one of those touches before shooting).

Exercise 5 (Diagram # 5)

Setup is the same as in exercise 4.
Continuous 3v1 with distance shots:

- As above, play starts with a 3v1.
- Now, however, attackers may also use the middle zone to build their attack, so that close-range shots also are possible.
- After shooting or losing the ball, the attackers and their defender return to the zone in front of their goal and the other group starts a new 3v1 in the opposite direction, etc.

Focus on

- Confident combination play (note that play is now in a 30 x 20 area; spread out offensively).
- Accurate shooting, even under opposition pressure (look up even before or as ball is passed to sight the keeper's position; "pass the ball" into the goal).

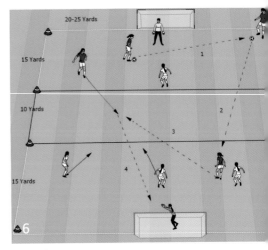

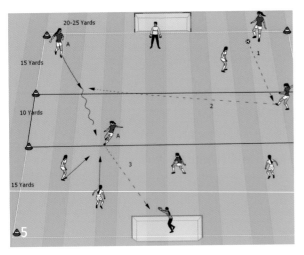

Exercise 6 (Diagram # 6)

Setup is the same as in exercise 5.
Long shot from a combination:

- As in exercise 5, play starts with a 3v1 in two zones.
- Now, however, attackers have yet another opportunity to score by passing to a "forward" (the single defender in the opposite zone), who acts as a target player. The target player tries to "lay off" balls to the middle zone for a first-time shot.
- Goals coming off combinations with the target player count double.

Variation

- Initially, and to make the exercise easier, the target player may not be defended with high pressure.

Exercise 7 (Diagram # 7)

Setup is the same as in exercise 6, except that we add a second defender in each zone, creating 3v2 situations in each zone.

3v2 with a long shot:

- Play now begins with a 3v2 in two zones.
- Attackers can pass to their two teammates in the zone in front of the opposite goal.

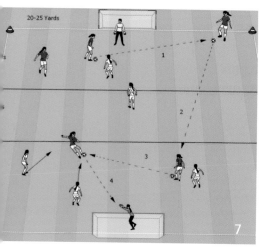

Variation

- Attackers can score on any type of combination, but shots made following the sequence described above count double.
- Lift all restrictions and play – and score – from a distance if possible.

Obviously the 5v5 game can evolve into an 8v8 game (with zones or without) played from goal to goal (with a 44-yard width) with the emphasis on well-taken shots from outside the box. These long distance strikes might be rewarded with a double count if they score, etc.

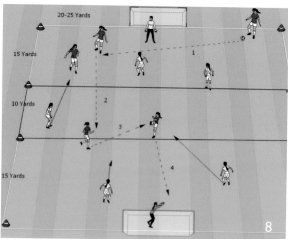

- The two forwards have two options for scoring: they can pass back to a teammate in the middle zone for a long shot; or they can shoot directly, either by beating an opponent 1v1 or through a combination effort with their twin striker.

Variation

- Only the two forwards can score.
- Same as above but one of the strikers from the second zone can move into the other zone to create a 4v2 situation.

Exercise 8 (Diagram # 8)

Setup is the same as above, but with two teams of five.

5v5 with special shooting rules:

- The two teams play without zones (a game of 5v5 on two goals with goalkeepers).
- To score, players must follow this sequence: An attacker must pass to a teammate in front of the opposite goal; this teammate passes back to another attacker for the shot (a three-man combination).
- Once the back pass has been made to set up a shot, the defense backs off to allow the attacker a clear shot.

Keep the Shot Low

Jack Detchon
NSCAA Senior Academy Staff

The following are shooting exercises. In all cases, you should emphasize low shooting for the following reasons:

- There will be more mishandles by the keeper as it is harder for the keeper to get to the balls;
- High balls are more reaction saves, and generally easier to keep out of the goal.

Exercise 1 (Diagram # 1)

Set up for exercises 1 through 7: In an area 44x36-yards, two teams of six players, two goalkeepers, supply of balls by each goal.

Organization
Goalkeeper throws (rolls) the ball at slight angle and player may not use more than one touch to shoot on goal; teammate in other line runs, under control (don't let ball rebound past you), to goal to clean up any rebounds. Players return to original lines. Goalkeepers distribute balls so that everyone shoots. Alternate shots from each goal.

Variation
Have players from each team count the number of successful goals from first exercise to last. Make it competitive.

Exercise 2 (Diagram # 2)

Organization
Goalkeeper services the ball at sharper angle, forcing the shooter to align hips and body to the goal. Again, shooting on first or second touch. First two teammates in second line follow up the shot, one centrally, second player running wide, both looking for rebounds. As soon as one ball is shot and play is over, group at other goal proceeds in the same manner.

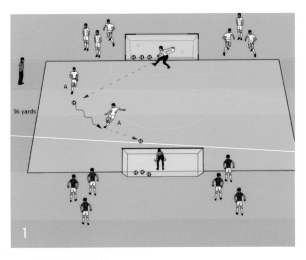

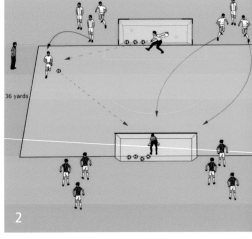

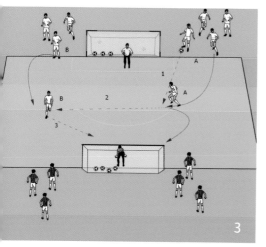

Exercise 3 (Diagram # 3)

Organization

First player in non-shooting line moves out to serve as target player with ball played in and laid off in a lateral/forward position. Shooter holds position so that he or she arrives to ball at proper time to deliver a shot within one touch. Target player turns and follows up misplays by keeper. Return to lines and second goal group repeats.

Exercise 4 (Diagram # 4)

Organization

Same exercise as above except ball is laid backwards for holding player to run onto for shot. This time ask that players hit ball with the outside of the foot. They should seek to spin or bend the ball on goal.

Exercise 5 (Diagram # 5)

Organization

Goalkeeper serves wide (as per exercise 2) and first player in second line runs to pressure shooter who must shoot with no more than one touch. Repeat from opposite goal.

Exercise 6 (Diagram # 6)

Organization

Instead of trying to combat the taking of the shot on no more than the first touch, the first player in second line tries to run to a point where a deflection of the shot is possible (Diagram # 5, run labeled 2).

Exercise 7 (Diagram # 7)

Organization

Opposite line sets up as target player and lays

6

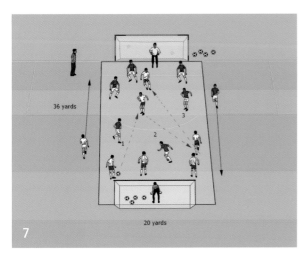

7

Stage 1

Five players must try to play ball off target player and shoot with no more than one touch. Five players in opposite end try to cut off angles for shot. Shooter tries to find openings with teammate ready to pounce on rebounds, caroms, etc. Game is continuous as long as ball is in play. Play over side or end line starts with goalkeeper of team in possession starting play. Team in possession seeks to spread play out to allow for shooting opportunities. Passing can be restricted to two touch or less.

Stage 2

Play 4v2 in each half of the field.

Exercise 9

Organization

Two teams of six play in 20x36-yard field. Two goalkeepers. Game is throw-volley-catch. Idea is to throw the ball low so that volley shots (or passes) are in order. Ball can be struck off throw either in air or on first bounce (half volley). Can also emphasize use of outside of foot volleys.

Repetition is the key

It should be emphasized that shooting exercises need to be designed for a good number of repetitions to take place (have plenty of soccer balls on hand) and that in each of these exercises there must be an emphasis on a quick examination of where an opening exists, getting the body (and shooting foot) ready and striking through the ball. Pressure must be applied by defenders to make the exercises realistic, and teammates must be ready to pounce on mistakes by the defense.

Editor's note: Jack Detchon currently resides in England following a successful stint as coach at Kenyon College (Ohio). He is a member of the NSCAA Academy staff.

ball off to shooter who must shoot with no more than one touch. Target player tries to run to spot to intercept, block, deflect attempt on goal. Repeat from opposite goal.

Exercise 8

Organization

12 players arranged in 5v1 games in each half of a 20x36-yard field. Two keepers. Supply of balls by each goal.

Shaping Runs Off the Ball

How to improve body positioning and the angle of runs

Douglas J. Williamson, Ph.D.
NSCAA Senior National Staff Coach

Most youth players, even those who play for highly competitive clubs, could benefit from increased tactical training in body positioning and the shaping of runs off the ball. The evidence for this judgment may be found in a number of sights that one can find repeated ad infinitum on American soccer fields. For example:

- Forwards sprinting to balls played down touchlines, backs to the goal, getting trapped against the line by defenders who do not allow them to turn

- Central strikers and midfielders checking back vertically (parallel to touchlines), limiting their vision and restricting their ability to play forward upon reception

- Forwards running full tilt away from the ball, parallel to the touchlines, forcing teammates to try to play low-percentage, over-the-top forward passes as the only option for penetrating a defense

- Flank players making runs that allow defenders to watch both the ball and the attacker, rather than bending away from the defender, so that he/she cannot watch both ball and player at the same time

- Flank players having crossing balls fly past them because they have run on a straight line toward the goal, rather than bending their runs in such a way that they can "frame the goal" and either collect a pass or finish with a powerful shot at goal

Some of the observers feel strongly that one of the major weaknesses of the American national teams is an inability to make creative and tactically astute runs off the ball. This is perhaps not surprising when one realizes that this is a characteristic of most of the play in our country at the youth level.

Rather than bemoan the obvious, it would seem that our task as coaches is to work to help our advanced players learn better body positioning and more effective attacking runs off the ball in the context of match play. There are many ways to do this, but this article will discuss three exercises that may help players improve their play in this area. The first exercise is a relatively simple passing and receiving session. The second and third exercises are more complex training sessions. Each exercise can be developed in such a way as to compose an entire training session, or portions of the exercises can be used as components of an extended practice.

The first exercise is a simple "windows" session. The standard space presumes 16-18 players and is approximately 44x35 yards in size. In the first activity in this session, the players in the middle of the field have soccer balls and play the longest possible instep-driven ball to a player in a "window," then follow the ball and get it back. What is essential at this fundamental stage of training is that the coach insists that the players following their pass to get the ball back check to the window at an angle, so that their first touch can be made facing into the bulk of the field (Diagram # 1).

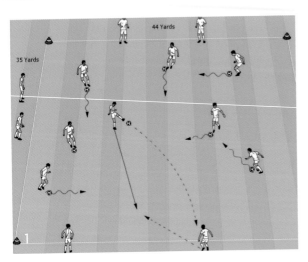

from the opposite team in the center of the field. The other players from the two teams stand in alternating "windows" around the perimeter of the field (Diagram # 3). The scoring objective for both teams is to complete seven consecutive passes to score a goal. Each time one of the teams has the ball, the contest is an 8v4 encounter, as the central players may pass to each other and to the "window" players on their team.

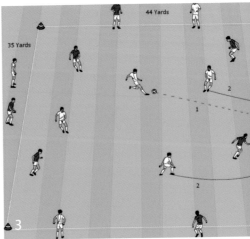

In the second activity, quite similar to the first, the players in the middle with the ball play a short pass to a window player, then sprint to the closest place on the perimeter of the field and receive a firmly struck pass across one's body before exploding off with the ball and then repeating the sequence (Diagram # 2).

This exercise may be helpful in teaching body position and the shaping of runs if the coach focuses his/her coaching points on how the central players move to get open to receive passes from each other and from the window players. The coach will thus focus his/her coaching points on opening one's hips to the field, on bending runs away from defenders, and on looking over one's shoulder to get a sense of pressure as one runs to the ball so one knows how to position one's body to take a first touch away from pressure or into open space.

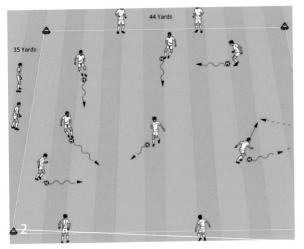

Once players have had the chance to practice some technical repetitions of the desired skills, the coach may progress to a possession game, with four players from one team and four players

The second exercise or training session to improve player runs and body positioning is one Tony DiCicco demonstrated at the NSCAA Convention several years ago. It is a "mandatory two-touch" passing and receiving session, usually utilizing a space of 25 yards long and 44 yards wide. The number and organization of players is usually

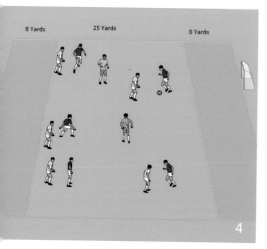

8 Yards   25 Yards   8 Yards

4

There are innumerable examples of how this exercise can be used to teach body shape, but let us mention just a few in this context. First, players in advance of the ball, because they have such a short field to work with, will need to check back to the ball at an angle so they can see the field and be able to take their first touch in any direction (Diagram # 5). Second, players at the back of the team will need to open their hips forward, rather than to the side of the ball, so that they can either change the point of attack or take a first touch into a pocket, or "seam," in the defense (Diagram # 6). Third, because space is at a premium, as the

4v4+2 or 5v5+2, with the "plus" players always playing on the attack (Diagram # 4). When Tony taught this session at the convention, he indicated that he had used it with the women's national team, playing 9v9+2 in the penalty area. This training idea can be used with a number of teams, primarily at the high school and college levels, but also including an advanced team of 10-year-olds. Often the players will need more space in which to operate successfully in this exercise.

The key to this session is that players must take two touches on each possession of the ball – not one, not three, but two. The idea is that players must be able to position their bodies in such a way as to be able to see the field and know where to take their first touch so they are taking that first touch away from pressure and/or into a space that allows penetration of the opposing defense. In the first stage of this progressive session, players must stop the ball on their second touch on the end line to score. In the second stage, players must stop the ball in the "end zone," with the ball entering the zone first. This simulates through passes in a match. In the third stage, players stop the ball in the end zone to score, but now the player must go in the end zone before the ball, which simulates finding target players in a match. In both stage 2 and stage 3, no more than one attacker and one defender may be in the end zone at any one time.

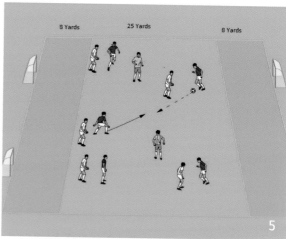

8 Yards   25 Yards   8 Yards

5

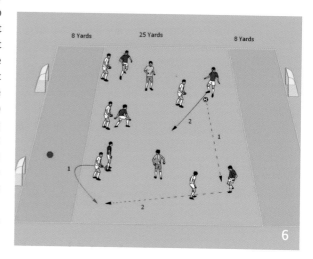

8 Yards   25 Yards   8 Yards

6

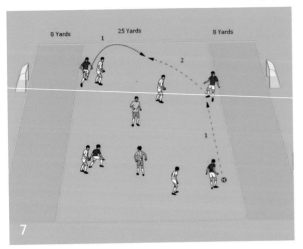

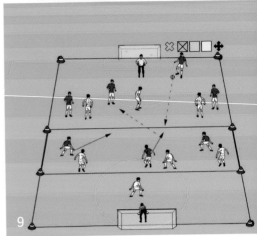

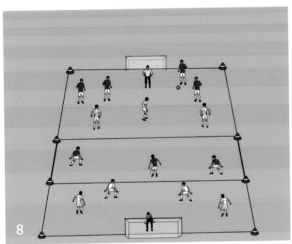

in their own defensive half of the field, including a goalkeeper defending a full-size goal, and three players in their attacking half of the field (Diagram # 8). The lines that are 18 yards from the goal constitute both the top of the penalty area and offside lines.

The first stage of this session is a possession game, with teams scoring points by playing the ball from the five to the three and back to the five. The players in the group of three are limited to a maximum of three touches on any one possession (Diagram # 9). This stage has tremendous value for teaching body shape and positioning. The back five, for example, must always be looking to shape their bodies in ways that accomplish multiple ends: maintaining possession; being able to play forward when defenders are not in the path of a pass; and being able to take penetrating touches forward when defenders have been split apart from each other. The front three, in order to be successful, must be checking away from the back five in such a way that they can run to the ball at an angle when a player in the back five looks up and indicates that he/she can play the ball forward. Then they must check to the ball in such a way as to be able to lay the ball off to a different player in the back five who may be more open than the original passer.

ball moves from one flank into the center, players on the opposite flank will be most successful in opening up the field if they bend their runs away from the person passing them the ball before that person actually receives the ball (Diagram # 7).

The third exercise can evolve into a full training session and is a favorite of Jeff Tipping, NSCAA's Director of Coaching Development. The space for this session is a field of 72 yards in length, marked off into 18-yard segments, and at least 60 yards in width, though the field could be as wide as 70 yards for older players. The basic organization of the session involves both teams having five players

In the second stage of this contest, goals are now scored by the front three scoring on the large goal (Diagram # 10). All players on the field, however, remain limited to their own halves of the field. An obvious benefit here is teaching the front three to play numbers-down, as they would often do in a match in the attacking third of the field. Body shape and angling of runs take on exceptional importance when a group is numbers-down in attack. Learning to make simple yet creative runs in tight spaces will help the front three exploit limited space in match situations.

The third stage of this training allows one player from the back five to come forward to join the front three after the back five have passed the ball across the half-field line (Diagram # 11). The most obvious benefit of this stage for teaching body positioning is in instructing the "runner" from the back five how to bend and use angle runs to stretch the field wide and unbalance the opposing defense. The fourth stage of this session is an 8v8 match with no zonal restrictions, and with the offside lines remaining 18 yards from each goal (does anyone remember this feature of the NASL?).

There are undoubtedly many other ways for coaches to teach players to improve their body shape and the angle of their runs in the flow of play; these are simply three of my favorites. Regardless of how we teach this subject, it is apparent that American players continue to need significant coaching in this aspect of attacking soccer. Coaches will need patience and players will need clear pictures and positive reinforcement from coaches if we are to improve our players' tactical awareness in this essential component of the game.

Receiving?

Be ready, be on your toes, have your feet positioned, be balanced, and know what to do with the ball

Wayne Harrison

*The best players understand the importance of correct preparation of both the feet and the body when receiving the ball. The coach can develop this awareness by using fast footwork drills, coordination drills and speed training. Here, Wayne Harrison offers insight into his **Awareness Training Method.***

Preparing the body, especially the feet, to receive the ball, to be balanced and to know what to do with the ball before receiving it are all among the most important components players must learn to be successful. And all of this must happen before the player even touches the ball.

Coaches work endlessly on what the players do when they have the ball at their feet but seem to ignore what players must do before they get the ball. So many players stand flat-footed with their head down and their body closed that they can't help but make a bad first touch and give the ball away.

Players need to be light on their feet, to be on their toes and ready to receive the ball. They also must have an open body stance so they have directional options, and they must know their decision-making options in advance of the ball before they can move quickly and efficiently.

This is critical for all players, for example, in a game in which they are closed down quickly by an opponent and need to have the correct foot preparation, thought awareness, and body positioning to get out of trouble with the right pass, run or dribble. But coaches spend little time on this important part of training.

Awareness training, fast footwork and coordination training go hand in hand. It is the link of the body and the mind. Coaches need to get the players to the stage where they instinctively "prepare their feet" to move and open up their body, where they see what to do before they receive the ball, where their first touch has an added purpose; not just simply to control the ball, but to control the ball to enable them to make their next movement successfully. This skill is critical whether the player wants to play a one-touch pass, a one-touch into space or one toward a teammate, then a pass (a two-touch pass in other words), or to run with it, dribble with it, cross it, receive and turn with it, or shoot with it.

This type of training is about making the right decisions at the right time while melding the body and mind. The objective of this training is to help the player receive and pass the ball quickly and effectively. This requires excellent footwork to decrease the time it takes to control the ball and maintain possession of it. The awareness method of training deals with the psychological aspect; the footwork is the transference and connection to this, initially without the ball, but ultimately with the ball.

© Thinkstock/iStockphoto/Fluid Illusion

All training is match specific. The Awareness Training Method is based upon developing a balance between ball handling and functional running and sprinting in combination with jumping, stopping and turning.

Changing stride length exercises will be especially important. Repetition of the exercises is important throughout the season on a weekly basis to develop good and correct habits regarding coordination, comfort in running, awareness of the efficient use of arms and legs in running and the synchronization of limbs. With this type of training, the intent is to develop a sixth sense in the players by teaching the players to use the right techniques at the right times.

The application of body coordination and speed work is particularly important in the 6 to 12 age group and will go hand in hand with an increased amount of technical skills training that leads into the Awareness Training Method of development.

General observations on running indicate the player's need to be able to adjust the stride length with ease in any situation and be able to adjust and vary the length of stride as the particular match situation dictates. When running, long strides mean less contact with the ground so the player is more easily knocked off the ball and unbalanced. It is better for the player to adjust the way he/she runs with shorter, quicker strides so there is more contact with the ground, less chance to be knocked off balance, and there is a greater chance that the feet are in the correct position when and where they need to be to receive the ball. Quick feet are essential for a player to be successful at soccer. Learning to use a shorter stride length on starting means the player gets away quicker.

Far too many players play flat-footed; they do not get their feet in place early enough or at all to run, change direction, or particularly to receive the ball and be able to control it with comfort and effectiveness. This training is designed to cure this big problem. It is about improving balance, foot coordination and speed.

Five to ten minutes of every session should be devoted to practicing this footwork at pace, without the ball. Then incorporate the ball as the players' skills improve.

The following routines are examples of circuits of cones that can be laid out to help players develop the aforementioned talent.

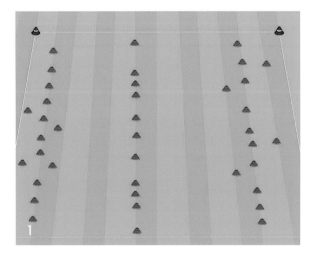

Fast footwork and coordination

To develop the Awareness Training Method in players, the coach must address the positioning of the players' feet before they have their first touch. Hence, the first session plan is focused on fast footwork. As with all the session plans, the session will finish with a small-sided scrimmage to ensure the players get to play with the ball but the focus for this session is work without the ball and before they receive it with their first touch.

Basic foot movement in and out of the cones is the best place to begin because it is easy for the players to have success, and it gives the players an idea of what you (the coach) are trying to teach

them. Below are different set ups designed to achieve this end.

- Three lines of players are in front of one of the lines of cones. The players run through the cones as fast as possible, changing stride lengths (as dictated by the cones) and staying on their toes for fast feet. Finish over the final five yards with a sprint (Diagram # 1).
- Begin with each player going one at a time, one behind the other without putting them under too much pressure. Have them do it slowly to get the rhythm. If they do it quickly, they may miss cones, and that would defeat the object of following the circuit set up and getting each step right.
- **Develop:** Once they are getting good at this, you can have two lanes of the same circuit set up and have a competitive race between two players. They must make sure they do all the foot movements correctly and do not miss any.
- Add new circuits to the session plan. Below are several different ideas you can use to keep the players focused during the session. (Diagram #s 2-5)
- Add a second circuit side by side so it is a race. Design your own circuits as long as the stride lengths and angles of movement are different to force the players to change their feet.
- Five to ten minutes of every session should be devoted to practicing this footwork at pace, without the ball. As their skills improve, add a soccer ball.
- Quick feet are essential for a player to be successful at soccer. Players must step between the cones with quick feet. The following routines are examples of circuits of cones that can be laid out to help the players develop this talent.

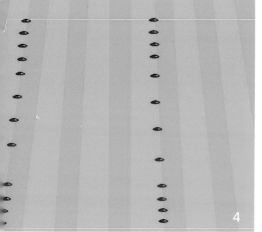

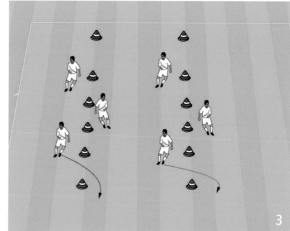

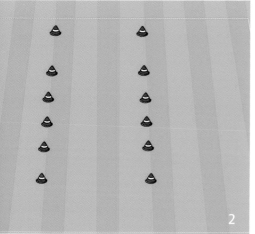

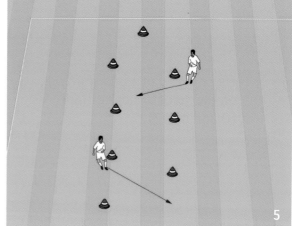

Developing fast footwork emphasizing the importance of the first step (Diagram # 6)

- Lots of quick-standing starts emphasize the importance of the first stride (emphasize also a short step). This is the most important stride as it is the explosive one to move quickly. In this routine, the players practice many of these. A player at each cone. The theme is a quick start and sprint and a quick stop. There must be a pronounced stop between runs as we are working on that explosive start. They all sprint forward one cone on command from the coach and stop quickly. Turn and sprint back together on command. Always run the way you are facing. First group just sprints and stops.
- Sprint forward one cone and stop but face the same way. The next command is to turn quickly and sprint back.
- Sprint to the side by turning at 45 degrees and sprinting.
- Jog backwards then turn at pace and sprint.
- Sprint to any cone; it can be a diagonal run now. Who is last? This is good for spatial awareness too. Where is the free cone?
- Sprint to two cones and stop at the second, sprint to three cones and stop at the third.

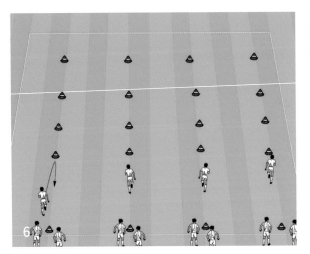

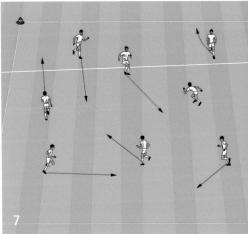

Change direction now but have them stand still at each cone for a fraction of a second so their next first stride is from a standing start.

Free running in a grid working on the quick explosive start (Diagram # 7)

- Let it go free now. Players can move anywhere. This now involves the players using anticipation, decision making, reaction and perception as well as coordination and fast feet to find space to move into without bumping into people.
- Peripheral vision development is starting to be introduced without the ball.
- Usual coach commands can be "start" and "stop" so they are practicing acceleration, deceleration, and lateral movement all in the one exercise.
- You can also use the commands "turn," "jump" (for a header), "check," "sit down," and so on for which they have to do a short sprint after the command then stop on the call "stop."

Variation on free running in a grid (Diagram # 8)

- Introduce balls and cones to the area.
- Players jog with a ball in and out of the cones until the coach commands a sequence of events. Players have to sprint and touch the cones or balls with their hands. Once the sequence is completed, they continue jogging.
- Variations:
  - Ball only once (as above)
  - Cone only once
  - Ball then cone once each

- Ball then cone then ball
- Ball then dribble it 2 yards and stop it then touch a cone
- Jump to head an imaginary ball then touch a cone
- Sit down then up and touch 2 balls

Developing fast feet with a fun game (Diagram # 9)

- Up to 5 players in a group with one of the players in the middle (could be three on the outside in a triangle, for example). Outside

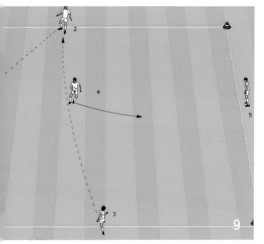

© Thinkstock/iStockphoto/Fluid Illusion

players need to pass the ball to another player. At the same time, try to hit the player in the middle below the knees with the ball.

- This forces the middle player to move their feet quickly and be well balanced and mobile. It is just a fun warm-up game for players to get them moving and focusing on fast feet and coordination.
- (3) Tries to hit (4) in the middle and (4) moves quickly out of the way. (2) Moves on the outside also to get possession of the ball. (2) Can try again to hit (4) or, as in this example, pass the ball to (1) for (1) to try, passing to (5) as a consequence of trying to hit (4).

- The area can be as big or small as you like; smaller means the player in the middle has less time to get out of the way and thus must be quicker. Maybe start up to 10 by 10 yards then reduce it to 5 by 5 yards, as they get better at it.
- Encourage players to pass quickly and accurately, making it hard work for the middle player. Rotate the players.

Team Techniques

Craig Brown
Scottish National Team coach

The former Scottish National Team coach is a frequent clinician at the NSCAA Convention. Here is a session that Coach Brown offered in his most recent visit at the 2009 convention in St. Louis.

Passing

Players are positioned as shown in four squads with a ball at two diagonally opposite groups. The front players take a touch and then play a weighted pass (1) across to each other. They move forward and, on receiving the other ball, pass it (2) to the front player of the facing group then follow their pass to the back of the facing group. The receiving player at the front of the opposite line passes the ball (3) to the new front player in the original starting position. The activity then resumes as before. Later, the exercise can be attempted at increased speed and with one touch only. Then, to encourage left foot passes, the exercise should be done starting at the two other groups.

Shooting

The shooting activity begins the same as the passing exercise above with an exchange of balls (1) from diagonally opposite front players. The next pass to the same front player of the facing line is a lay-off (2) to enable the receiving player to dribble forward (3) and shoot (4).

After shooting, either the player or goalkeeper plays the ball to the side of the squad on his right where other spare balls should be located. This helps to ensure that the exercise flows without interruption. He then joins the end of the opposite squad in the passing activity.

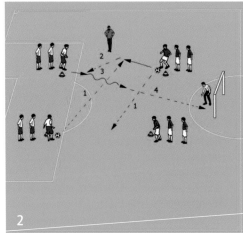

Crossing and Finishing

A further progression moves the activity into a "crossing and finishing" exercise. The first pass is an exchange (1) as above. Then, instead of laying the ball off inside, it is played wide (2) for the receiving

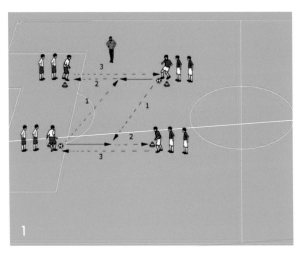

player from the front of the opposite group. Having played the ball out for the "winger," the player who initiated the exercise moves forward as a striker to finish the cross from the other squad. The winger dribbles (3) the ball into a wide position before crossing (4) for the striker's finish (5). After shooting, the player joins the end of the squad straight and opposite from where he started (6).

The new front players take another ball and recommence the activity with the opening diagonal pass.

there is no defined width in the playing area. Play naturally comes back to the focal area – the goal that is being attacked!

The (real) goalkeepers may be introduced from the beginning or after the players have played for a time with 2 defenders in goal. When the 'keepers are in goal the 2 from the goal line move to the cone behind the goal and rest in preparation to be joined by their colleagues who are defending the goal line as the two defenders in the 4v2.

Center Goal Game

The game is played 4v4 with the possession 4 starting at the cone 35 yards from the goal. They play against 2 outfield defenders and two other defenders who must remain on the goal line. The goal is designated with two corner flags as shown in Diagram # 4. In order to control the start of the play, it is a good idea to have all 4 players do an exercise (i.e., 3 press ups) before they start playing. The 4v2 exercise should result in a goal attempt after which all 4 defenders take the ball to their starting cone on the other side of the center goal. The defending team changes the 2 defenders with 2 "goalkeepers." The coaching opportunities in the 4v2 activity are limitless, and it is suggested that

Shaping a Team in a 4-4-2

Activity #1

Set up: 8v4 Cross Running

This is an 8v4 exercise with the middle 4 players playing in both directions. For fitness work, it can be used on a full-sized field, but the penalty box to penalty box distance can be equally demanding and better for teaching.

Instructions

Shown in the Diagram # is the middle team playing north and south with the red team. When the attack is over, either by a successful attack or the defending team winning possession and

team operates with the – white /blue – middle four and their own two strikers against the back four and two strikers of the opposition – the gray team. This numerical superiority should result in a successful attack. On winning the ball, the defenders should attempt to pass back to their goalkeeper or clear up field or out of play. They do not initiate an attack, or counter attack at this time. The coach controls the exercise.

Coaching Points

The defending team, supplemented by the neutral midfield players (who could have changed to their own positions prior to the new movement), now play against the original six. The game proceeds from end to end allowing the coach to make relevant points and introduce attacking and defending set piece arrangements.

playing the ball back to their 'keeper or putting it out of play, the middle 4 players change places at speed as shown, A with C and B with D. The game resumes on the signal of the coach when the change of positions has been undertaken successfully. The blue – whites play with the gray. After a 10-minute period of hard work, the middle 4 players change with one of the other "teams" of 4.

Coaching Points

When playing in the other direction, the middle players change positions – SPRINTING – wide right, A changing with C, and B changing with D. The 'keeper holds the ball until the change is complete.

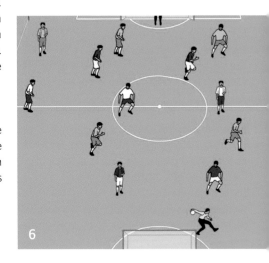

Activity #2

Set up: Shaping a Team In a 4-4-2 Formation

Using the 70-yard field, teams are set up in three colors. On either end there is a back four and two strikers. In addition, there is a middle four playing with both teams.

Instructions

The 10v6 game is started by a throw-out from one goalkeeper who initiates the nature of the play specified by the coach (i.e., up, back, and through with center striker). The back four – reds – of this

Developing Passing Skills – 5v2

Dave Nicholas

Drill: Five players arrange themselves in a circle, approximately 10 yards in diameter. The size of the circle will vary depending on the players' ages and abilities. Within the circle are two defenders. The five players should play one or two-touch passing while attempting to keep the ball away from the two defenders. The offensive player who makes a mistake (i.e., ball out of area, too much pace on the ball, failing to control the ball) changes places with the defender who has been in the middle the longest. The first pass is always free, thus assuring that the drill gets underway.

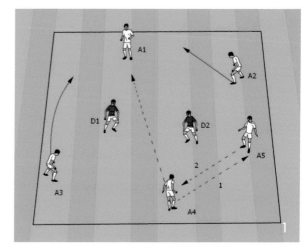

This is a drill that can be used in warm-up, but initially there must be some instruction. Following are some of the coaching points that need to be covered either in initial instruction or in subsequent practices.

Near Support: The players on either side of the player in ball possession are most important. They must be in a correct position for support by the time the player passed to receives the ball.

Do not wait until he receives it! Anticipate! The supporting players should almost be in a square position to support, while being as close as their skills will allow   (Diagram # 1). The proximity of the defender is a consideration in terms of distance. Such positioning will result in a good many square passes, which are possession passes. Possession is one objective of this game.

Far Support: While the near-supporting players are trying to disrupt the defensive arrangement with quick, short passing, the plays on the far side of the circle are looking for the best position "away" from the ball that will allow for a pass to come to them between the two defenders. This drill

builds the ability for the players to combine for the penetrating ball. In Diagram # 1, we see that A1 has opened up for the ball, illustrating this principle.

For this to take place, the 2-3 players in close support are involved with quick, short passes. 3-5 passes will hopefully lead to penetrating pass opportunities.   More passes will allow the two defenders to concentrate their efforts into a small space and deny the penetrating pass. Also, small spaces tend to limit play by the attackers, with play becoming very predictable.   As the longer, penetrating pass is made, the two players closest to the receiver immediately take up their close support once more and try to repeat the same rhythm.

Rhythm: Players ignore half of the field. This is evident in this exercise. If a player is receiving a ball from the right and his back is turned to the left half of the circle, he has cut his options in half. He must "front" the whole circle, opening up his body position so that he can see all of his possible

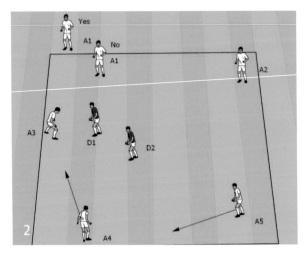

passing outlets (Diagram # 2).

Feinting: In the previous example, the player will probably have to play the ball back to the right, thus being predictable. If he faces the entire circle, he could go left or right. With a quick foot, hip or shoulder movement in one direction (properly timed), he could unbalance the defender and play the ball in either direction.

Technique: Obviously, various aspects of passing are going to emerge. The ball must be played behind a supporting player, and subsequently lost, which means the player making the pass becomes a defender. Passes should be properly weighted. The strength of the pass is a judgment to be made by the passer. Again, if the ball is hit with too much strength (speed), it is the player of the ball who takes the middle of defense. Finally, players should strive for variety in their passing, using different parts of their feet. This lends itself to feinting and quicker foot movement, with resultant greater speed and anticipation in the 5v5 game.

Other Coaching Considerations

- Use players who play around each other (strikers-midfielders; midfielders-backs: right side, central or left-sided players) together in 5v2.
- Make competitions out of the game (most

penetrating passes in groups in five minutes).
- Use keepers as middle two defenders (with rest).
- Limit to one touch.
- Let the game move its location, with no stoppages for switching of attackers, to middle with play continuous but with a limit of a 10-yard radius in effect as the group moves about.

Quick Feet (5v2): Because of the limitation of space in this drill, you will begin to identify the better players on your team just through the use of this drill. Almost without fail, the poorer players will find themselves in the middle, defending against the ball. Part of the problem may lie in technique (poor control on reception or poor control in passing). Also it may be as a result of poor decision-making.

But players must build more time for decision-making by improving their "speed": playing speed in this case. The faster the control can take place, the more time is on hand to decide which passing technique to apply to the particular defensive problem to be overcome. So in control, passing (and dribbling), and quickness of feet is important.

I have a couple of favorite ways of developing this particular area of concern. The first practice has nothing to do with the 5v2 exercises. However it can serve as an indicator of the level and the improvement of quickness, as well as helping indirectly to improve the level of play in the 5v2 exercises.

Start with one foot on the ground, bearing one's weight, and the ball of the other foot touching the top of the soccer ball. With a hopping motion, switch feet. Continue to repeat this movement. Everything must be done on the balls of the feet. Don't let the players get back on their heels. Demand speed with this drill. I have found that high school players should be able to touch the ball 90-120 times in 30 seconds if concentrating. Times can be varied in this drill, with limits of 10-30 seconds. Drilling longer than 30 seconds brings muscle fatigue that spoils the technique.

Continually using this technique in practice will stimulate the neurological pathways necessary to improve quickness.

We can also work on quickness by implementing a condition on the exercise. Every player must touch the ball twice every time it comes to them – no more, no less. After the player touches the ball once, a split-second will elapse before the second touch is possible. Strive to reduce the time between touches. By adding the mandatory second touch, the player's time and space is reduced. A defender now has a split-second longer to close down the player in possession.

The major fault of the players in this exercise is that they kill or stop the ball on the first touch. They must redirect the ball with the first touch, while maintaining the ball with their own space. However, here it is important to remember that feinting comes into play. He can play the ball back to the right (depending on the defender's position) with the inside of the left foot, the outside of the right foot, or he can back heel it.

Decision-Making: In the last example, which part of the foot is used? Which pass is made? Before a player is able to constantly make correct decisions, he must have certain tools at his disposal. We, as coaches, must give the players the opportunity to practice the types of passes being discussed. Without acquiring these skills, players will lack the necessary confidence to quickly enact a decision. Also striving to improve quickness of feet allows players more time to analyze the situation and make the correct choice. (More time sometimes means a fraction of a second; sometimes that is all that is necessary.) We must encourage players to "observe" the field while the ball is in motion. Upon receiving the ball, decision-making is made easier as the brain has already "taken" several pictures and has made a decision as to what is the best pass to make in relation to teammates' positions and the alignment of the defense.

Again, a coach can perhaps spot, in the 5v2 game, those players who have trouble with making the right decision – usually they have trouble with making the right decision – usually they are in the middle! By reviewing the players' options in the 5v2 game, the coach can begin to appreciate their thought process and help the player to make more correct passing decisions.

Changing Decisions: Sometimes a "mind set" is developed by the player, but because of the speed of the game, it is no longer in effect as the ball approaches the player. In any case, even if the decision is changed by circumstances, the player must move to the ball. He can then use a second touch of feinting or both to buy time for a new decision to emerge. By demanding that a player move to the ball, the first rule of ball possession is instilled in 5v2.

Reading the Game: After viewing your team playing the game for several practices, you will see that they all perceive the game differently. Unfortunately, perception is one area of the game that is innate. It can be improved but not as readily as other aspects of the game. By improving the concentration of players and working on their anticipation, a coach can perhaps overcome the lack of a player's innate ability to "read the game."

Concentration: This is an area of the game that can be improved by 80%. To improve concentration, we must give players very specific tasks. In the 5v2 exercises, we can diversify the demands of concentration by imposing different conditions but only one at a time. Examples would be: one-touch passing, two-touch passing, five passing equal one goal, all passes with the outside of the foot, etc. In other words, players are not just playing but improving their concentration levels.

Anticipation: Anticipation is yet another area that can be drastically improved. Experience is certainly a factor in the development of anticipation, but one can begin to train players to Feinting their own movements and look for cues from the opponent's movements.

We have thus far only examined the offensive principles underlying the exercise. However, in order to create a realistic challenge for the five offensive players, the two defensive players must be taught their individual roles and responsibilities, as well as how to function in tandem.

Pressure: As soon as the first "free" pass is made, it is essential that one of the two defenders put pressure on the player in possession. If no pressure is applied, the player in possession and his immediate support should play a series of short passes until a defender is drawn to them. There should be no "diving in" or overcommitment unless there is a guarantee that the ball will be won. In fact, in this particular exercise, defenders should utilize all their tactical plays to win the ball and, if possible, remain on their feet throughout.

In approaching an opponent who has the ball, a defender must be ready to "check" his forward rush and momentum abruptly. Just as his opponent, the defender is trying to leave open various options in order to instill some decision-making in the mind of the attacker, for if he is unsure of the defender's next movement, the game is suddenly more difficult. The defender can fake a tackle, he can follow the pass, or he can anticipate and intercept the pass.

Angle-Distance: Two considerations at this point are:
- How close do we get to the player in possession?
- What is our angle of approach? Distance is dependent on the defender's and/or attacker's ability.

However, the defender should be close enough to tackle in case of poor control by the attacker and close enough to prevent/intercept a forward pass. (This is usually in the region of the 4-6 feet

from the attacker.) In approaching the player, the defender must be examining his position by considering several factors: Where is his covering player located? What is the relative strength of the attacking players, i.e., which are the weaker players? In which direction does he anticipate the play to move? Which are the attackers' good feet? In general, we might state that if the defender approaches the attacker straight on, the attacker has the option of playing to either his right or left. We must therefore teach the defender to "shepard" or "channel" play in the direction we want the play to go.

Cover: What is the role of the second defender? The one thing the defenders are trying to prevent is the "through ball," i.e., the pass played between the two defenders. The second defender therefore should not mark an opponent as he would present a "square/flat" formation (Diagram # 3), and while his partner pressures an opponent, he must provide cover (Diagram # 4).

Again, the question arises; how far behind the pressuring defender and at what angle does the second defender play? In terms of distance, the abilities of the players have to be taken into consideration. In a normal game, the second player should be close enough to intercept/tackle the

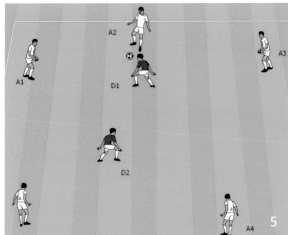

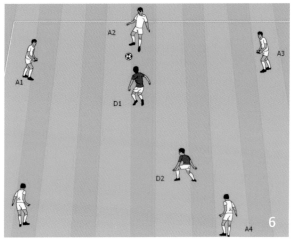

onrushing attacker. In our particular exercise, where there is no attacker dribbling, we still want to train the covering defender to be aware of this aspect of distance. In general, he should be 6-8 feet behind the pressuring defender. In looking at the covering angle, several aspects are considered, but above all, a "through ball" must not be allowed.

In Diagram # 5, the pressuring defender has assumed a straight-on approach. The second defender has overplayed slightly to the left, and the ball will probably be played to A3. In Diagram # 6, the pressuring defender has overplayed to the left, with the covering defender playing slightly to the right. Again, the ball will probably be played to A3. In Diagram # 7, both will again probably be played to A3.

Remember, in stating that the ball will "probably" be played in a certain direction, the game of soccer is a game of "cat and mouse," where the attacker is aware of the defender's ploys and is trying to do other than the expected and vice versa.

The difference between Diagram # 5 and 6 is that C, the pressuring defender, will move with the pass to A3 as he is the nearest defender while in Diagram # 6, the covering defender is closer so he is the one to apply the pressure to A3 with the other defender now assuming the covering role.

Communication: In this exercise, communication is vital, especially in the early stages. Players may eventually play more instinctively once they are more familiar with the tactics of the game and their teammates. However, for the time being, the covering defender, in general, should be "talking" to the pressuring defender.

Note: If you are working on defensive principles, do not play one-touch passing, as defenders will not have time to pressure and cover and therefore the coach will not have the opportunity to correct.

Anticipation: We also now refer back to anticipation. Let us look at Diagram # 7 again (it could apply to 5 & 6 as well). If A2 looks up and sees both players overlapping on the same side, he will probably play A3. But this could be a deliberate ploy by the covering defender. For once A2's head goes down and his foot initiates the backswing motion, the covering defender is already moving toward A3. This early movement by the covering defender should always take place before A3 receives the ball. The difference in time may be all an attacker needs to shoot or play a forward pass in a game. In this case, the covering defender has deliberately set up this play and is anticipating the next move.

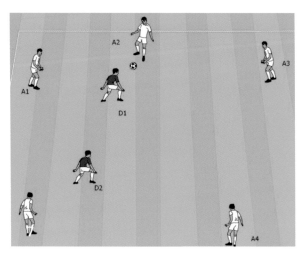

Decision-Making: Just as the defenders are trying to outwit attackers, the opposite is also true. With this in mind, defenders must never challenge with only one option in mind. They must have a back-up plan should the attacker do something unpredictable. As was discussed earlier, a short, but very valuable amount of time passes before a second option can be initiated and enacted. However, the process can be sped up if the back-up option has already been initiated and is ready should the primary option be discarded.

In continuing the last notion, the pressuring defender can reach out with one leg to block a lateral pass by the attacker, but he must be ready

to recoil and assume a good defensive position if the attacker is faking a pass and brings the ball back to the other side.

Other Versions

6v2 (Diagram # 8)

The placement of the players is the same as that for the 5v2 exercises, with the addition of an extra attacking player who plays within the circle of five. The outer players still become defenders should they make an error, but the designated middle attacker stays in for a specific period of time, regardless of errors.

8v3

Seven attackers form a circle (approximately 25 yards across) with three defenders inside the circle, as in the previous exercise.

Note: In any of these exercises, the coach can select the size of the playing area. This size will be determined by the age and ability of the players, plus the specific objective of the exercise.

By adding the "inside" attacker, in both 6v2 and 8v3, the exercises become more position-related.

© Thinkstock/iStockphoto/Fluid Illusion

The inside player can offer constant close support to the player in possession, i.e., play as a midfielder. On the other hand, the player may position himself away from the ball and, playing as a striker, "show" himself at the approximate support angle, but more distant than in the previous example.

Summary: While 5v2 is fun and a simple warm-up, it is an exercise that initially demands that all the principles and subtle tactics involved in the game be taught. Thereafter, the development of the game and the fun involved is as far-reaching as the players' imagination and creativity.

Open Play

Another variation allows a ball that has gone outside the area to be played back into the area with a one-touch pass by the attackers. The defenders can, however, intercept this return pass.

Dribbling

Frans Van Balkom

Millions of people all over the world of different races, backgrounds, and cultures have one thing in common – love and passion for the great game of soccer. Why is this?

One reason is that soccer can be tremendously exciting for players and spectators alike! A player is challenged in many ways during the game. He must make numerous decisions, has to be creative, and can express himself totally when playing. Spectators play the game mentally. The numerous tactical possibilities and the great skills of the players make watching a game, at a high level between two competitive teams, a very exciting affair. Even though soccer is a team sport, the success or failure of the team depends a great deal on the individual performances of the players.

In no other sport are more skills needed and displayed than in soccer. The one skill that excites spectators more than any is the art of dribbling. A dribbler uses individual dribbling skills combined with feinting, coordination, speed, timing, creativity, and surprise when taking on opponents.

One player who is one of the best examples of that and whose dribbling skills and style of play are admired all over the world is the great Argentinean player Diego Maradonna. His dribbling skills were masterfully demonstrated in the '86 Mexico World Cup, especially in Argentina's games versus England and Belgium when he dribbled past their entire defenses and scored. Since the early days of soccer, spectators have been fascinated by great dribblers in action. Players like Northern Ireland's George Best, the Dutch player Johan Cruyff, Brazil's Garrincha, the Spanish player Gento, and the most famous of all, the Englishman Sir Stanley Matthews. Matthews was knighted by the Queen of England for the role he played in promoting soccer and sportsmanship. He still played soccer at the highest professional level until late in his 40s', exciting spectators and players alike with his dazzling runs and great finishing passes.

In soccer, various methods can be used to create an opening to get behind an opponent's defense, but nothing is more exciting than watching a player using dribbling skills to take on defenders to create an opening for himself or set up a scoring opportunity for his teammates.

Dribblers have always played a big part in the attacking game but never before has there been more need and demand for players who have the individual skills and ability to take on defenders than in today's game!

Today's Packed Defenses

The reason for this is that most teams are very defense-oriented and, once ball possession is lost, they fall back into their own half of the field en masse. Once they start to apply pressure, they press the man with the ball and the supporting players around the ball, making it very difficult for attackers to find room for either a pass or a dribble. Under such conditions, playing the ball successfully behind the opponent's defense is almost impossible. Short combinations become more and more difficult once the opponent starts to apply pressure.

A team that has the players with the skills to shield and play the ball around until the opponent's defense is fairly disorganized now needs a player with the ability to take on defenders to create an opening.

© Thinkstock/iStockphoto/Fluid Illusion

are very predictable and lack dribbling and attacking skills.

- Another important factor is that the game at high levels has changed tactically, especially from a defensive point of view. Much more pressure is put on the player with the ball, especially when inside the opponent's defensive half of the field. Being pressured by two or three players at once is normal and opportunities to pass off near the ball are hard to find.

- But, most damaging of all, there are many coaches who only seem to be concerned about having a winning team. In many cases, players are discouraged to take on players or even forbidden to do so, because of the risk of possibly losing the ball.

- Lastly, the lack of knowledge on the coach's part regarding development of skills plays a major role.

In many games, teams that dictate play and attack almost non-stop lose because they cannot find a way to create openings in the opponent's wall of defenders. More and more of their players are pushed up to join the attack and, when ball possession is suddenly lost, the opponent then finds plenty of space to successfully counterattack and sometimes score!

Despite the fact that there is a tremendous need for players who can deal with tight marking defenses, there are hardly any dribblers around. Why is this? A number of reasons can be suggested. Some of them include:

- Dribblers and generally skillful players suffer because of the excessive physical play, which has been brought into the game. Luckily everyone is starting to realize the importance of good skillful players and excessive, vicious play is no longer tolerated.

- The tactical team concept of "play safe, don't lose ball possession," has led to boredom and is partly to blame for creating players who

Principles of Coaching Individual Skills

Volunteer youth coaches cannot be praised enough for the time and effort they spend helping young people in their general soccer development. However, they could achieve much better results, especially in regard to developing individual skills (including dribbling), if they would coach according to the following principles:

- The coach must be able to demonstrate the skills and moves.

- The coach must understand how to develop and build up a dribbling program in combination with other skills.

- Allow/encourage players to use dribbling moves in practice and in games.

- Demand that players be creative and use dribbling moves in games.

- Teach players a number of different dribbling moves. This will help them select the moves they feel confident with and which they can

© Thinkstock/iStockPhoto/Fluid Illusion

Dribbling

In the eyes of opponents, successful dribblers are very unpredictable and are masters of the art of feinting. A player who tries to take on (dribble) opponents each time he has possession of the ball becomes predictable, will frequently lose the ball, and exposes himself to injury.

Successful dribbling actions are enhanced by the support and behavior of the dribbler's teammates. A player in ball possession must have various tactical options when in ball possession because if opponents know that his only option and aim is to dribble, their defensive task becomes much easier.

It is also helpful when a team is able to play the ball around. Good support, near and off the ball, helps a great deal in setting up players to make good dribbling runs. A sudden action of a dribbler catches defenders sometimes unprepared and by switching and changing ball sides frequently, the opponent's defense will be stretched, and become unbalanced and the chance for successful dribbling occurs.

Dribblers who can create openings against tightly packed, high-pressuring defenses are vitally important in today's modern game.

Dribbling Moves

There are a great number of dribbling moves – some very simple, others complex. When using them, they are combined with others skills, such as feinting, shielding, etc. To dribble successfully, speed and timing are important. A player may learn up to 40 different moves but will usually rely on special/favorite moves when under real pressure. One of the most acclaimed dribblers ever, Sir Stanley Matthews, was known for using only one special move. He varied that move a good deal. The move was named after him and is known as the Matthews Move!

use successfully in realistic game situations. A player who has the ability to regularly use two or three different moves successfully in games is a big asset to the team.

- The dribbler must have the full approval of the coach in regard to dribbling.
- The best age to develop skills is 11-14 years old.
- Learning dribbling skills must be part of every player's general basic skill training program.
- Young players who show that they possess the basic fundamentals to become exceptionally good dribblers should be given all possible support and encouragement.
- When developing a player's dribbling skill, the coach must, at the same time, develop the player's tactical knowledge. Once he has mastered the moves, he must learn when and when not to take on players. All dribbling actions must be in the best interest of the team and be part of the team concept. Discipline and tactical awareness are vitally important and must be demanded and taught by the coach.

By allowing players to practice moves regularly, their timing and feeling for when and how to use the moves improve. To become a successful dribbler, continuous practice and repetition of the moves is very important.

Everyone can learn all the moves. Some learn faster than others, usually because of better coordination. But not everyone can be equally successful when using the moves. Personality, character, inborn physical attributes like power and speed, and other factors play a big role in how successful a player will be as a dribbler.

A coach must know and understand each player's ability regarding dribbling. A good team is a combination of various types of players, each playing a big part in the building of a successful team, and the coach must be aware of their strong and weak points in order to get the best possible results.

Move #1 – Push Left, Sprint Right
Dribble ball with right foot toward an oncoming player. Push ball with instep of right foot past left side of opponent (to dribbler's right), and sprint past his right side to collect the ball behind him.

Move #2 – Scissor
There are a number of scissor moves. The Single Scissors, behind, over, and around the ball are some. One of the most effective is the one around the ball and is as follows: Dribble the ball with the right foot toward the opponent's right side. Step with right foot, from the inside, around ball (the right foot passes between the ball and the left leg goes around the front of the ball and is planted on the right side of the ball). Place right foot down and play ball with outside of left foot past opponent's right side. Especially effective when close to opponent as ball is shielded from the opponent.

Move #3 – Double Scissors
Dribble ball with right foot. Take a small step with right foot toward the right, over and past ball.

Take a big step with left foot to left, past the ball, then play ball with outside of the right foot past opponent's left side and accelerate.

Move #4 – Matthews Move
Start this move with a dead ball. Place left foot next to ball and lean left. Lift right foot off the ground and push the ball slightly inside (toward the left) with the inside of the right foot. Then push off with left foot and play ball with opposite of right foot to right past opponent's left and sprint past him to collect ball.

Move #5 – Circle Around Ball
Dribble with right instep. Then circle with right foot from outside (right foot moves to the right, comes back across the front of the ball and back toward the body) around the ball. Play the ball again with instep or outside of right foot and accelerate.

Move #6 – Cap Under Body
Dribble with right foot. Cap ball with instep of right foot back and toward left foot. Then play ball with inside of left foot past right side of opponent and accelerate.

Move #7 – Swivel
Dribble with right foot, feint cap with right foot and drop right shoulder. Then cap ball with left foot back and across body to right side and play ball with inside of right foot to right side past opponent's left side and accelerate.

Move #8 – Pulling the V
Dribble ball with right foot at an angle toward opponent's right side, forcing him to step to his right. Then pull ball with sole of right foot back toward you, pivot on left foot and play ball with inside of right foot to right at an angle past defender's left side and accelerate.

Move #9 – Outside Inside
Start moving at a slow pace. Play ball with right foot alternating with inside – outside. Right foot is kept off the ground and short forward hops are

made on the left foot. Ball is played with inside of foot on outside of the ball and with outside of foot on inside of the ball. After about 10 ball touches, suddenly push outward, or cap ball inward, and push off with left foot accelerating sideways and forward (on angle), beating opponent on right or left side.

Move #10 – Roll Off

Dribble ball with right foot, step with sole of right foot on top of the ball and roll ball outward. Then push the ball with the inside of the right foot across the body to the left. Put right foot down and play ball with outside of left foot to left past defender's right side and accelerate.

Methodical Build-Up of Moves

- At the beginning, all skills are learned with a dead or slow moving ball at a slow pace without any kind of pressure. Each player has one ball.
- Players practice moves at high pace and work in pairs.

Players perform same move at same time, beating each other.

- Two players use one ball. In the beginning,

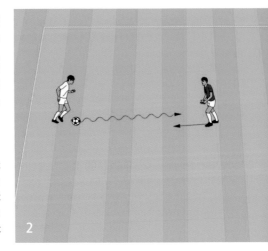

player "B" is passive (does not try to win the ball). Later, "B" is allowed to move forward, put pressure on "A" and attempt to win the ball from "A".

- Four attackers (X), each with a ball and moving in a counterclockwise direction, attack two defenders. At first, defenders are passive (standing); later, they may attempt to win the ball. Defenders, in attempting to win the ball, can only move to the left or right (not forward or backward). A defender who wins the ball changes place with the attacker who lost it.
- Six players – three attackers (X), three defenders (O). A single defender defends along

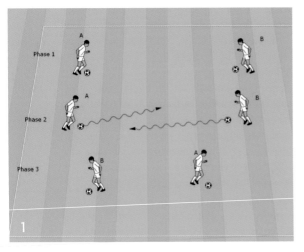

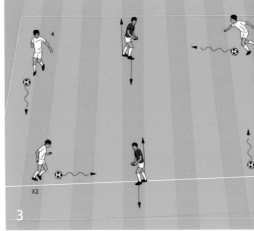

a line (5 yards) against a single attacker. O2 and O3 wait their turn by a cone at either end of the line. After O1 defends against X1, O2 comes in to defend against X2, etc. If the defender wins the ball, he changes places with the attacker. When all three attackers have played 1v1 from one direction, they then attack from the opposite direction.

- Combine dribbling moves with shielding and finishing work in restricted area 30 by 20 yards. 3v3 and a goalie, using goal at one end and a line between cones on other end as targets. Team in attack uses individual actions and combinations to score a goal. When a goal is scored, the attacking team keeps ball possession and attack line between cones. When ball is dribbled over line, attacking team attacks goal again. Defenders must allow attackers 2 yards to come out once they dribble over line.

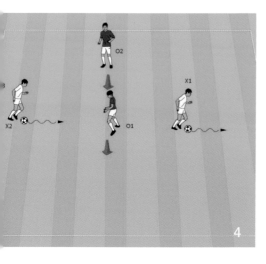

- 3v3 and a neutral player (Y) using two goals in a 30 by 20 yard confined area. Combine dribbling with shielding, feinting, finishing, and counterattack. Neutral player plays with team in ball possession.

- Same as #7 but neutral player plays with team defending.

- One server (Y) and three attackers play vs. four defenders and goalie in confined area of 40 by 30 yards.

Objectives: Attackers – Server dictates pace and controls attack. Attackers work on actions, ball possession, combination play, and finishing. Stressing individual actions is especially important. Objectives: Defense – Winning and keeping ball possession counterattack over line. After 10 minutes, attackers change role with defenders.

- 8v8 playing across one half of field using 2 goals.

7

8

Objectives: Use individual actions in combination with feinting, shielding, finishing, and counterattack. Also, work on slow build-up, switching sides and pressuring.

Once players have learned and are able to use skills at a high pace, all dribbling must be performed in combination with all other skills in realistic game situations. A good deal of time must be spent during practice playing various types of games with and without goals such as 2v2, 2v3, 3v3, 3v4, 4v5, 5v6, 8v8, and finally, players using dribbling skills in regular 11v11 games.

The Art of Crossing

Jeff Tipping
Former Director of Coaching NSCAA

O f the 101 goals scored from open play in the 2006 World Cup, 46 were from restarts and 20 were scored from crosses (16 from the right and four from the left). The FIFA goal breakdown looks like this:

Crosses	20
Combination Play	16
Defense Splitting Passes	18
Solo Efforts	16
Diagonal into the Box	7
Exceptional Finish	11
Defensive Error	3
Rebound	8
Counter Attack	2

It is not surprising with defensive systems becoming ever more sophisticated that attacks frequently come from wide positions that result in a crossed ball.

There are basically two kinds of crosses employed from flank positions. The first, and by far the most common these days, is the so-called "early cross," which is delivered from positions around the corner of the penalty box (Diagram # 1). The second cross is the "goal line cross" delivered from approximately the junction of the goal line and penalty box (Diagram # 2).

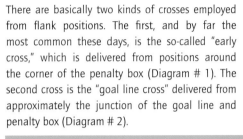

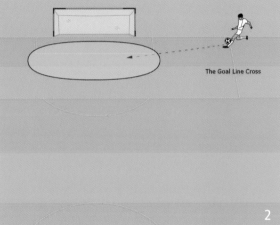

The Goal Line Cross

2

Early Cross

1

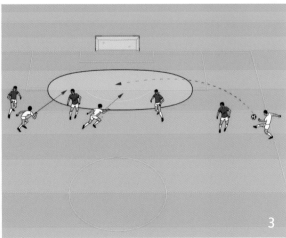

3

The major reason the early cross has become so popular is due to the development of the zonal or "flat" back four. The emergence of the flat back four in the United States and the virtual elimination of the sweeper system has opened up an "offside" space between the backs and the goalkeeper when the back line pushes up maintaining its zonal-shape (Diagram # 3). This is the space exploited by the use of the early cross.

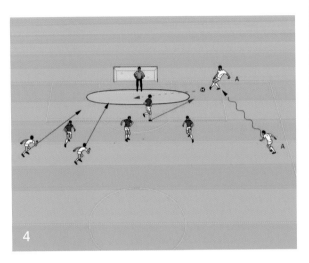

4

Ten or fifteen years ago, a sweeper occupied this space (Diagram # 4) so flank players would frequently dribble to the goal line and cross the ball to the top of the six-yard box or the far post. Without a sweeper occupying that space, the flank player can now cross the ball much earlier. The key tactical elements a flank player must take into account in executing the early cross are:

- A clear space between the back line and the goalkeeper.
- The defenders have been turned and are moving back toward their own goal.
- The flank player is in a position where the ball can be delivered with the necessary "hook." The closer the flank player gets to the goal line, the more difficult it becomes to hook the ball effectively.

- The presence of forwards in and around the penalty box (Diagram # 5).

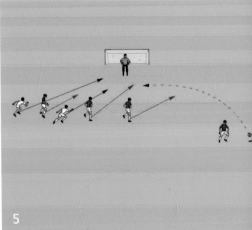

5

Hooking the Ball

Eliminating the goalkeeper is a vital aspect of any cross. Delivering the early cross with spin or "hook" achieves this objective. The key technical aspects in deliver a hooking ball are:

- Striking the ball with an in-to-out motion, i.e., striking the ball on the right side with the right foot, left side with the left foot.
- Striking the ball with the toe up. This contributes significantly to the hooking effect. Toe down will make the ball go straight.
- Hips facing forward. It is quite important that the player does not turn the hips in toward the goal too much as this will tend to deliver a straight ball.

The Delivery

The perfect delivery arrives in the space between the retreating backs, attacking forwards and the goalkeeper with spin. The perfect height is between the player's shin and chest. This makes it almost impossible for the defender to easily clear the ball and easy for the attacker to stoop or dive and head it in. Anything above the chest makes it easier for the defender to flick the ball on into the neutral space. If the defenders and attackers are at the top of the penalty box, the crossing players should deliver the ball to the space between the penalty spot and the six-yard box, commonly called the "second six-yard box." (Diagram # 6).

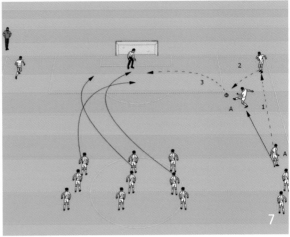

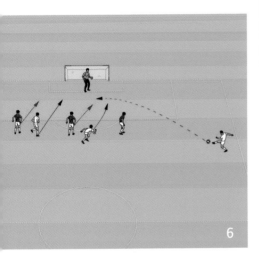

The second six-yard box is, generally, just too far for the goalkeeper to come out for the interception but close enough for a forward to redirect the ball into the goal without significant technical demands. The crossing player is urged to deliver the ball into the space – the emphasis is on the forward to get into space and connect with the ball. If forwards are slow or reticent to get into second six, they need to be forcefully reminded that this is their responsibility.

Coaching Exercises (Diagram # 7)

Organization – Flank players in wide positions with a supply of balls. The rest of the players arrange themselves in three lines. The flank players pass the ball forward (Pass A) to a "rebounder," who plays the ball back to the flank player (Pass B). The central players begin to move forward with bending runs. The rebounder plays ball back slowly,

and the flank player meets and hooks the ball into the vital area (Pass C). It is easier to bend a ball that is rolling toward you, and it is recommended that coaches begin with this artificial condition to ensure spin and to give players success. It is critical that the flank players begin slowly and that the coach carefully observes the practice to make sure the technique is correct.

Stage 2

Adding two defenders and taking away the "rebound" player can develop the practice further. A cone is introduced about 10 yards outside the penalty area and two flags are introduced in the wide areas. In this exercise, the "rebounders" become defenders who begin at the 10-yard cone (Diagram # 8). The central players play the ball to the feet of the flank players and begin their attacking movement by moving in a pre-determined manner. The flank attacker receives the ball and begins dribbling forward. The key condition here is that the defenders cannot retreat past the 10-yard cone until the flank player physically goes past the touchline flag. This will create a delay just long enough to allow a space to open up behind the back two and the crossing player can hook the ball into the vital area (Diagram # 9). Two new

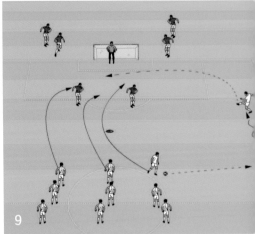

defenders rotate in on every new sequence. Repeat
– To avoid collisions, keep goalkeepers in their own
six-yard box!

This practice is developed into a full 9v9 game in
the NSCAA Advanced National Diploma. To access

details and sites of upcoming Advanced National
diplomas, visit the residential courses section of the
website or call the National Office.

Cultivating Talent in Young American Soccer

Players between the ages of 7 and 13

Horst Wein

Here are some thought provoking ideas for running a youth soccer program:

1. Consider the exclusive use of a number 4 ball for all players aged between 8 and 13 years in their training sessions and competitions. The WHO (World Health Organization) also demands it for health reasons, and the world of soccer for facilitating the young children to acquire technical skills and achieve a superior tactical learning.

2. Use the many variants of Mini Soccer with 4 goals (instead of attacking one centralized goal, the ball has to be kicked in one of two goals, separated by no less than 12 yards) with the purpose of systematically stimulating the perception skills, a capacity that has to be considered as a base for correct decision-making and execution of technique.

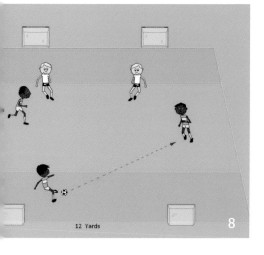

12 Yards

8

3. Regularly organize different competitions, tailor-made to the mental and physical capacities of the young kids, such as a Soccer Triathlon, 3-on-3 or 4-on-4, a Mini Soccer Pentathlon, a Goalkeeper Decathlon, a Decathlon for Soccer Players or a Heptathlon). To be able to stimulate the game intelligence of our young players, it is necessary to offer them more than a single official competition in one season. Competing in the same season in several competitions that are different from the traditional ones will improve their capacity of adaptation and their flexibility of the brain. In all these competitions, the participation, the enjoyment, the recreation and fun are more important aspects than winning.

4. For children 10 and 11 years old, the season should be divided in two parts. In the first half of the season, a competition is played without giving points away or establishing a classification table. In the second part of the season, a championship is played with 3 periods of 15 minutes and an interval of only 5 minutes in which the coaches may exchange their commentaries with the players. Coaching from the sideline is forbidden.

5. Allow substitutions in all youth competitions as happens in basketball, volleyball, or hockey, i.e., the same player may be taken off and return as often as the coach prefers. The "rolling substitution" generates within the group of players a much better coexistence, avoids overloads, and furthermore allows better communication as the coach may take a player

off the field to give him any technical-tactical advice.

6. In order to cultivate important but often forgotten aspects like "fair-play", sport ethics and perfect behavior toward the opponents, the teammates and the referee, each team receives the opportunity to present to the referee after the end of the game one golden card with the name of a player written on it. This player always has to be named from the opposite side. In case nobody has demonstrated fine sportsmanship, no card is handed to the referee. At the end of each season, the player who received the most cards from the opponents is considered sportsman of the season.

7. To lessen the percentage of the anaerobic effort in a game played on the full field, convince the authorities to prohibit 11-a-side competitions for children between 7 and 13 years. Competitions with 3, then 7 and later 8 players on the field increases its dimensions the same way as the fewer players in a team increase technically, tactically, in their perception and understanding of the game.

8. Publish and diffuse sufficient teaching information to make sure that in each preparatory session the 7- to 13-year-old players are exposed for half an hour to multipurpose motor activities that improve their level of coordination.

9. Allow in all youth competitions between 8- and 13-year-old players a rule that states that a team that is losing with a difference of 4 goals (0:4, 1:5, 2:6, etc.) can introduce one additional player into the game to force the winning team to continue to try hard and put their best efforts in.

10. Regularly supervise the development work carried by the Soccer Schools of Initiation with

the purpose of protecting the young talents through the systematic application of the proposals listed here.

11. Convince the teachers of the importance of using soccer activities as an educational instrument to improve the children's technical, tactical, visual, cognitive, and physical capacities.

•   Healthful habits toward the practice of sport,

thus maintaining and improving their health.

- Teaching them to efficiently occupy their leisure time with sport activities, offering enjoyment and pleasure.
- Contributing to the development of the personality of each one of the young players.

12. Consider as recommended schools only those Soccer Schools of Invitation of the State Soccer Federation which apply the philosophy and the recommendations exposed here. If they fulfill the norms imposed by a certification committee, they will have the right to use the badge of the Federation near the name of the school. Through this procedure, the selected schools attract the interest of the parents and the public and will benefit from:

- Free insurance
- Discounts in the acquisition of sport material
- Free access to special coaching seminars or days organized by the federation for their teachers
- Help in connecting with other institutions (interchanges)
- Help in the organization of sport or cultural events, etc.
- Help with medical issues to detect any potential risk for the player's health

13. Create a manual that orients the teachers on how to periodically communicate with the parents and how to collaborate in the important task to support their ethical, moral, physical, and intellectual growth, and leave aside the material interests that the consumer society wants to impose on the world of youth soccer.

14. A teacher of young talents who always wins with his or her team will lose at the end. So what? He or she has done everything to assure his or her own professional future and not the one of his or her talented disciples. In youth soccer, we say:

" To win one cup less means frequently to win more than a promising talent".

© Thinkstock/Stockphoto/Fluid Illusion

Chapter 2:
Tactics

The 1v1 Situation: The Foundation

Raffaele Tomarchio

Raffaele Tomarchio is the resident coach at www. ICoachSoccer.ca. This article was published in the January-February 2010 Soccer Journal.

It is no secret that one of the most important situations during a soccer game is the 1v1 match-up. During the course of a game, attackers have to decide whether to beat an opponent by dribbling past him or her or passing the ball, while defenders try to prevent opponents from getting near the goal and scoring. To be effective in the 1v1 situation, each player must have a good overall technical and tactical understanding. In many cases, the outcome of a game is a direct result of the various 1v1 opportunities the team is able to win.

During the exercise of 1v1, each player can experience, analyze and solve individual tactical situations while attacking and defending. Furthermore, players come to understand the level of their ability, both what they do well and where they need work.

On the attacking side, players who have good dribbling abilities combined with quickness and a combination of moves and fakes will be successful in beating an opponent. On the defending side, good speed, determination and physical ability are the key ingredients for good defense. What follows is a series of 1v1 exercises that reflect the basic 1v1 situations. These are presented in a "guided discovery" teaching style.

General guidelines

Attacking after the ball is won

What does a player do when receiving the ball in these situations?
- Back to the opponent's goal
  - Pass back
  - Turn to attack defender

- Facing the opponent's goal
  - Beat the defender
  - Get into position to shoot

- In front of the goalkeeper
  - Score with a direct shot on goal
  - Dribble to the keeper to score a goal

Defending after the ball is lost

What does a player do after losing the ball?
- When chasing the opponent
  - Adjust running speed to the speed of attack
  - Time the tackle
- When trying to win the ball
  - Delay the attack
  - Channel the opponent wide
  - Time the tackle

1v1 with two goals and two keepers with the attacker in possession (Diagram # 1)

Attacker's Objectives
- Beat the defender for shot on goal

Defender's Objectives
- Slow down the attacker and channel outside

Organization
- Groups of six alternating attacking and defending. In a 15 by 20-yard grid, an attacker in possession of the ball takes on a defender and tries to score a goal. The attacker must cross the midline to score.

Attacker's Solutions
- Look for the direct path to the goal
- If the defender gives space, shoot
- Try to unbalance the defender to get a shot

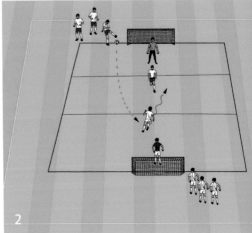

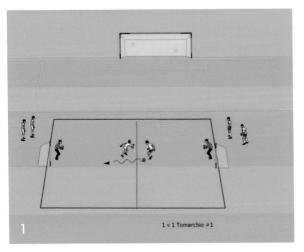

1 v 1 Tomarchio #1

Defender's Solutions
- Get in a line between the ball and the goal
- Assume a good defensive position – sideways on
- Adjust to the speed of the attacker
- Think: Can I win the ball?
- Think: If the attacker shoots, can I block it?

Coaching Points
- The coach asks the players: What went right? What went wrong? Why? What adjustments must be made?

1v1 with goals and two keepers (Diagram #2)

Attacker's Objectives
- After receiving the ball, the attacker attacks the goal frontally looking for a shot

Defender's Objectives
- Prevent the shot on goal
- Channel the attacker to the outside

Organization
- Groups of 6 to 8 players alternating attacking and defending. In a 15 by 20-yard grid divided into thirds, the defender kicks the ball to the attacker, who, after receiving the ball, will attempt to score a goal. If the defender wins the ball, he attacks the goal. **Variation:** The defender can win the ball only in the mid third.

Attacker's Solutions
- Good first touch and control the ball
- Go straight at the goal
- Use a change of pace and change of direction to beat the defender
- Before taking a shot on goal, look at the keeper

Defender's Solutions
- Meet the attacker as far from the goal as possible
- Adjust your speed to the attackers speed
- Channel the attacker to the side by using proper body position – sideways on
- Look for a bad touch from the attacker

Coaching Points
- What went right? What went wrong? Why? What adjustments need to be made?

1v1 with two goals and two keepers with the attackers back to goal (Diagram #3)

Attacker's Objectives
* After receiving the ball from his defensive goalkeeper with his/her back to goal; the attacker tries to turn the defender and shoot on goal

Defender's Objectives
* Prevent the attacker from turning and channel the attacker to the side line

Organization
* A group of 6 to 8 players alternating between the attack and the defense. In a 15 by 20-yard grid, the goalkeeper throws the ball to the attacker, who will try to turn and shoot

Attacker's Solutions
* Check back to the ball to create space and attack the ball
* If the defender is not close, turn and attack the goal
* If the defender is closing down the attacker, shield the ball and try to turn the defender for a shot on goal
* Before the shot, look at the keeper

Defender's Solutions
* Do not be so tight that you can be turned – do not allow turn
* Can you win the ball?
* Channel the attacker wide

Coaching Points
* The coach asks the players: What went right? What went wrong? Why?
* What adjustments are needed?

1v1 on two small goals (Diagram # 4)

Attacker's Objectives
* Beat the defender and score goals

Defender's Objectives
* Prevent shots on goal
* Channel attacker away from the goal

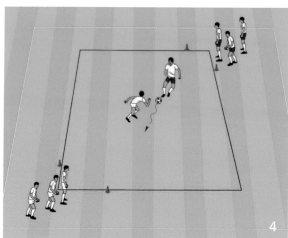

4

Organization
* Two groups in pairs alternating attacking and defending. In a 15 by 15-yard grid, the player with the ball has 30 seconds to beat the defender. If the defender wins the ball, he/she has what is left of the 30 seconds to score.

3

Attacker's Solutions
- Quick, tight ball control
- Go straight at the defender
- Use change of direction and body feints to get around the defender
- Shield the ball if necessary

Defender's Solutions
- Meet the attacker as far from goal as possible
- Adjust your speed to the attacker's speed
- Channel the attacker wide by moving sideways on body position
- Win the ball and attack

Coaching Points
- The coach asks the players: What went right? What went wrong? Why?
- What adjustments are needed?

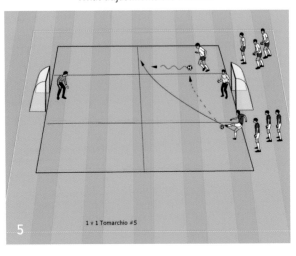

1 v 1 Tomarchio #5

1v1 toward a goal and keeper working on the recovery run (Diagram # 5)

Attacker's Objectives
- After receiving the ball, use a good first touch and attack the goal for a shot

Defender's Objectives
- Put pressure on the attacker by running to get goal side and in a good defensive position

Organization
- Two groups of equal numbers alternating between attacking and defending. In a 30 by 30-yard grid divided into three zones, the defender passes the ball to the attacker. The defender will recover to a goal side position and attempt to prevent the shot. The attacker can shoot only when he/she passes the middle line.

Attacker's Solutions
- Quick control of the ball with a good first touch
- Go straight at the goal
- Stay in front of the defender with good body position
- Look at the keeper

Defender's Solutions
- Run quickly at the attacker using an angle that will enable you to get into position between the attacker and goal
- Channel attacker outside
- Prevent the shot
- Tackle the ball

Coaching Points
- The coach asks the players: What went right? What went wrong? Why?
- What adjustments must be made?

1v1 with a frontal approach to a goal and keeper (Diagram # 6)

Attacker's Objectives
- Beat the defender
- Shot on goal

Defender's Objectives
- Delay the attacker
- Channel the attacker wide
- Block the shot
- Win the ball

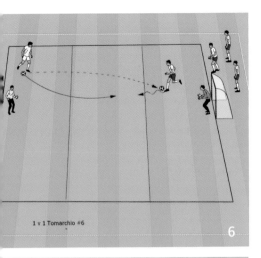

1 v 1 Tomarchio #6

6

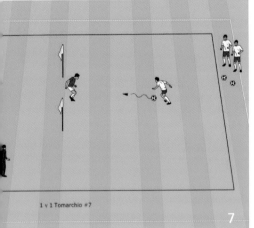

1 v 1 Tomarchio #7

7

Organization

- There are two groups of equal numbers in a 20 by 20-yard grid split into three zones as shown with a goal with keeper on both sides. The defender passes the ball to the attacker who is in the third zone. The defender runs out to prevent a shot. **Variation:** If the defender wins the ball, he can attack the other goal.

Attacker's Solutions

- Quick control of the ball with a good first touch
- Go straight to goal
- Look at the keeper
- Take a shot – even while under pressure

Defender's Solutions

- Go quickly toward the attacker sideways
- Channel the attacker wide
- Prevent the attacker from getting into the shooting zone
- Prevent the attacker from shooting

Coaching Points

- The coach asks the players: What went right? What went wrong? Why?
- What adjustments need to be made?

1v1 through the gate for shot on goal (Diagram # 7)

Attacker's Objectives

- Get through the gate for a shot on goal

Defender's Objectives

- Channel attacker away from gate
- Prevent the attacker from getting through the gate
- Prevent a shot

Organization

- In a 20 by 20-yard grid, an attacker in possession of the ball tries to go through a 10-yard gate that is guarded by a defender. If the attacker gets through, he/she can shoot.

Attacker's Solutions

- Draw the defender away from the gate
- Get through the gate
- Shoot on goal

Defender's Solutions

- Channel the attacker away from the gate
- Prevent the attacker from going through the gate
- Prevent a shot

Coaching Points

- The coach asks the players: What went right? What went wrong? Why?
- What adjustments are needed?

© Thinkstock/iStockphoto/Flup Illusion

Many other exercises can improve the 1v1 confrontation. The coach should make it competitive, fun and informative. The 1v1 situation should be part of the development plan at the early ages.

Encourage experimentation and creativity with young players. The defensive part of the exercise is equally important and should be introduced early. Enable the players to discover the different problems they face by asking questions and allowing the players to find solutions.

General points of methodology and organization
- From easy to more difficult tasks
- From known to unknown
- From simple to complex
- Lots of repetition and variations

General coaching points for attackers
- Go straight at the defender
- Be in control of the ball
- Unbalance the defender with feints
- Change direction
- Change speed
- Have a positive attitude

General coaching points for defenders
- Close the space between you and the attacker
- Slow down the attacker
- Get the attackers head down
- Channel the attacker wide
- Wait for the right moment to tackle

Training the 2v1 Situation

Raffaele Tomarchio

Making the 2v1 situation a regular staple of any development program for the age groups of 8-12. This is part one of a two-part series on the 2v1. This was originally published on Icoachsoccer.ca and in the March-April 2010 Soccer Journal.

Introduction

The 2v1 situation represents the basic starting point in developing team play. Compared to the 1v1, it is a more complex situation with different elements for players to consider.

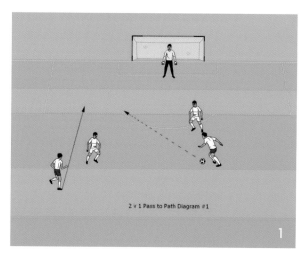

2 v 1 Pass to Path Diagram #1

The 1v1	The 2v1
• Myself (The Player)	• Myself (The Player)
• The Ball	• The Ball
• The Opponent	• The Opponent
	• The Teammate

From the tactical point of view, this situation helps in the development of two important individual tactical elements: **passing and support**.

When **passing to Man**, the player receiving the ball does not make any movement to space, communicating that he/she wants the ball at their feet.

When **passing to Space**, the player receiving the ball makes a movement to the space, communicating to the player in possession of the ball his/her intention to receive the ball in his/her running path so that he/she can gain proper control of it. A good pass must be accurate, with good pace and correct timing.

Passing (Diagram # 1 and 2)

Passing is a technique used by two or more players to transmit the ball from one player to another. Although there are different ways to pass the ball, there are two types of passing:

- Passing to Man
- Passing to Space

Support

Support is the ability of players to move and get in the correct position to receive the ball. Knowing how to pass the ball and putting yourself in a good position to receive it goes hand in hand for a successful attacking play. In 2v1 situations, players are stimulated in solving the various problems presented by the activity and to make the correct decisions to solve them.

Player's Decision Making in the 2v1 Situation

Player with the ball	Player without the ball
• When to pass	• When to get open and support
• Where to pass (feet or space)	• Where to get open to support
• How to pass the ball (trajectory)	• How to get open to support

2v1 Training

When designing and executing training exercises, the coach must follow the proper coaching methodology by:

- **Identifying the exercise objective.**
  The exercise should be designed with a clear objective in mind (see list below).
- **Setting up the exercise.**
  The coach, as a facilitator, should set up the area where the exercise is going to take place.
- **Explain the exercise to the players (demo).**
  Players need to understand what the requirements and rules of the exercise are. Explanations should be simple and concise, with a possible demonstration.
- **Allow enough time to practice the exercise (repetitions).**
  Players must have enough time to practice a particular exercise (many repetitions).
- **Using proper progressions.**
  From simple to complex, time pressure, handicaps.
- **Observe and Correct.**
  Take time to observe the activities and provide the proper correction through "demos."
- **Evaluating the exercise.**
  See what works ,and make proper adjustments if needed.

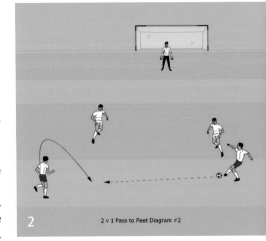

2   2 v 1 Pass to Feet Diagram #2

2v1 for a shot in front of the goal (Diagram # 3)

Area: 15x20
Age group: U8-U12

- Players take turns on attacking a goal defended by two players, a keeper and one defender.
- Defender's starting position is in the middle.
- Players rotate roles.

Progression: Players need to take a shot within a time limit.

2v1 Objectives Progression	Progression
• 2v1 for shot on goal	• Limiting the defender time
• 2v1 to win space	• Defender inside the playing space
• 2v1 to keep possession	• Defender with a handicap

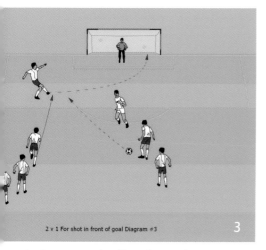

2 v 1 For shot in front of goal Diagram #3

3

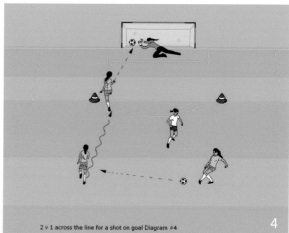

2 v 1 across the line for a shot on goal Diagram #4

4

2v1 across the line for a shot on goal (Diagram # 4)

Area: 15x20
Age group: U8-U12

- Pairs take turns on attacking a 12-yard wide goal line with a defender. If they beat the defender, they can take a shot on goal.
- Attackers score one point if they are able to cross the line and keep control of the ball.
- One point is also earned by scoring a goal.
- The line defender cannot move forward or backwards, but can move sideways. Defending pair changes only if they win the ball.

Which pair can score more goals in 10 minutes?

2v1 + 2v1 for shot on goal (Diagram # 5)

Area: 15x20
Age group: U8-U12

- This is a continuous game.
- Two players attack a goal defended by a keeper and a defender.
- The defenders starting position is in the middle of the field.

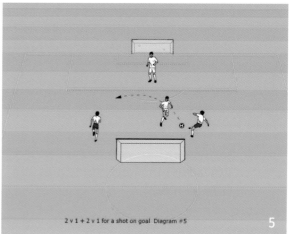

2 v 1 + 2 v 1 for a shot on goal Diagram #5

5

- After each attack, teams change roles.

Which team can score more goals in 10 minutes?

2v1 to win space across the line – Defender limited on the line (Diagram # 6)

Area: 15x20
Age group: U8-U12

- 2 teams of 2 players take turns attacking a 12-yard wide goal with a defender.
- Attackers score one point if they dribble across

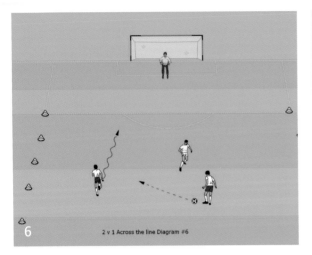

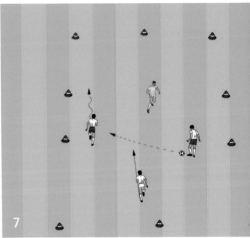

the line while keeping control of the ball.
- The defender cannot move forward or backward, but can move sideways. Teams take turns on attacking and defending.

Who can score more points in 10 attacks?

Progression: Make the goal smaller

2v1 across the line – time pressure (Diagram # 7)

Area: 15x20
Age group: U8-U12

- 2 teams of 2 players take turns on attacking a 12-yard wide goal with a defender.
- Another defender is placed 5 yards behind the attacking team and will try to win the ball as soon as play starts.
- Attackers score one point if they dribble across the line keeping control of the ball.
- The line defender cannot move forward or backwards, but can move sideways. Teams take turns attacking and defending.

Who can score more points in 10 attacks ?

2v1+2v1 across the line (Diagram # 8)

Area: 15x20
Age group: U8-U12

- 2 teams of 2 players take turns on attacking two 12-yard wide goal with defenders.
- Attackers score one point if they dribble across the line while keeping control of the ball.
- Defenders cannot move forward or backwards, but can move sideways. Teams take turns on attacking and defending.

Who can score more points in 3 minutes ?

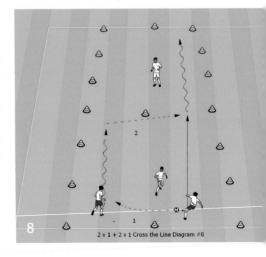

2 v 1 + 2 v 1 Cross the Line Diagram #8

2v1 to keep possession – 2v1 in a square (Diagram # 9)

Area: 15x15
Age group: U8-U12

- Two teams of 2 players each play against each other.
- The team in possession plays against one player from the other team inside a 10x10 grid, while the second player waits outside.
- How many consecutive passes can they complete before the ball is intercepted or goes out of the grid?
- After one try each, the team with most passes scores a point.

First team to score 5 points wins.

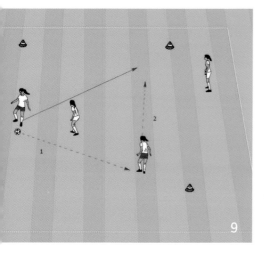

2v1 grid to grid (Diagram # 10)

Area: 15x30
Age group: U8-U12

- Inside 2 grids placed next to each other, two teams play two 2v1 games. The objective is for one team to pass the ball to the other team in the other grid.
- Each pass = one point.
- Change roles

Progression

Before passing the ball to the other grid, they must complete at least 3 passes in their own grid. Now, I would like to take a look at the coaching points of the 2v1 situations. In order to help our players, we must know the technical and tactical elements of each situation, recognize mistakes players make and create training sessions to correct them. These are the standard 2v1 situations that players encounter during a game:

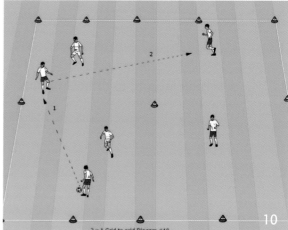

2 v 1 Grid to grid Diagam #10

2v1 for a shot on goal or to win space (Diagram # 11)

The elements of the 2v1 are:
- The ball carrier
- The supporting player
- The defender

In these situations, the player in possession of the ball is the one with the decision making power. In pursuing the goal of this exercise, this player has to decide whether to dribble the ball past the defender, use the help of the supporting player in order to get in a shooting position, or advance the ball.

Option #2: Pass to supporting player

Option #1: Dribble past defender

11

12

2 v 1 Dribble Diagram #12

Decision making to dribble or pass

The ball carrier will decide whether to dribble or pass the ball based on the position of the defender.

To Dribble (Diagram #12)

If the defender takes a central position in respect to the ball carrier and supporting player, then the ball carrier will continue to dribble the ball toward the available open space, and eventually (by changing pace to advance the ball past the defender) to deliver a shot on goal.

Coaching Points to Dribble
- Ball close to body
- Change of pace

To Pass to the Supporting Player (Diagram #13)

If the defender comes out and challenges the ball carrier by closing down the space in front, then the logical option is to pass the ball to the supporting player to advance the ball to the shooting zone for a shot on goal.

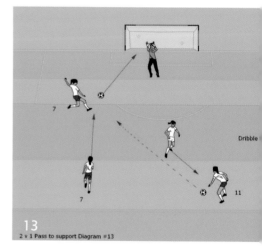

13

2 v 1 Pass to support Diagram #13

Coaching Points to Pass to a Supporting Player
Ball Carrier
- Pace on the ball
- Pass to the receiving player's path
- Time of the pass

Supporting Player
- Receives ball with the foot farthest away from the ball
- First touch to set up shot

Common errors players will make

Players are too close (Diagram #14)

Many times, especially in the younger age groups, the players' starting position is too close to each other, making the defender's job to win the ball easier.

Coaching Points

- The starting position of both players needs to be as wide as the grid allows
- After the start, the players should maintain distance apart from each other

2 v 1 Supporting Player Position - Incorrect - Player is in offside position Diagram #15   **15**

mon Errors: Players are too close Diagram #14   **14**

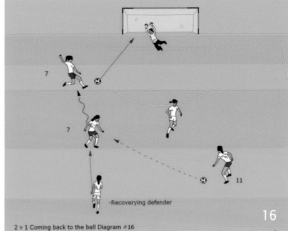

2 v 1 Coming back to the ball Diagram #16   **16**

Supporting Player Position

Even though the supporting player has the correct width in relation to the ball carrier, sometimes his supporting angle might be wrong. In **Diagram #15** with #11 in possession of the ball, #7 takes a forward position in relation to #11. This creates a problem for #11 because the defender #2 may intercept.

In Diagram #16, #7, aligns his position with the ball, giving #11 a better passing angle #7 can now run to it and use the momentum to run past a possible recovery attempt by #2.

Coaching Points

- Supporting player to stay wide with the line of the ball
- Supporting player to time his/her run

Supporting player receiving the ball (Diagram #17)

When receiving the ball, the supporting player must receive it with the foot farthest away from the ball. Many times, especially when the ball comes from the right side, players tend to use their "comfortable" right foot instead of their left foot, making the control of the ball difficult, as the ball can roll over their foot, hence losing possession. When using the opposite foot, the inside part of the foot is used, which makes it easier to control the ball.

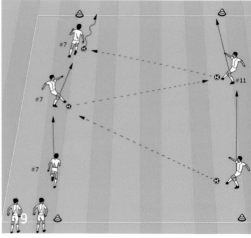

The supporting player receiving the ball must receive the ball with the foot farthest from the ball. In this case, the left foot.

17

Corrective Exercises

2v.0 Dribble and Pass (Diagram #18)

Area : 15x20
Age group: U8-U12

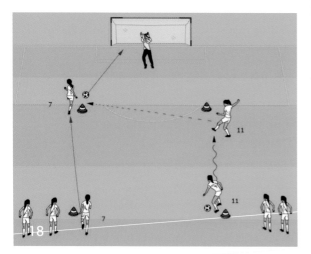

18

#11 dribbles the ball to the cone. When he reaches the cone, he will pass the ball into #7's running path then change roles.

Coaching Points
* Keep ball close to body
* Players to stay wide
* Time of the pass
* Quality of the pass
* Supporting player to receive with the foot farthest away from the ball
* Quality of the shot

2v0 Pass to Path (Diagram #19)

Area : 15x20
Age group: U8-U12

19

#11 starts play by passing the ball to #7's running path. #7 receives the ball and does the same as #11.

Coaching Points
* Players to stay wide
* Quality of the pass
* Time of the pass
* Supporting player to receive with the foot farthest away from the ball
* Quality of the shot

2v2

Jim Lennox
NSCAA Director of Coaching Emeritus Hartwick College

Jim Lennox, director emeritus of the NSCAA Coaching Academy, presented the following session to the NSCAA coaching staff at its in-service program held at Nova Southeastern University in January of 1999.

The following are ways in which the coach can make play more predictable in coaching 2v2 exercises. I will describe the objective of injecting the variable into the coaching scheme and show, by example, expected outcomes for the players involved.

I.   2v2 on 20 x 35-40-yard field to small goals

An obvious means for the two attackers is to try and spread the two defenders so that the first attacker can penetrate on a line or to a goal via the dribble (Diagram # 1). Failing that, the goal here is for the team with the ball to penetrate through the use of combination play. A through pass (if defenders are

square, Diagram # 2) might be "on" as might a 1-2 or wall-pass — if the defender can be committed by the first attacker and the second attacker can support at the proper angle and distance. If the first attacker is pressured and turned, that player can initiate a takeover maneuver with the second attacker or under the same circumstance, the

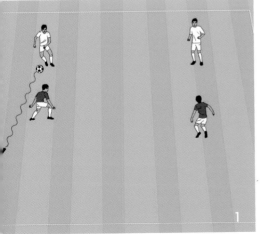

4

When the space is a longer rectangle, the coach is emphasizing vertical play. The attackers attempt to use the space behind the defenders with long through passes or passes over the top. The defenders must deal with tracking the attacker's vertical play. Fitness is also an objective here (Diagram # 5).

second attacker can make an overlapping run to relieve pressure (Diagram # 3). The coaching objective for the two defenders is to coordinate their movement to pressure the ball and cover the space.

The 20 x 35-40-yard space is ideal in that it allows the coach to train the players on both sides of the ball. The 40-yard length allows for penetration while the 20-yard width encourages the defenders to "squeeze" the attackers and win the ball for themselves (Diagram # 4).

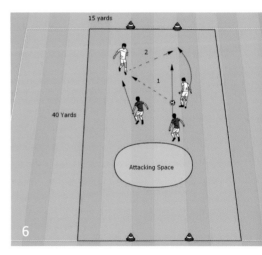

15 yards

40 Yards

Attacking Space

6

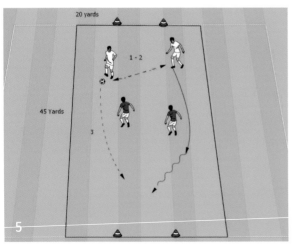

20 yards

45 Yards

1 - 2

3

5

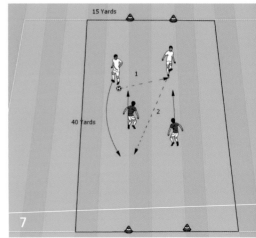

15 Yards

40 Yards

1

2

7

III.   2v2 on 15 x 40-yard field to small goals

Here the objective is for the attacking team to possess the ball, draw the defense to them and then penetrate to goal. Patience with the ball is critical here and if penetration is not "on," then the attacking team must play the ball back to a supporting teammate (Diagram # 6) and seek to establish space behind the defenders for the attack to take place in. The defending team must seek to high pressure the ball in this situation (Diagram # 7).

V.   2v2 on 35 x 40-yard field to small goals

Add two servers on the width of the field to play with the team in possession of the ball seeking to play the ball wide where the servers are limited to two touches. They seek to serve balls into the area for strikes on goal (headers, volleys). Defenders will work on defensive heading (Diagram # 9).

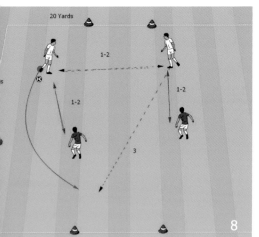

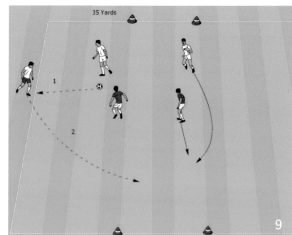

IV.   2v2 on 20 x 30-yard field to small goals

Here, with the field shorter, the emphasis is on tight technical play. A lot of lateral play with more square passes for possession due to the limited space behind the defenders. Lateral 1-2 movements and takeovers will dominate the combination play. The idea of the first attacker will be to find the right moment to play flighted balls behind the defense for the supporting attacker to run onto and collect or shoot at goal. Defenders must cope with lateral play, keep pressure on the ball and cover their attempts to deny penetration (Diagram # 8).

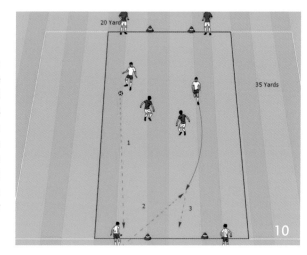

VI.   2v2 on 20 x 35-yard field to small
        goals

In the next exercise, position target players at
either side of the goal on each end of the fields for
the attacking team to use. Two attacking players
seek to play balls to target players (limited two
touches) at end of the field who then play balls
to either attacker for shots on goal. Defenders
attempt to track the runs, not ball watch and deny
penetration (Diagram # 10).

VII.   2v2 on 20 x 35-yard field to small
        goals

In this exercise, instead of using target players,
position the support players on the sidelines.
Because the support players are on the sidelines,
the coach is emphasizing possession by the two
attackers. From possession, there will be opportunities
to achieve penetration (Diagram #11). Again, the
defenders must pressure and cover each other as
they deny penetration.

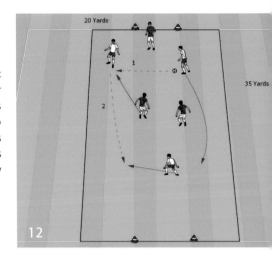

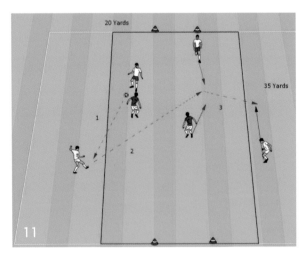

VIII.   2v2 on 20 x 35-yard field to small
        goals

In this exercise of 2v2, we add target players for
each team into the field. Once the ball is won, the

designated target player plays in advance of the
ball. He or she does not try to score or defend. Both
teams of two will have their own target player. The
coach can limit target players to two touches.

The two attackers use their target as they did in
practice number V. This is basically a recreation of
midfield players playing to the feet of front players,
but playing on the field, not in an advanced
position near the goals (Diagram # 12). As with all
these exercises, defenders try to pressure and deny
penetration.

IX.   2v2 on 20 x 35-yard field to small
        goals

The supporting player now plays behind the two
attacking players and is limited to two-touch play.
Each team has a support player. The objective is to
possess the ball 3v2. The support player becomes
the goalkeeper when the team is not in possession
of the ball. The object of the support player is to
seek through passes in combination play and also
to change the point of attack. Defensively, the
support player cannot run in advance of the ball or
try to win the ball (Diagram # 13). Defenders must
perform their function of denying penetration and
watch for opportunities to pressure the support
player.

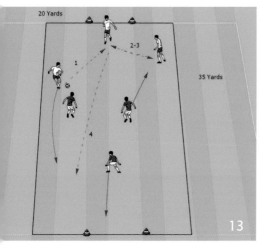

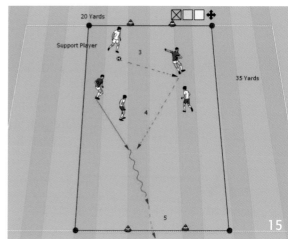

X.   2v2 on 20 x 35-yard field to regulation goals

In this variation, the free player must support the team in possession of the ball from a back of ball position. When one team gains possession, that team must keep possession until the support players run behind them to create a 3v2 (Diagram #14). The objective is to penetrate for shots on goal (Diagram #15).

I have used the group tactical exercise 2v2 to demonstrate how a coach can manipulate the variables of an exercise to elicit desired playing behaviors. Any number of players may be used, 3v3, 8v8, 3v2, etc.

Typically, the coach will alter the size and number of goals, use of target and support players both outside and inside of the playing area, limit the number of touches, and finally, define zones within the playing area. The permutations and possibilities are limited only by the imagination of the coach.

Editor's note: Jim Lennox has coached at Hartwick College since 1976 and has directed the Hawks to numerous NCAA Division I Tournament appearances and the national title in 1977.

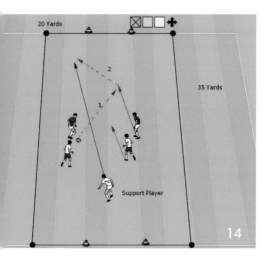

Combination Play for Attackers

Distinct movements and passes can achieve positive results

Tom Rowney
Oregon State University
March-April 1996

Acombination play may be defined as a distinct grouping of movements and passes, typically involving two or three teammates, that create and/or exploit space. Probably the best known and most widely practiced combination play is the wall-pass (Diagram # 1). But there are a number of others that can be used to take advantage of a particular alignment of defenders and attackers and can be accomplished through a variety of angles, with lateral, vertical or diagonal runs.

Editor's Note: In the Diagram #s that follow, unless otherwise noted, each individual square represents a 10-yard by 10-yard area. A broken line indicates the movement of the ball; a solid line indicates the movement of a player. The purpose of this article is to illustrate the types of combination plays that can be utilized and how those plays might be practiced to achieve positive results in the game.

Type of combination plays

Based on the above definition, we can categorize the following combination plays into distinct groups:

- Penetrating wall-pass, set-up wall-pass, wall-pass fake and spin, pass and spin
- Takeovers
- Reverse-pass combinations
- Over-fake and over-fake spin
- Overlaps
- Third man runs

Practice session

Practice sessions for combination plays should maintain a logically sequential teaching emphasis. The initial emphasis should be on teaching the technical and movement requirements in situations that are pre-arranged by the coach. This can be accomplished through basic grid work where correct repetition of plays is of paramount importance. Practice should then move on to small-sided or squad games that stress the need for players to recognize when the alignment or "shape" of defenders and teammates predisposes the situation to execution of a particular combination play. Finally, at the more advanced levels, players should be expected to actively create (by their movement and positioning) situations that force opponents into an alignment where a combination play will produce a successful outcome. This can be accomplished in 11v11 game sessions, as well as in squad games.

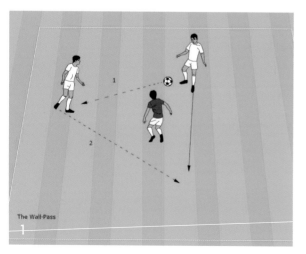

The Wall-Pass
1

The following, therefore, outlines a logically sequential coaching session that includes:

- Theme-related warm-up
- Basic grid practice
- Small-sided game
- Squad game
- Regional practice/11v11 game.

The practices that follow will need to be divided into a number of separate sessions – the number of sessions will depend on the developmental level of your team. Furthermore, while these practices may be used for midfielder player functional practice (since the combination plays are the same) we have chosen to integrate finishing work into the practices for two important reasons:

- Combination plays are used as a means to an end. The "end" (an attempt on goal), therefore, should be included in the practice.
- Including finishing work provides for a more economical use of practice time.

Warm-up

The theme-related warm-up includes the whole squad in a 50x50-yard area. The squad is divided into two equal-number groups with one group arranged outside and evenly spread around grid area and the other inside the grid as in Diagram # 2.

The warm-up begins with the inside player conducting a combination play with any outside player. After the combination play, the participants change places. Combinations should not be undertaken with the same teammate each time. To simplify instructions for beginning or intermediate players, places need not be changed after completion of the combination. Places can be switched after a one to two-minute period.

The coach should encourage verbal communication from insider players, particularly at the beginning levels where players should only need to say the name of a teammate (i.e., "Yes, Jane!"). In more

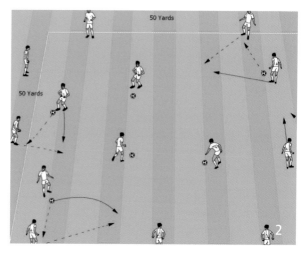

complicated moves, where the combination is on the blind side of the supporting player the combination player should be indicated to the teammate what needs to be accomplished, (e.g., "Over, Jimmy") to let the teammate know to leave the ball.

The following combinations are conducted for a period of one to two minutes with a period of stretching between changes. Players inside the grid start with a ball each and compete the following:

- **Wall-pass combination** Move toward a player on the outside of the grid and complete a wall-pass. After receiving the return pass, the ball is played back to the wall player, who moves into the grid area changing places with the teammate. The new inside player now finds a different outside player with whom to conduct a wall-pass combination (Diagram # 2).

- **Pass and spin combination** Move toward a player on the outside of the grid. As the ball is played to the outside player, spin to receive the return pass into place. After spinning and receiving the ball, play the ball back to the outside player and change places (Diagram # 3).

- **Over-fake combination** The same as above, but the ball is returned softly back to the feet of the inside player who allows the ball to run across the body or through the legs while turning. The receiving player should dip the shoulder toward the wall before turning. After the turn, play the ball back to the outside player and change places.

- **Takeover combination** In Diagram # 4, an inside player communicates and completes a takeover with an outside player. The player previously in possession moves to the place outside the grid vacated by the teammate. Progress to practicing the faked takeover where the player in possession "dribbles" post the teammate rather than allowing the teammate to take over possession

- **Reverse-pass combination** The inside player communicates with an outside player and completes a reverse pass combination using the roll-back, heel, flick-pass, or instep technique. The player previously in possession moves to the place outside the grid vacated by the teammate (Diagram # 5).

- **Two-Person overlap combination** In Diagram # 6, the inside player plays a pass to an outside player (who moves slightly into the grid area to receive the pass). The passer then overlaps around the teammate and receives the return pass. The overlapping player returns the ball to

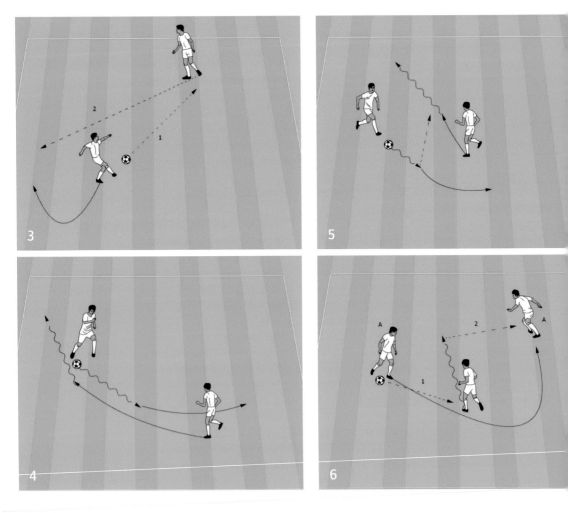

the teammates and moves to the place outside the grid vacated by the teammate.

Warm-up progression

The warm-up progresses by dividing players into groups of three and increasing the grid area, if required, to accommodate squad size. One member of the group positions outside the grid area with a ball while the other two work as a pair inside the grid area (Diagram # 7)

• **Over-fake combination** An inside player communicates with an outside player to receive a pass. The inside player allows the pass to run across the body or through the legs to inside partner behind. After allowing the ball to run through, the player should spin to receive a possible pass from partner in possession. The player now in possession keeps the ball and changes places with the outside player. The outside player moves inside to make a new pairing with the remaining inside player, as in Diagram # 7.

• **Three-person overlap combination** In Diagram # 8, an inside player communicates with an outside player to receive a pass. The other inside partner overlaps the outside player who moves into grid area. The inside player

receiving the initial pass plays a second pass to the overlapping teammate. The overlapping teammate (now with the ball) changes places with the outside player.

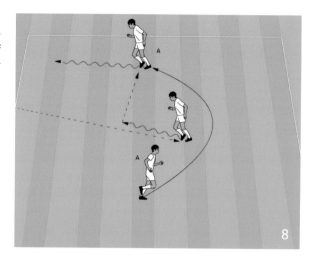

Basic grid practice for two-person combinations

After completing a warm-up with a variety of combination plays, the practice can progress to basic grid work in which the coach prearranges the situation so that players, through repetition, can focus on the technical and movement requirements of the play.

In Diagram # 9, two groups of 2 (attackers) v. 1 (defender) with a goalkeeper are arranged in a 30x20-yard grid. Each group of three should alternate after completing a combination play.

Initially, the coach should condition defenders to a passive role where the defender does not attempt to stop the combination play. An alternative to passive defending is to require the defender to defend one aspect of the play only. For example, in the penetrating wall-pass play, the defender may be conditioned to defend the dribble only. Progression to a more realistic defensive role can be made as combination plays are learned. At

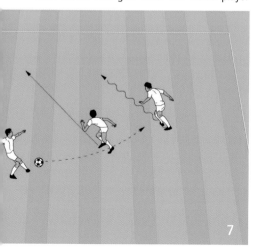

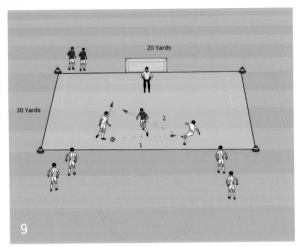

9

Penetrating wall-pass

The penetrating wall-pass is used to get around an immediate opponent and exploit the open space behind that opponent (Diagram # 9 above). In any 2v1 situation, a good defender will "drop off" in an attempt to delay the attack and keep both attacking players in sight. In this case, it is vitally important that the penetrating player draws the immediate defender "in" toward the ball, i.e., commit the opponent by attacking the opponent at speed. In the initial stages of practice, however, the defender can be conditioned to commit the penetrating player at speed.

this point, the attacking players must determine whether to continue the combination or to fake the combination and select another option. Players should practice faking combinations if the defense reads the situation correctly. For example, the penetrating player in a wall-pass should dribble if the immediate opponent attempts to cut out the initial pass. In any case, players should be regularly reminded that combinations function to create and/or exploit space – it is not necessary to complete a combination if the initial movements of teammates and opponents have created a better alternative.

The pass to the wall player is made at a point as close to the defender as possible but not so close that the defender has the opportunity to intercept the pass. Making the initial pass in mid-stride (particularly with the outside of the foot) is preferable, as this will allow the player to maintain and build on existing momentum. As the pass is made, the penetrating player should accelerate past the defender into the space behind and prepare to receive the return ball. If the defender moves to cut out the initial pass, the penetrating player should dribble past the opponent.

The above practice organization can be used for all of the following two-person combinations – the wall-pass, wall-pass fake and spin, takeover, reverse-pass, and the two-person overlap.

Coaches should encourage the use of a variety of techniques (push-pass, instep, or outside of foot) for playing the initial and return ball while advocating the use of the best technique given the situation. The choice of technique for the initial pass will depend on the penetrating player's stride pattern and the location of the ball at the point of contact.

Wall-pass combinations

The wall-pass involves two teammates – the penetrating player (initially in possession of the ball) and the wall player – and can be divided into four distinct variations:

- The penetrating wall-pass
- The set-up wall-pass
- The wall-pass fake and spin
- The pass and spin.

The choice of technique for the wall player will depend primarily on the body position as contact is made, the location of the ball as it arrives, and the required timing of the return pass. Competency in a variety of techniques will allow for a variety in the timing of the return pass.

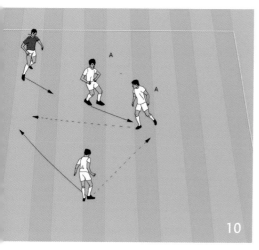

Set-up wall-pass

In the set-up wall-pass, the wall player is typically used to lay off to or set up a teammate for a dribble, pass, or shot (Diagram # 10). It is a combination that works well in preventing opposing defenders from covering dangerous space or combining to rectify a numbers-down situation. In Diagram # 10, the covering defender shifts toward the receiving player to prevent the player from turning with the ball. This creates space, and in our practice set-up, a shooting lane for the penetrating player. When playing the ball off, the wall player often needs only to control the ball rather than pass it in order to "set it up" for a teammate. Furthermore, more advanced players can and should practice this play with the wall player moving in one direction while "laying off" the ball in another direction with the use of a reverse pass.

Wall-pass fake and spin

Wall-passes in tighter situations are often more effective than those conducted over a greater area. This is because when the distances between combining teammates is greater, defenses have more time to read and adjust defensive shape to the counter the play. In such situations, the wall player may find it more beneficial to fake the wall-pass and spin with the ball.

The wall-pass fake and spin (Diagram # 11) is a particularly useful faked combination. If the isolated defender reads the return pass and attempts to intercept it and/or shift across to close down the penetrating player, the receiving player should fake to play the return pass but allow the ball to run across the body or through the legs and turn with the ball to attack the scoring area.

At the more advanced levels, the penetrating play may "draw" the defender by loudly demanding the return pass. Alternatively, the wall player can communicate an intention to make a return pass before spinning with the ball. Either way, the wall player must anticipate the movement of defenders and react accordingly.

As the teammate spins in possession, it is vitally important that the penetrating player continue his or her run into the scoring region. This will provide support for his or her teammate and will leave the player well placed to finish off any rebounds. Players who learn to keep their runs going in this way score more than their fair share of easy goals.

Pass and spin

The pass and spin is another variation on the basic wall-pass. In Diagram # 12, the ball is played into a tightly marked player who has checked to receive the initial pass. The receiving player returns a first time ball to his or her teammate then spins into space behind the defender to receive the final pass. The pass and spin is most effective when the spinning player is tightly marked and the initial return pass is played the first time.

Takeovers

The takeover combination involves two players – one in possession of the ball – and can occur when teammates attack the same space. In Diagram #13, the player in possession is making a lateral run across the preparation area (the area 20 to 30 yards from the goal) while the supporting player makes a run along a line parallel to and behind the teammate in possession. As the players come together, the possession player "leaves" the ball for his or her teammate to take and penetrate into the space behind the defender. In almost all takeover circumstances, the player in possession must be moving the ball with the "off-defender" foot, i.e. the foot farthest from the immediate defender. A common mistake in this combination is for the

possession player to "pass" the ball to the receiver at the last second, rather than letting the receiver "take" the ball.

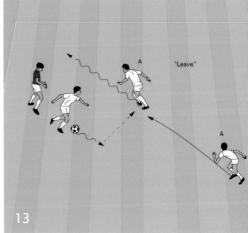

Coaches should stress that, in a takeover combination, the function of the possession player is to protect the ball from opponents until the takeover is complete. Both the possession and receiving players should accelerate out of the take-over phase and continue to penetrate at pace.

A variation of the takeover can be accomplished when the possession player allows the ball to run into the path of a teammate resulting in a first-time

shot or pass (Diagram #14). In this move, the player releasing possession must step aside from the space that his or her teammate is attacking.

A final option for attacking teammates is to fake the takeover. This occurs when the player in possession keeps possession by dribbling past his or her teammate. Faked takeovers are particularly effective at the advanced levels of the game where opponents are more attuned to reading and adjusting to combination plays.

Regardless of the variety of takeover possibilities, coaches should emphasize that, whenever a player with the ball runs toward or across the line of another teammate, or a player without the ball runs similarly toward a teammate in possession, both must anticipate the opportunity to complete a takeover.

Reverse-pass combinations

Takeover and reverse-pass combinations are similar in terms of the types of combined runs that paired teammates can undertake. The difference is that in reverse-pass combinations the receiving player typically attacks space vacated by the teammate in possession, and the ball is actually passed into the vacated space (rather than "taken over" by the receiving player).

Reverse-passes can be accomplished with the outside of the foot or a flick pass, the instep, a roll-back with the ball of the foot or the heel. In Diagram # 15, the supporting player attacks the space vacated by a teammate in possession. The ball is played back into the place – using one of the above techniques – for the supporting player to run on to.

An option for the player in possession is to fake the reverse-pass in an attempt to gain extra yardage on the immediate opponent and continue in possession of the ball. A faked roll-back with the

ball of the foot is a particularly effective deception. Another alternative is a fake to play the ball back with the instep of one foot while playing the ball with the other, used with great success by Peter Beardsley of Newcastle United and England.

The two-person overlap

The overlap can include two, three, or more players. Diagram # 16 depicts a typical overlapping combination between two players facing one defender. The penetrating player passes to, and then makes a run around, a teammate to receive a pass in the space behind or the other side of the defender. If the defender closed down the receiving player, the pass can be made to the overlapping player. If the defender moves to prevent the pass to the overlapping player, the receiving player can maintain possession by dribbling inside the defender. Again, communicating an intention to complete an overlap will enhance the deception if the receiving player decides to dribble past the defender.

Three-person combination play

In Diagram # 17, two groups of 3v1 with a goalkeeper are arranged in a 30 x 20 yard grid. The coach should condition the defenders to be

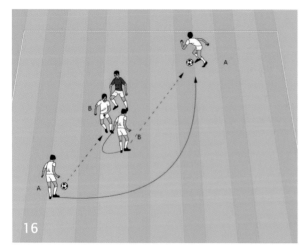

16

goal. The spin should be undertaken as quickly as possible but not so early that the defender reads the fake.

The receiving player must carefully consider the timing of the run into the space behind the faking player. If the run is too late, the player will not reach the pass. If the run is too early, the player might over run the pass or may lose momentum which may be needed to beat the defender.

Over-fake and spin

The over-fake and spin involves three players and is a logical extension of the previous move in which the faking player spins to penetrate into the scoring area to receive a return pass. As in the previous combination, the fake player feigns receiving the ball but lets it run across the body or through the legs to a receiving teammate behind.

Advanced players can develop this combination and the previous one by chipping the original pass directly to the receiving player with the receiving player volleying, chesting or heading the ball down for the spinning teammate in Diagram # 18.

passive. This practice organization can be used for all the three-person combinations in this section – the over-fake, the over-fake and spin, three-person overlap and the third-man running activities.

Over-fake or "dummy"

The over-fake combination is also known as the "dummy" and involves three players – the passer, the fake player and the receiving player. Diagram # 17 depicts a typical over-fake move in which the fake player feigns receiving the ball and lets it run to the receiving player behind. The faking player should finish the fake by spinning away toward the

17

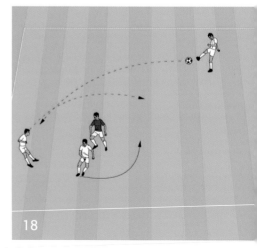

18

The three-person overlap

More intricate overlapping moves can be constructed to include three players for advanced groups (Diagram # 19). Such overlaps are beneficial in developing the timing of runs and passes.

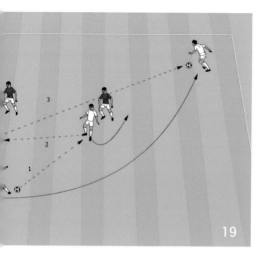

a crossover play while a third plays a penetrating pass to one of the original teammates who has continued to attack the space behind the defenders.

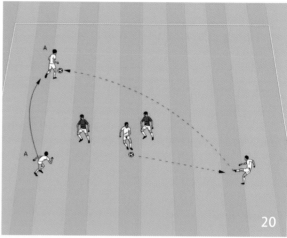

Third-man runs

A third-man run is a general or catch-all term used to describe any three-person combination play including, but not limited to the overlap and over-fake outlined previously. Specifically, it incorporates those situations in which a second or third pass in a sequence finds a third teammate with the ability to exploit space.

For any three-man run combinations to be successful, three things must happen:

- Opponents must initially be focused in the vicinity of the ball
- Both the possession player and the penetrating player must be aware of exploitable space
- Runs and passes must be timed with precision.

Diagram # 20 depicts a typical third-man running combination in which two teammates complete

Small-sided games

Once players have a solid understanding of the timing and technical requirements of a variety of combination moves, practice can progress to small-sided games. Small-sided games (and the following squad games) should be used to encourage players to recognize when the alignment or shape of defenders and teammates pre-disposes the situation to execution of a particular play.

Diagram # 21 depicts a 4v4 game with goalkeepers with two attackers against one defender who are restricted to an assigned half in a 60 x 30 yard field. Attacking players are required to complete a combination play or faked combination play before a shot can be taken. At the initial levels of practice, the defenders may be conditioned to stay goal side until an attacking player takes the first touch. The offside law may also be off. When the defender wins the ball, he plays it to a teammate on the other side of the grid. Goalkeepers may play to defenders or attackers.

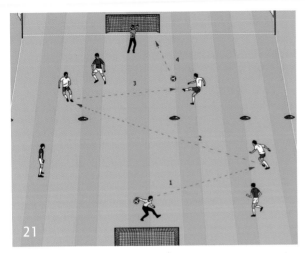

combination in any region in the field, four points for combination play that leads to a shot on goal, six points for a combination play that leads to a goal, and 10 points for having two combination plays in a row, i.e., a wall-pass with an over-fake combination!

The focus of this practice (and the following regional and 11v11 game practice) is for players to recognize the opportunity to select and accomplish the right combination or faked combination play given the situation and to correctly execute the chosen play with respect to the timing of runs and passes. Players should be encourage to "set up" a particular combination with movement, passing and positioning – in other words, be proactive rather than reactive.

The practice is progressed by adding players to produce a 6v6 with 3v2 in each half of the field. In this practice, a defender in possession is initially allowed to pass and move into or run with the ball into the other half of the field creating a 4v2 situation. Practice is further progressed by restricting all players to their assigned half of the field.

As players develop, they should be encouraged to "set up" a particular combination with their movement and positioning and be required to maintain a high level of concentration; a momentary lapse could mean the loss of a scoring opportunity.

Squad game

Once the players are comfortable with combining in grids and small-sided games, progress can be made to more dynamic and game-like squad games. For our theme, the squad is divided into teams (from 4v4 and up) in a regular game with no restrictions. The number of players in the squad determines field size. Players can be conditioned to complete a number of combination plays before shooting. It is also recommended that the coach introduce a point system in which, for example, two points are awarded for a combination play or faked

Regional and 11v11 game practice

Practices using the regional or 11v11 format are probably the most important. This is because the angles and distances are most game-like. Practice at the regional level takes place in one half of the field but should be focused in what might be called the preparation area of the field that is 20 to 40 yards from the goal.

Diagram # 22 shows a regional practice where four attackers play against three defenders and a goal keeper. To start this in a realistic way, the ball is initially played to a defender who clears the ball to an attacking player. The attacking players then must complete a single or series of combination plays before a shot can be taken.

The coach should emphasize the need for movement and tight passing, as teammates get closer to the opponent's goal. If the defending team wins possession, they must combine to get a teammate across the mid line with possession of the ball. The practice continues by adding players to each team until the teams are at full strength.

Since this provides for the most realistic game situations and allows the coach to integrate the teaching and learning that has taken place previously, the final progression in any theme practice should be 11v11.

Tom Rowney made this presentation at the NSCAA Convention in Philadelphia in 1995. He is the head women's coach at Oregon State University. He serves as the NSCAA State Director for Oregon. He holds the NSCAA Advanced National Diploma and the USSF "A" License.

At this level, the overall focus should be to:

- Gain an understanding of where on the field combination play might be attempted. Attempting combination play in one's own penalty box carries considerable risk, while to do so in the opponent's box has more benefit.

- Encourage players to attempt combination play when the opportunity arises.

- Encourage players to create opportunities for combination play by their movement and positioning.

- Encourage players to make correct decisions with regards to options or faking combination play. Remind players that faking a combination play is just as effective as a real combination play.

- Emphasize that combination play is a means to an end – scoring goals.

Recognizing the Moment

Coaches can help players improve anticipation, become faster in decision-making

Wayne Harrison

As coaches, we must teach players to establish in their minds what to do with the ball before they receive it, not after. Encourage players to look before they receive the ball to be aware of their options in advance. For example, if a player only has enough time to pass the ball with one touch, he needs to know where his pass is going before the ball arrives. By improving anticipation, coaches help players become faster with their overall decision-making.

Anticipation begins with awareness. At every instant, your players must observe where the ball is coming from and how it is traveling (in the air, on the ground, quickly, slowly, etc.). They must also have the ability to look beyond the ball, maintaining an awareness of the relative positioning of teammates and opposing players, and the direction in which each player is moving. The following coaching points will help you improve your players' awareness of their surroundings:

- **Keep your head up.** Avoid looking down at the ball, and consequently not observing what is around and where players are in relation to each other.
- **Look before receiving.** Anticipate the next pass before you receive the ball by looking over both shoulders and thinking ahead. With younger players, equate this concept to a bird on a fence looking around.
- **Maintain an "open" body stance.** Do this by turning "side on" (half turned) for greater peripheral vision and by taking an angle of support that allows you to see most (if not all) of the other players on the field.

- **Focus on the first touch.** Relax as you receive the ball so you can control it quickly, and move the ball away from pressure on your first touch to create more space and time.
- **Communicate to help the receiver.** Use brief phrases like "man on," "turn" and "time" so that players on the ball know whether or not they are about to be pressured by the opponent. Practice this type of verbal communication during non-competitive activities to simulate game situations.

Anticipation also requires imagination. To anticipate their future options, players must first be able to imagine how their teammates and opponents are likely to react following each touch of the ball. They must also have insight into the use of the ball and how various techniques can be employed to both control the ball and play it into different spaces. The next set of coaching points will help cultivate imagination and creativity among your players.

- **Change pace.** When you receive the ball, accelerate with it to get away from near-by defenders.
- **Change direction.** Turn with the ball on your first touch to move off at new angles. A change of direction can be especially effective when combined with a change of pace.
- **Look for opportunities to take a "big first touch."** Before the ball arrives, look for spaces away from both your current position and nearby opponents. Play the ball into these open spaces on the first touch to "get behind" the defense quickly.
- **Move off the ball to provide support.** Once you have made a pass, look to support others

in possession so you can receive the ball again. Avoid standing still or "admiring your pass" since this effectively takes you out of the game. Move aggressively to support the next pass as the ball is traveling to a teammate.

- **Switch the play.** Let the ball run across your body to change direction and switch play, saving a touch by using your upper body to Feinting your movement and the pace of the pass to help you. Recognize the available space behind you before you receive the pass.
- **Take advantage of crossover runs.** Instead of relying solely on the pass, create deception through take-overs and "fake-overs." Use your inside foot to exchange (or keep) the ball, and accelerate away from the crossover point as a decoy run.
- **Alternate between one- and two-touch play.** Change the attacking rhythm frequently so that players must always think two (or more) moves ahead of the current situation. Supporting players must quickly find angles off each receiving player so the ball can be delivered with just one touch.
- **Play without communication.** Challenge your players to think for themselves with no help from others – no verbal or non-verbal help such as calls of "man on," "turn," clapping or pointing.

The training program is designed to develop players' composure when in possession of the ball, to increase time on the ball by anticipating situations ahead of time, to decrease the time needed to move the ball, by having total awareness of all players around them, and by encouraging players to use their imagination in their use of the ball and by allowing them to make their own decisions.

The point is not to have players playing at 100 miles an hour and playing one touch all the time but to teach them to be aware of the options before they receive the ball. Then, they can decide, does the ball need to go one touch; do I need to hold onto the ball for longer until another option opens up; is this the time to run with the ball or dribble with it?

The coaching ideals are designed to help the players give themselves as many options as possible and then decide which one to use at any given moment. They are not designed to discourage dribbling with the ball nor running with the ball while keeping possession yourself (because many of the sessions encourage the quick movement of the ball between players, especially one- and two-touch play), but to help identify when dribbling or running with the ball, for example, would be the right option to use. One of the biggest problems in youth soccer is that when there is a moment to play one- or two-touch, the moment is lost because the player isn't yet aware of this option – he or she is too busy controlling the ball and then looking to see where the players are. By then, it is too late. They may dribble or run with the ball to get out of trouble, but the best option of the quick one- or two-touch pass was lost. Your players must rely on their anticipation, imagination, and awareness to aid their decision-making process. At any point in time, each player must decide the following:

The decision-making thought process – what happens to each player as the ball arrives?
- Observing where the ball is coming from
- Observing how the ball is coming
- Knowing where their teammates are
- Knowing where the opposition players are
- Deciding what the player should do with the ball and the appropriate technique or skill to use
- Observing where to play the ball
- Deciding when to play the ball
- Deciding how to play the ball
- Deciding why a given choice is best

If a player is being closed down as he/she receives the ball, the player may have to determine the answers to these questions before the ball arrives. Otherwise, with time on the ball, he/she can wait for the right moment depending on the positions of teammates and the opposition. This is when reaction plays a part in the process. As the other players move about the field of play, they constantly create new situations for the player on the ball to assess and respond to with the correct pass, dribble, run, shot, cross and so on.

To put these concepts into practice, it is best that you follow a training progression that begins with "shadow play." These types of activities lack pressure from an opponent, and thus allow a developmental program to take place without a loss of possession caused by defensive pressure. Although there are no defenders, shadow play should include other players who effectively simulate pressuring situations by working in the same area. This stage of the progression will give your players a chance to develop composure on the ball, which is a critical element for future success.

Next, introduce opposition, initially using an overload situation (such as 5v2 or 6v3). During this stage, reinforce the idea of "playing ahead of the game" by looking beyond the ball to anticipate future options. Encourage players to remain composed with the ball and relax under pressure, while also using correct technique to perform each task efficiently and effectively. The players must pay particular attention to the first touch of the ball.

Finally, you should include full-scale practices to put players in the pressure situations they face on the field in regular team play. The coach must try to build into the player each observation as it happens. Over time and with much practice, the player learns to assimilate each observation more quickly until eventually they all combine into one in the mind.

Players must be both psychologically and physically prepared to meet the demands of the game. Their development in these respects will be ongoing throughout their playing career and will be further influenced by the experience gained from every coaching session and game played. The degree of improvement a player attains using these methods depends on his commitment (in terms of repetition of practice and belief in the system) and level of ability.

Do not expect results overnight. Players have to be patient in learning this approach as it takes time and great concentration to develop. But, in the end, they should benefit from improved decision-making that allows them to work ahead of the opposition.

Identifying Levels of Awareness

1. Start with only one team to simplify the process for the players as an easy introduction to the idea. Then divide them into two teams once they are starting to master the idea. Have the players stand still and pass the ball around the group. They must look before they receive the ball to see where they are passing. Make it two- then one-touch.

2. To ensure they are looking, have the players call the name of the player they are passing to before they pass the ball. When they don't call the name, you know they haven't looked ahead of the ball. Observe which players can't do this and allow them two touches and more time and look to see how they improve with practice.

3. Develop: Have two teams and have them pass to opposite colors so there are fewer choices, so the players have to be even more aware of where they are passing before they receive

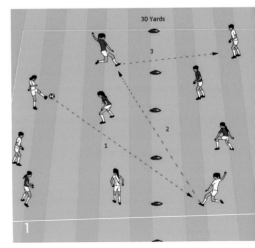

the ball. Introduce two balls to the session, then three and so on. Have players continue to stand still and not move to keep it simple. Have them begin to move around the area slowly to make the decision-making more difficult as players are harder to find.

Two Teams Playing Through Each Other

1. This is the basic beginning of the A.I.A. session where we have all the players moving freely passing and moving within their own team. Divide the group into two teams again. Begin with one ball being passed around a team and, as they become proficient, introduce another ball to increase their A.I.A qualities.

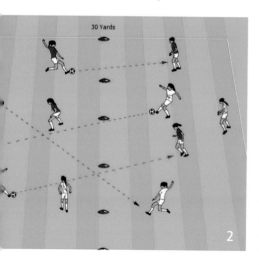

2. Have the teams play throughout both grids to spread the play out and get the players comfortable and composed. As they improve, you can change it to playing in one grid only so there is less room to work in and things happen more quickly. This is a test of their A.I.A. ability.

Technical/Tactical Design
The following information and coaching points form the basis of what the session is designed to achieve.

- The players must play with their heads up (so they view what is around)
- Look over the shoulder before receiving the ball
- Body stance is open to receive the ball.
- Awareness of teammates' positions on the field before receiving the pass
- Awareness of opponents' positions on the field before receiving the pass.
- Move the ball on the first touch away from pressure into space (or one-touch transfer). Receiver moves the ball away at an angle off the first touch
- Passing to space to move players into a better position on the field
- Passing to the player's feet
- Turns/dribbles, one-touch, two-touch, free play, etc.
- Communication (verbal, physical or through eye contact)
- Angles/distances of support
- To increase competitive edge, passer pressures receiver by closing them down after the pass

As you practice with your team, do not try to develop all the previous key coaching points in one session. It may be that you have to spend several sessions on just establishing the first key point of getting the players to play with their head up and not looking down at the ball when they have it. Once you believe you are getting success with this, only then should you move to working on the second point in your next practices. This process of learning is the same as in the introduction where there are several things the player must think about even before they receive the ball, beginning with seeing where the ball is coming from and so on, up to the selection of the pass.

Two Teams Playing Through Each Other then Becoming Competitive

1. Once the players "get it," it is time to introduce a competitive element to the game. Have one ball to play with and make it a possession game. Introduce another ball so each team has

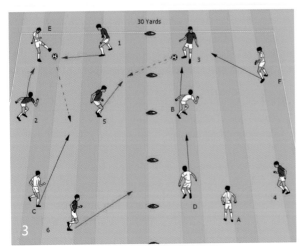

30 Yards

keep possession of. This means the players are constantly looking around the area they are playing in, focusing on keeping two balls. As soon as a player receives and passes on one ball, they are looking to receive and pass the second ball and so on.

5. Above, each team has a ball to keep possession of and at the same time try to win possession of the ball they haven't got.

6. Observe: (C) and (D) make movements to support (E) to keep the ball, at the same time (B) and (F) close down (double team) (3) on the other team in possession of the other ball.

two balls to focus on at the same time so one team's players can be defenders trying to win a ball back and at the same time be attackers having possession of the other ball.

7. Observe: (1) and (2) close down (E) to win back the ball and (5) and (6) move into space to support and receive a pass from (3).

2. It may be that a particular player is involved In trying to win a ball back but has to be aware that other teammates have possession of the second ball and he/she may have to adjust thinking and positioning instantly if a player looks to pass the second ball to him/her. This helps the mind prepare for instant transitions from attack to defense and defense to attack. They need to be aware of changing their focus; one second trying to win a ball but the next making themselves available to receive another ball from a teammate already in possession.

8. Continue by adding a third ball. Awareness must be really sharp now with so much to think about; which balls we have in our possession and consequently where we have to position ourselves to keep possession, but also, which balls we do not have and how we need to work to try and win them back.

3. On changing from a defender to an attacker by receiving the second ball that this player's team has possession of, this player must think about where the other players are who are free to pass to in order to keep the momentum of the game going. Going back to the A.I.A. principles, this player has to know where the ball is going before receiving it to have the best chance of keeping possession of this second ball.

9. Decision-making now is being tested to the fullest capacity. Do I support the balls we have, do I defend to win back the balls we do not, do I change mid-stream as the opportunity presents itself? Every player needs to be aware of all these options. When we go back to one ball with two teams playing simple possession, the A.I.A. instincts of the players should be more developed and sharp.

Numbers Game: Passing in Sequence

4. The next stage may be that the team wins back the first ball so they have two balls to

1. Players and only one ball to begin. Players must pass in sequence, i.e., (1) passes to (2); (2) passes to (3); (3) to (4) and so on to (8) who passes to (1) and we begin again. You

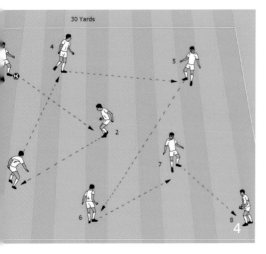

can have players static to begin, then have them passing and moving.

2. Player receives from the same person and passes to the same person each time. This develops great awareness of time, space and player positions. Continuous work on and off the ball.

3. Awareness of where the player you receive from is and where the player you pass to is. Because of this, players begin to anticipate the pass to them and where it is coming from. Also they must look to where it is going to (where is the player they are passing to?).

4. We are trying to create a situation where players are looking two moves ahead, not just one. For instance as (1) is about to pass to (2), (3) should be looking to support (2) for the next pass already, looking two moves ahead before the ball leaves (1). At the same time, (3) should be looking to see where (4) is.

5. Peripheral vision development results from this. You may ask players to make it difficult to find them by lots of movement off the ball to test their teammate's vision.

6. Variation: Use two balls, then three balls at the same time. Start with a ball at (1) and (5)

then at (1), (4) and (7). To keep the sequence going, players must move the balls quickly with few touches, hence their peripheral vision development improves dramatically. As soon as they have passed one ball off, the next one is arriving so quickly that thinking is needed to make the correct decisions.

Transition Game: Defense to Attack and Attack to Defense

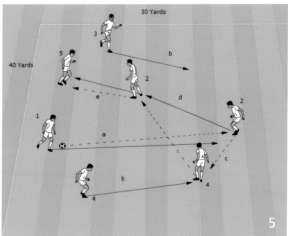

1. There are two teams and one ball with players passing to anyone. Passer (1) plays the ball to the receiver (2). The passer (1) then becomes a defender and must pressure receiver (2).

2. Receiver (2) must work a 1-2 around the defender (1) with a support player. Try to establish support on both sides of the receiver so there are two options available to support (3 and 4).

3. Work on angles and distances of support (triangular support), timing of the pass depending on the closeness of the defender, quality of the pass (preferably off the front foot to aid the Feinting of the pass). Receiver accepts 1-2 from support player (4), passes to a new receiver (5) and becomes the new defender and the cycle begins again.

4. Routine: a) (1) passes to (2) and pressures; b). (3) and (4) move to support (1) (thinking two moves ahead); c) (2) passes to (4); d) (2) runs around (1) to receive (give and go); e) Now (2) passes to (5) and becomes the defender.

5. Variation: Increase number of balls, passing to opposite color only but support from same color, i.e., pass opposite, support same. Quick decisions required. Passer plays the ball to receiver and closes down as a defender; receiver must move the ball away first time or draw defender in and move the ball off at an angle away from the pressure.

Specific Peripheral Vision Coaching Sessions

This is a simplified set up to get initial understanding. Increase numbers as previously shown in two teams of six. We started earlier with one ball and six players for example so each person on the ball had five choices to make and that was easy. Now we must identify one and only one pass and try to make it. That pass is to the person who runs outside the zone. This player is the free player (unmarked). The session goes as follows:

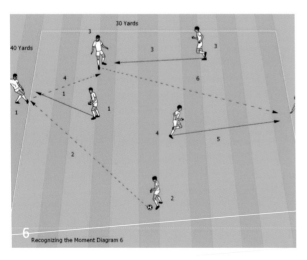
Recognizing the Moment Diagram 6

1. Player (1) runs outside the area (perhaps after several passes within the zone). Player (2) on the ball sees the run and must pass to (1). As (1) is about to receive (as the ball is traveling to him or her), (3) moves into a position to support (1), showing anticipation and awareness. As (3) receives the pass, (4) makes a run out of the area.

2. (3) has already seen the run by (4) and passes. (4) brings the ball back in and the game continues. This is an indicator of how quickly players recognize the run and consequently make the pass.

3. Hence players are beginning to look one and two moves ahead of the ball. It doesn't need to happen so quickly in terms of the next player running outside, but it serves as an example. The run can be likened to a penetrating run into the attacking third where the player hasn't been picked up or tracked and is in a great position to attack and score if the passer sees them and makes that pass.

4. Within the zone there are many choices of pass but as soon as a player makes the run outside that is the pass to make. The coach can determine the tempo of the game, e.g., to avoid too many running out at the same time, the coach can signal to an individual player to move out without the others knowing so only one at a time goes out.

5. Once the free player is outside and waiting for a pass, see how many passes are made inside the zone before someone sees the right pass, i.e., to the outside player. This is an indication of which players play with their heads up (good peripheral vision) and which do not (poor peripheral vision or even none at all).

6. The fewer touches on the ball the player needs to get the ball there, the greater their anticipation of the run. One touch is the ultimate aim, to reach the point where the ball is traveling to the player at the same time

another player makes their run out; they see the run and make the pass at the same time.

7. More touches means more reaction time needed and in a game situation this may mean the player being caught in possession before they get around to making the pass. Initially the coach may see several passes made within the area while a player stands and waits outside until someone sees them; this will happen less and less as you practice and as the players improve their peripheral vision. The exciting part of this is when the coach sees one of their players make the right pass quickly in a game situation due to the work they have done in this session.

8. Variation: Introduce defenders to this session but maintain the attacking overload.

Passing/Support and Running with and without the Ball: Long Passing

1. You can use various numbers of players at each end of the grid in this sequence. Pass and move in own grid until eye contact with a player in the other grid (or a call), then play a long pass to that player.

2. Balls are constantly changing grids; players have to have awareness in their own grid to

receive the ball, but also awareness of when a pass is on the way from the other grid (must have head up and be constantly looking around to see this). If they don't observe where their own teammates are or where those in the other grid are, they won't be successful with this so they must play with their head up and have the ability to look away from the ball as well as at it, observing all the options that are available both in their own grid and the other one.

3. Conditions: Ball can't bounce between grids for chipped or lofted passes, or must be driven along the ground with pace for quick passing.

4. Develop running with the ball across the grids. Pass and move within own grid, then a player picks a moment to run and takes it. Keep balance of balls in each grid. Can start with one in each; try to avoid two in one grid at once. Increase to two balls per grid.

5. Long pass, then follow the ball (supporting the pass) into the other grid so not only balls are being transferred but also players. Players must move as quickly as possible to support in the other grid.

Passing then Supporting the Pass

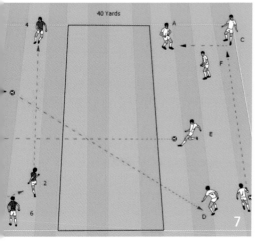

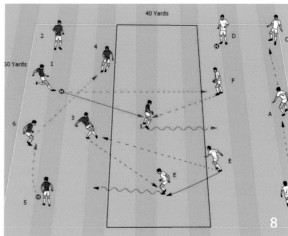

Third Man Running Development

6. Variation: The type of runs to be made are straight or diagonal runs. Diagonal passes and straight runs, and diagonal runs and straight passes as above or diagonal runs and diagonal passes. Equate the situation with how to make it difficult for defenders in a game to mark players who make different types of runs.

7. If a player makes a run and doesn't receive a pass, then they work their way back into their own grid. Relate the move to a player making a forward run, they don't get the pass, they work back, draw a defender with them and then another player makes the run into the space left to receive a through ball.

8. Receiving and turning: A player moves out of the area and positions side on at an angle to receive and turn (looking before receiving) and take the ball to the other grid. The same can happen on the other side.

9. Give and go (movement in two's): A player moves into the neutral zone (with a third man running off the ball) and another player on the ball passes to them. The passer then follows and receives a pass back (a 1-2 move) and then passes the ball into the other grid, both

players move into the other grid and join in. On entering, the existing players in this grid must balance things and look to break in twos the other way as soon as possible.

10. Introduce a defender in each grid. 4v1 – only one ball per grid. As the number of players involved increases so do the number of balls used. So at times, two players can be making moves across the free space from the same grid at the same time, hence there is constant movement between grids. The players will get good at passing and moving and being able to look beyond the ball and at the same time making quick decisions the more they practice this session.

Passing and Support Directional Target Game

1. Start with two balls and two teams passing and playing through each other with no opposition. Develop by having two balls per team to work with. Have the players play in a relaxed yet composed way. Develop this into a competitive game.

2. This is a 4v4 target game (you can vary the number of players). Players must get the ball to their own end targets; if they do, they retain possession as a reward. Before they can go back to a target, they must pass the ball back into their own half of the field. Targets have two touches and can pass to any of the four players. Players can use support on the outside (1 or 2 touch). Inside players have no touch restriction.

3. This is an intense workout with little rest. Keep it short so players perform with quality, rotate outside players in. If a team wins the ball back in their attacking half, they can go directly to their targets (same as regaining the ball in the attacking half and shooting for goal).

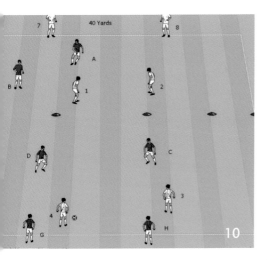

4. Observe the attacking team: recognize the movement off the ball. For example, to work the ball into their own half, see if the players make runs early. Some should support short and some long so the target has choices.

5. Observe the defending team: See if they are stuck to the ball or if they recognize runs off the ball and track players making runs away from the ball into the other half.

6. To lessen the workload and keep everyone involved, have players switch with targets and outside players when they pass to them.

If done properly with the correct progression, the Target Game can be a useful tool to teach your team a number of very important concepts.

Attacking as a Team and as Individuals
* Creating space by running off the ball to receive or help a teammate receive.
* Developing quick support play, working angles and distances incorporating switching the ball using the side players.
* Passing long and short to targets and to teammates.
* Receiving and turning in tight situations and dribbling in 1v1 situations.

* Lots of touches on the ball for the players in this practice.
* Quick decision-making is required in this session because the numbers are small, the area tight and the transitions rapid.

Defending as a Team and as Individuals
* Pressuring players on the ball to regain possession.
* Supporting pressuring players and tracking runners off the ball.
* High pressure to regain possession in the attacking half to be able to go straight to the target to score.

The coach can also teach transitions from defense to attack and attack to defense, quick decision making and improved concentration as the transition takes place. The players also learn about interchange of position, how to play the target and how to support the ball. The coach can concentrate the drill on one of these areas by changing the conditions. A change of conditions changes the focus of the game. For example:

1. No restriction on touches, then three, two or one touch, but only if it is okay to do so. Introduce a neutral player to create a 5v4 overload in the middle if players are having trouble with possession.

2. Interchange of players outside to in, inside to out, as they pass the ball observing the quality of the pass and the first touch of the receiver.

3. For quick transition, have one teammate at each end so you are attacking both ends but once you have passed to one target, you keep possession and must try to get to the other target. You can't go back unless the opposition wins the ball, then you get it back. Only then can you go back to the same target.

4. To lessen the workload and keep everyone involved, have players switch with targets and

outside players when they pass to them. This causes a constant transition of players and improves the player's concentration. The team can only score if they get an overlap, crossover or 1-2, etc., during the build up.

5. No talking so players have to rely on their own vision to play.

6. Players move into the target zone to receive the ball so we don't play with actual targets; different players can then become the target player.

7. Man-Marking: Have the players man mark so they must track a player when they don't have the ball and they must lose their marker when they have the ball. This is a good test to see who is working hard and who isn't as they have a designated job to do. You, as a coach, can see who works to get free of their marker and who works hard to prevent the player they are marking from getting the ball.

As coaches, we must teach players to establish in their minds what to do with the ball before they receive it. Players must look before they receive the ball to see their options. These activities are designed to increase player anticipation and, as a result, player awareness. Players must learn to read the game. This includes how the ball is arriving, from where it is arriving, where the opponents are, where teammates are and what is beyond the ball. The following activities suggest methods to move this type of training into total team training and the development of positions and team shape.

Small-Sided Game 8v8 Developmental Session with Composure Zones to Aid Development

1. Overload at the back. Two forwards can't encroach into the 5-yard composure zone. Defenders pass ball across the zone under no

pressure until one is free to run it out. Attackers can now try to win it back.

2. Players stay in own zone to keep their shape. Support in front and behind.

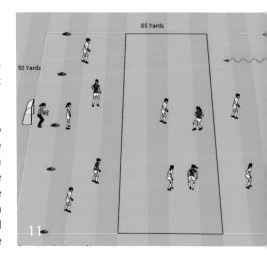

3. Open it up so players can move between zones.

4. Defenders can take the ball back into the composure zone for safety, and this encourages spreading out and playing from the back. Be patient, keep possession, go forward at the correct moment.

5. Defenders: spreading out, running with the ball, passing the ball, supporting the keeper, keep possession, decision-making.
Midfield: receiving and turning, switching play, linking play, runs, keep possession, creating space, decision-making.
Forwards: as above, also supporting short and long, diagonal runs in front of the ball, holding the ball up, lay offs, dribbles\shots, quick decision-making.

6. As ball advances, players at the back move up. Keep checking positions and shape of the team.

7. To get full game started, have one team standing still and let the other team play through them to get a feel for how to build up the play.

8. Develop this by having both teams with a ball each playing through each other where they are not under the pressure of losing the ball.

Development into a 3-2-2 System

1. Play offside from thirds. Players interchange between zones one at a time, always returning to original set-up. Check the balance of the team with and without the ball. Create a 3v2 in midfield zone with player (2) moving up. Could play the ball into attacking third and maybe player (6) joins in to make a 3v3.

2. Player (2) fills his place in midfield. If the team loses possession, players either drop back in or you can develop the session to include pressing to regain the ball. (For example, if a team is losing the game, go high-pressure and leave three players in attacking third, two in midfield third and two in defensive third. DEVELOP.

3. Condition: can only score if all players are over the defensive third line. Keep compact vertically.

4. Restrict number of touches on the ball (if they are able to do so) to encourage quick passing and to improve the speed of decision-making.

5. Vary play by encouraging defenders to pass directly to the forwards: midfield players can then support them facing the opponent's goal (easier to support than to receive and turn with the ball).

6. If you have problems making the session work with equal numbers, then reduce the game to an 8v5 situation using one forward, one midfielder, two defenders and a keeper on the opponent's team until the players are comfortable, then go into the full workout.

Positional Development

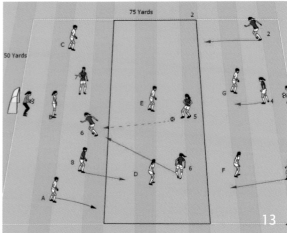

Coaching Points

1. Player (5) is on the ball. (8) comes short to receive, defender tracks, space is created in behind. Player (6) does a diagonal run to receive the pass.

2. If defender-marking (8) stays (doesn't track 8), (5) can pass to (8)'s feet who can turn and attack 1v1, or (5) can play it wide.

3. In possession, (3) and (4) push out to leave opponents offside.

4. **Transition** — we lose possession and, for example, (6) and (5) finish in front of (8) and (7) up the field; (8) and (7) defend midfield.

Possible Passing Options

5. Player (5) on the ball. Three possible options to pass forward (e.g., to (6), (7) or (2) who continue the runs). If (5) cannot make this pass, (5) can go to the side to (8) or back to (3), (4) and the keeper to keep possession until the situation allows for a forward pass again (you won't obviously get all these options to pass but it shows how it can work).

6. Caution: in attack, be aware of quick counter-attack if opponents win the ball, i.e., we have a 2v2 at the back.

7. Discussion: you can get so much work into this session; every time you look, there may be a new situation to discuss. Choose a theme and stick with it. When you have established it with the players, only then move onto another theme.

Training Session to Practice Team Shape

1. Two balls, a ball each team, shadow play, but with opposition to play against. Each team takes up their positions based on the position of their own ball, not the opponents'.

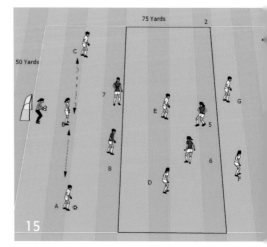

2. Effectively, there are two separate games going on. Initially, have the players stay in their thirds to establish a team, then open it up. Have a game with two balls being used to play.

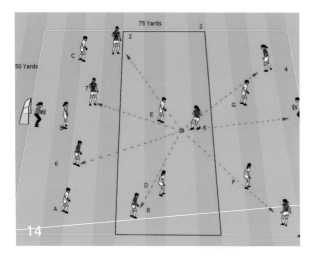

Sharpening Field Vision

Players can learn to study the field through exercises

The following are some technical-tactical exercises developed and presented at the 1999 NSCAA Convention.

The coaching exercises focus on how coaches can help improve players' field vision.

Exercise 1, presenter: Matt Driver, technical director, South Jersey Barons. Diagram # 1

- 25 x 40-yard field divided into two halves.
- Two teams of six, players numbered from 1 to 6.
- Each group has two balls and plays in its own half.

Passing by numbers
- Each group dribbles both balls simultaneously. Each player must pass to the next in numerical sequence: 1 passes to 2, 2 to 3 ... 6 to 1, etc.
- Same as above, but with three balls in motion at once. Players 1, 3 and 6 start with balls.
- Same as above, but both groups play simultaneously in the same (slightly larger) half.

Variations
- Three groups of four playing simultaneously in the same space.
- Same as above, but with two or three balls per group.

Exercise 2, presenter: Matt Driver. Diagram # 2
- 30 x 20-yard field.
- Three teams of four, with different color jerseys.
- Three balls.

8v4 with three balls
- Two of the groups team up as outside players (attackers) to keep the three balls away from the third group as long as possible.
- If the defenders win a ball, they immediately return it to the attackers.
- Each defender keeps track of his wins. After three minutes (and on active rest period), a different group rotates into the middle. Which group ends up with the most wins?

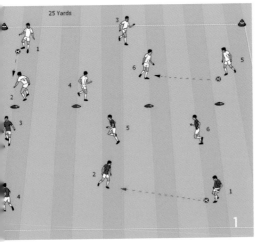

© Thinkstock/iStockphoto/Fluid Illusion

Variations
- 4v2, free play, but with two balls at once.
- Players limited to two touches.

Exercise 3, presenter: Tony DiCicco, head coach, U.S. Women's National Team. Diagram # 3
- 25 x 35-yard field.
- Three teams of four, with different color jerseys.
- Extra balls provided.

8v4 in three groups
- Two of the groups team up as attackers to keep the ball away from the third group as long as possible.
- If the defenders win the ball, players immediately switch roles. The defenders become attackers, and the attackers who lost the ball become the new defenders.
- The 8v4 continues uninterrupted while two of the groups team up as attackers to keep the ball away from the third group as long as possible.
- If the defenders win the ball, players switch roles immediately.
- Because the teams are of different sizes, the situation is constantly changing; when the

team of two is in the middle, it's 6v2, otherwise it's 5v3.
- Attackers' touches are limited according to the situation; they can play freely when it's 5v3 but have only two touches when it's 6v 2.

Variations
- Attackers limited to two touches regardless of the situation.
- Field size adjusted according to skill level.

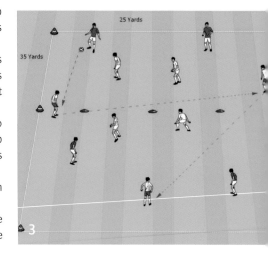

The Neutral Player Concept

Alan Maher

A coaching technique that can ensure successful practice sessions

One of the devices used by coaches to ensure that the objective of a soccer training sessions is achieved is to use certain restrictions so that the technique or tactic that is the focal point of the session has a good chance to be successful. One coaching technique that is highly successful is the use of the neutral player. Following are some ways in which the neutral player concept can be incorporated into your practices.

What is a neutral player? It is the extra player who always plays with the team with the ball. Why use the neutral player in training? In a game where a team gains ball possession, it immediately tries to gain numerical superiority. Players must learn to recognize this and take advantage. The transition from defense to attack must be quick and efficient. The real measure of a team's effectiveness is how it can exploit the capture of the ball and put itself into the opposing teams defensive third. In practice, when both teams have even numbers, the players struggle to maintain ball possession. Use of the neutral player aids in teaching these transitional and tactical skills. What are the functions of the neutral player? To give the attacking team numerical superiority and to help in the organizational transition of shifting from defense to attack.

During training, the neutral player (NP) must wear a vest or shirt of a different color so he/she can be easily recognized. The NP cannot be marked man to man. The NP cannot score goals and should be rotated often. The NP plays like a regular field player with certain guidelines or restrictions that are imposed by the coach. This article will provide examples of how these restrictions can be imposed. Restrictions may include:

- When a team gains possession of the ball, the first pass must go to the NP. This pass allows the neutral player to control the flow of the game.
- NP must pass to the team in control of the ball
- NP must dribble before he/she passes the ball
- NP must take two touches
- NP must take one touch
- NP's first pass must be square or back
- NP's first pass must be forward
- The NP must touch the ball before the attacking team can score
- The NP must change the point of attack

As noted, the coach must determine what restrictions are to be applied. Typically, two-touch passing comes before one-touch passing and changing the point of attack.

On the Sidelines

The NP does not always have to play on the field. He/she can play on the sideline or end line. The players on the sidelines (sideline NPs) of the training field have certain duties and responsibilities:

- The sideline NP cannot enter the field of play
- The NP must pass to the team in control of the ball
- The NP must remain stationary in a corner or assigned area
- The NP must run along the sideline following the ball
- The NP must pass to another NP if changing the field of play is the objective
- As an option, the NP can pass to another NP if the pass to a field teammate is not possible

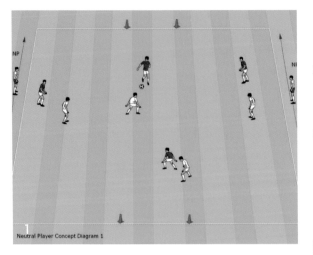

Neutral Player Concept Diagram 1

and 40 inches wide
- Combination of both

2. **Line soccer**
   - Score by dribbling over the end line
   - No score if passing or shooting over end line
   -

3. **Keepaway:**
   - Score by combining on a given number of passes, i.e., 5 passes = 1 point
   - Score by maintaining ball possession for a given period of time

Again, the coach must determine the duties and responsibilities of the NP. In Diagram # 1, you can see the NPs on the sideline.

Types of Games

There are three types of games that can be played using the NP methodology.

1. **Games with goals**
   - Regulation goals – what the players face in a real game
   - Mini goals – cones can serve as goal markers; these goals should be between 36

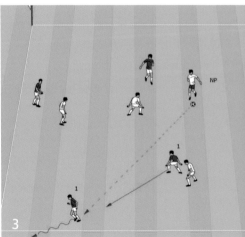

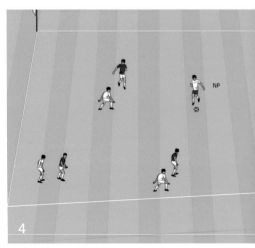

Field Size

The size of the field should vary according to the age and experience of the players. A good rule of thumb is to multiply the number of players on one team by 10 yards. Thus a game of 2v2 should be played in an area 20 yards long or 5v5 in a 50 yard long field. The field should be longer than it is wide. For our above examples: 20 x 15 and 50 x 40.

Going to Goal

With regulation goals, use goalkeepers. With mini goals, no goalkeepers are to be used. Field players cannot stand in mini goals.

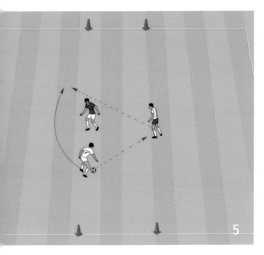

Toward Mini Goals 1v1 (2v1)

Two opposing players have support from one NP

Objective: Use the neutral player to penetrate and score
Number of Players: 3
Field size: 30 yards long by 15 or 20 yards
Rules: NP may pass the ball only to the player with last ball possession.

One Against One (3v1)

Two opposing players have support from two NPs

Objective: Seek and use support on both right and left
Number of players: 4
Field size: Length 40 yards, with width of 25 or 30 yards
Rules: The NP can pass only to the player who last possessed the ball. NP may not pass to other NP. NP must first pass to other NP.

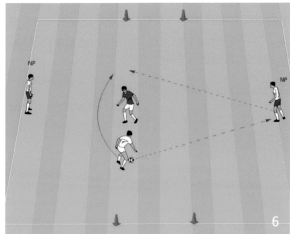

One Against One (3v1)

Two opposing players have support of a NP on each touchline

Objective: Seek and use support to the left and right
Number of players: 3
Field size: Length 30 yards, with width of 20 or 25 yards
Rules: NP may pass the ball only to the player who last possessed the ball. NP may not enter the field of play. NP may not pass to opposite NP. NP must pass to opposite NP.

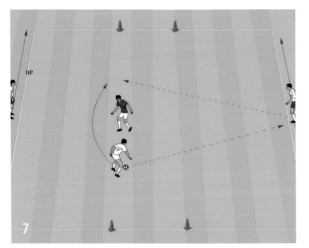

Going Toward Regulation Goals One Against One (2v1)

Two opposing players have support from two neutral goalkeepers; that is, the goalkeepers return the ball to the player who was last in possession.

Objective: Use neutral player to penetrate and score!
Number of players: 4
Field size: Length 20 yards, with width 20 or 25 yards
Rules: Neutral keepers must return the ball only to the player with the last ball possession. Field players must attack both goals.

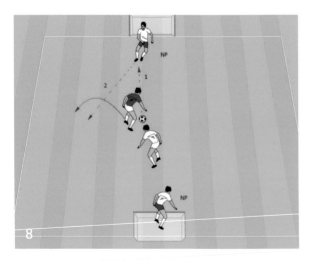

One Against One (2v1)

Objective: NP must pass the ball only to the player with the last ball possession
Number of players: 3 field players and 2 goalkeepers
Field size: Length of 30 yards, with width of 20 or 25 yards
Rules: NP may pass the ball only to the player with last ball possession

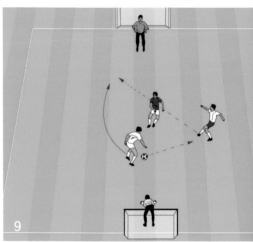

One Against One (3v1)

Objective: Use NP to penetrate with the ball by way of pass combinations
Number of players: 4 field players and 2 goalkeepers
Field size: Length 40 yards, with width of 15 or 20
Rules: NP must stay in his/her half of the field. NP may pass ball only to the player with last ball possession. Goalkeepers must release the ball to his/her teammate. Look for quick penetration.

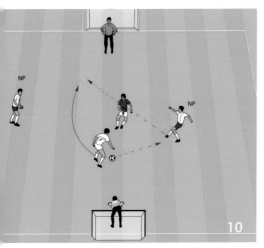

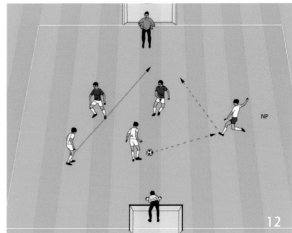

One Against One (3v1)

Two opposing players have support of a
neutral player on each touchline

Objective: Attack the goal with support on both
sides
Number of players: 4
Field size: Length 20 yards, with width 15 yards
Rules: NP may pass the ball only to the players
with last ball possession. GK'ers must release the
ball to his/her own team
Very important: The 1v1 games are very
demanding. Rotate players often.

Two Against Two (3v2)

The attacking team has support from one NP

Objective: Penetration by quick combination play
Number of players: 5 field players, 2 goalkeepers
Field size: Length is 50 yards, with width of 20 or
25 yards
Rule: The first possession pass by either team must
go to NP

Two Against Two (4v2)

The attacking team has support from two NPs

Objective: Penetration by quick combination play
Number of players: 6 field players and 2
goalkeepers
Field size: Length of 60 yards, with width of 30 or
35 yards
Rules: The first pass must be to a NP. NP must play
behind the attacking team as playmaker. NP must
play ball with one touch. NP can only square or
back pass.

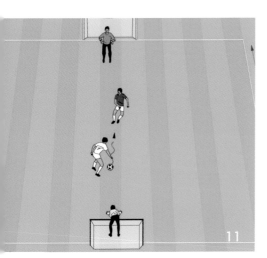

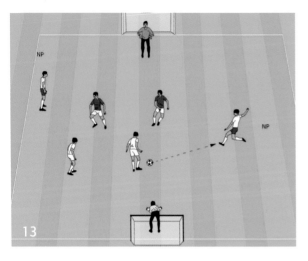

Remarks: After two minutes, the NPs must replace a team on te field. The NPs must stay even with the ball.

Summary

As coaches can see from these few examples, the use of the NP in training of teams can be very valuable. A reminder to all coaches that the exercises in themselves are valuable but must be prescribed based on the age and playing maturity of the team.

These games have stressed combination play. But a coach need use only his/her imagination to incorporate the NP into other training games.

Alan Maher has had a long and storied career in the world of soccer. He has published many articles and soccer books. He has been a strong advocate of the Dutch soccer culture.

Two Against Two (4v2)

The attacking team has support from a NP on each touchline

Objective: Attack the goal with support on each side
Number of players: 6 field players and 2 goalkeepers
Field size: Length is 50 yards, and width is 40 yards
Rules: Both NPs must stay off field of play. Goalkeepers must release ball to his/her own teammates.

he Neutral Player Diagram 14

Small Group Practice

If well planned, they can be very valuable

Rolf Mayer
This was first published in the April 2000 issue of *Success in Soccer*.

Suggestions for practice

No small-group practice, no matter how interesting and carefully designed, can replace practice with the full team. Coaches need to remind players of the benefits of regular practice, penalize them for absences and constantly work to improve participation. The best way to attract and motivate players is engaging, "play-oriented" practice.

The following sample exercises are most appropriate for the main section of the practice session. **Remember:** Small-group games (even old favorites like 4v2 and 5v2 keep-away games) must come after a warm-up period (running and stretching).

Small practice groups mean exercises with small groups. With regard to training efficiency, this actually can be advantageous. However, the coach must also keep in mind that small-group practice is considerably more intense, physically, for the individual players. Always combine short exercise periods with long, active rest periods.

This also means that a small-group practice session should always close with a cool-down period to help players recover.

Player absences aren't the only reason to have small group practices. The following exercises work just as well in special sessions scheduled outside regular practice times.

Small group training – six players without goalkeeper

Exercise 1 – Diagram # 1
*   15 x 15-yard field marked with cones

4v2
*   Six players play 4v2 in the field.
*   Depending on their skill level, certain players may be assigned specific roles.

Playing time
*   15-20 minutes

Variations
*   Direct play
*   Two-touch rule
*   Two touches required

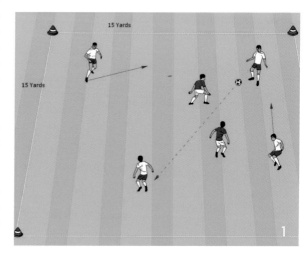

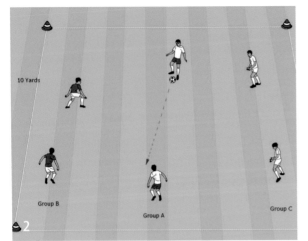

Exercise 2 – Diagram # 2

- Two 10-yard-long lines about 30 yards apart

2v2v2 on dribbling lines

- Group A attacks against B first, attempting to dribble across their end line (=1 goal).
- If B wins the ball, they attack in the other direction, on C's end line.

Playing time

- 2 x 5 minutes with a two-minute active break (jogging) between rounds

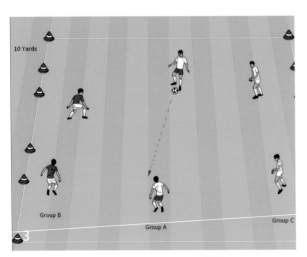

Exercise 3 – Diagram # 3

- Same as above, except with two small (2-yard-wide) goals on each end line

2v2v2 on two small goals each

- Same as above, except the groups now try to score on their opponents' goals.

Playing time

- 3 x 3 minutes with two-minute active breaks between rounds

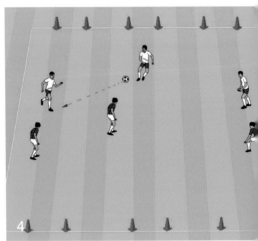

Exercise 4 – Diagram # 4

- Three small goals on each end line of a 30 x 20-yard field
- Two teams of three

3v3 on three small goals each

- The attackers can score on any of the opposition's three goals (focus on shifting the area of play).

Exercise 5

- 3v3 on two five-yard goals
- 20 x 25-yard field
- 3v3, with one defender playing goalkeeper

Small group training – six players and goalkeeper

Exercise 1 – Diagram # 5

- Each player stands outside the penalty area with a ball, facing a goal with goalkeeper.
- The goalkeeper sets out cones for the different shooting exercises.
- Playing time is 15-20 minutes.

Shooting exercises

- Players take turns executing various shooting exercises.
- Starting at the inside right position, players dribble through a slalom and shoot.
- Players dribble around two cones set up on the penalty area line, then shoot.
- Players shoot at a sharp angle.

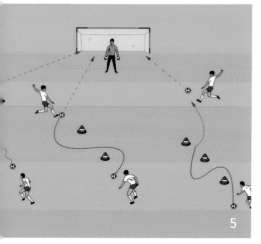

Exercise 2

1v1 from various angles

- The six players divide into pairs and play 1v1 on the goal, starting at various positions.
- If the defender wins the ball, he shoots (or else passes to the goalkeeper, who passes back to him. Partners switch roles after each round.

Exercise 3 – Diagram # 6

- A 30 x 35-yard field is marked in front of a goal with goalkeeper.
- The players divide into three groups of two.

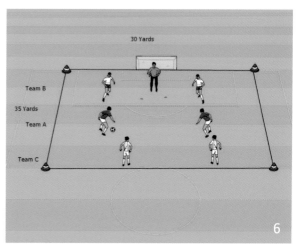

2v2v2 on one goal and one dribbling line

- Group A attacks against B first (2v2), attempting to score on the goal.
- If B wins the ball, they attack against C in the opposite direction and must dribble across the end line to score.
- If C wins the ball, they attack against A, and so on.

Playing time

- 3 x 5 minutes with five-minute active breaks (jogging) between rounds

Exercise 4 – Diagram # 7

- A field twice the size of the penalty box is marked in front of a goal with goalkeeper.
- The coach divides the players into two teams of three.

3v3 on one goal with goalkeeper

- Group A attacks against B first (3v3), attempting to score on the goal.
- If B wins the ball, they must first dribble or pass briefly out of the field.

7

8

- Afterwards, the teams switch roles, and B starts an attack on the goal.

Playing time
- 4 x 3 minutes with 2-minute active breaks (jogging) between rounds

Variation
- Team A tries to score on the goal, while B tries to keep the ball as long as possible.
- They switch roles after each round.

Small group training – six players and two goalkeepers

Exercise 1 – Diagram # 8
- All players stand in the center circle with one ball each.
- Goalkeeper A stands in a 10 x 10-yard square on the sideline, Goalkeeper B is in the goal.

Shooting exercise with goalkeeper pass
- The first player dribbles, then kicks a pass in the air to Goalkeeper A, catches the ball and throws it back into the path of the player, who has started running toward the goal.
- He dribbles the ball a short distance, then shoots.
- The next player in the center circle then starts the next round.

Playing time
- About 20 minutes

Variation
- The goalkeeper rolls the ball into the path of the shooter, who must shoot on the first touch.

Exercise 2 – Diagram # 9
- Two goals with goalkeepers are set up on the endlines of a field twice the size of the penalty box.
- Two teams of three; each player picks an opponent from the other team. One pair takes positions in the field.

9
Small Group Practice Diagram 9

1v1 on two goals with four passers

- The pair on the field start playing 1v1 on the two goals.
- The attacker may pass to all four players outside the field to help him set up a shot, but the outside players must play one-touch.

Playing time

- 45 seconds per round

Variations

- The attacker may only pass to his two teammates.
- The attacker may pass to any of the four outside players, but if he passes to one of his teammates, he must immediately switch positions with him.

Exercise 3 – Diagram # 10

- Same as above, except two pairs take positions on the field and the third stands outside the field, one player on each sideline.

2v2 on two goals with two passers

- 2v2, the attackers try to score on the opposition's goal.
- They may pass to the two outside players to help build their attack.
- After 90 seconds and an active rest period (jogging), the outside players replace one of the pairs on the field.

Exercise 4

- Free 3v3 on two goals
- 3v3; the attackers try to score as quickly as possible.
- Three three-minute rounds, with active breaks between rounds.
- For more skilled players, touches may be limited.

Small group training – seven players without goalkeeper

Exercise 1 – Diagram # 11

- Within the penalty area, the players divide into two teams of three.
- The seventh player remains neutral.

3v3 + one neutral player maintaining possession:

- The attackers try to maintain possession of the ball as long as possible.
- They can also pass to the neutral player as necessary.

Playing time

- 2 x 3 minutes with a two-minute active break (jogging) between rounds

Variations

- Limit the number of touches.
- Attackers can score by dribbling across the opposition's endline.

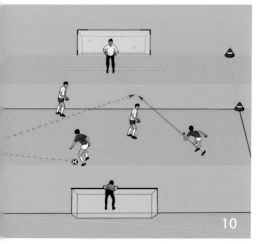

10

11

Exercise 2 – Diagram # 12

- The neutral player joins one of the teams, creating a 4v3 situation.
- The field is twice the size of the penalty area.
- Two small goals are set up on one end line, four on the other.

4v3 on two or four small goals

- 4v3 on the two end lines.
- The three-player team defends two goals; the other team defends four.
- The four-player team is limited to three touches; their opponents have unlimited touches.
- After each round, one player from the four-player team switches sides.

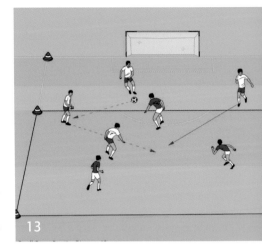

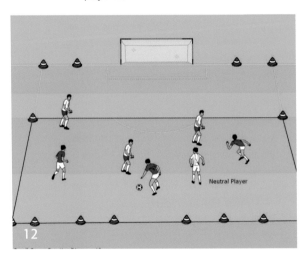

Playing time

- 4 x 3 minutes with two-minute active breaks (jogging) between rounds

Variations

- Touches are unlimited for all players.

Exercise 3 – Diagram # 13

- In the same field as above, a five-yard-wide goal is set up in the normal position.
- A 10-yard dribbling line is marked on the opposite end line.

4v3 on one five-yard goal or dribbling line

- 4v3 on the two end lines.
- The three-player team defends the dribbling line; the other team defends the goal.
- When the four-player team is on defense, one of them must play goalkeeper.
- The four-player team is limited to three touches; their opponents have unlimited touches.

Playing time

- 4 x 3 minutes with two-minute active breaks (jogging) between rounds.

Small group training – seven players and one goalkeeper

Exercise 1 – Diagram # 14

- One goalkeeper positioned in a normal goal.
- The other players stand in a square marked with cones at the intersection of the sideline and centerline, with one ball each.

Shot after goalkeeper pass

- The first shooter juggles the ball, then dribbles briefly toward the goal and passes it in the air to the goalkeeper.
- The goalkeeper catches the ball and throws it back to the shooter, who runs to meet it, controls it and shoots.

4v3 on one goal and one dribbling line

- Team A attacks against B on the goal with goalkeeper.
- If B wins the ball, they counterattack on the dribbling line.
- After each round, one player from the four-player team switches sides.

Playing time

- 4 x 2 minutes with two-minute active breaks (easy run) between rounds

Variations

- Adjust the width of the dribbling line according to players' skill levels.
- Set up two small goals instead of the dribbling line.

Exercise 3 – Diagram # 16

- The field is twice the size of the penalty area.
- A goal with goalkeeper stands on one end line, and two five-yard dribbling lines are marked on the opposite endline.
- The coach divides the players into two groups:
  o   Group A: three players
  o   Group B: four players

- The next player starts the next round.

Playing time

- 20 minutes

Variation

- The goalkeeper rolls the ball to the shooter, who shoots off the first touch.

Exercise 2 – Diagram # 15

- The field is twice the size of the penalty area.
- A goal with goalkeeper stands on one endline, and one five-yard dribbling line is marked on the opposite endline.
- The coach divides the players into two groups:

3v4 on one goal and two dribbling lines

- Team A attacks against B on the two dribbling lines.
- Team A has unlimited touches and includes the goalkeeper as "sweeper" in their attack.
- Team B is limited to three touches.
- After each round, one player from the four-player team switches sides.

Playing time

- 4 x 3 minutes with two-minute active breaks (jogging) between rounds

Small group training – seven players and two goalkeepers

Exercise 1 – Diagram # 17

- The field is twice the size of the penalty box.
- A goal with goalkeeper is set up on each endline.
- The coach divides the players into two teams of three. The seventh player remains neutral.

3v3+1 on two goals

- The two teams play 3v3 on the two goals.
- The attackers can pass to the neutral player as necessary.

Playing time

- 5 x 3 minutes with two-minute active breaks between periods

Variations

- All players are limited to three touches.
- Both teams have unlimited touches, but the neutral player must play directly.
- Attackers are only allowed to shoot after a wall-pass.
- Only the neutral player is allowed to shoot.

Exercise 2 – Diagram # 18

- The field is the same as above.
- The coach divides the players into two teams:
  - o Team A: three players
  - o Team B: four players

3v4 on two goals with goalkeepers

- Team A attacks against B on the goal with goalkeeper.
- A can include the other goalkeeper in their attack, but Team B cannot.
- B is also limited to three touches.
- After each round, one player from the four-player team switches sides.

Playing time

- 4 x 3 minutes with two-minute active breaks (jogging, stretching, juggling) between rounds

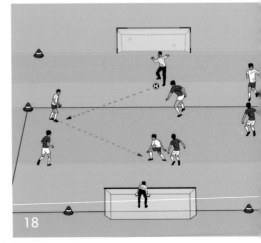

19

Exercise 3 – Diagram # 19
- The field is the same as above.
- Teams also remain the same.

3v4: scoring vs. maintaining possession
- When Team A has the ball, it can attack on either goal, with unlimited touches.
- Team B attempts to keep the ball as long as possible and can include both goalkeepers; however, they are limited to three touches.
- After each round, one player from the four-player team switches sides.

Playing time
- 4 x 3 minutes with two-minute rest periods between rounds

Variation
- For more advanced players, limit the four-player team to two touches.

© Thinkstock/iStockphoto/Fluid Illusion

Off the Shoulder Movement for Strikers

Wayne Harrison
November – December 2008

It is important for coaches to take time to work with their strikers individually and in small groups to teach them the correct movement(s).

Individual Striker Movements – Diagram # 1

The three possible movements of strikers:
- **Short to go long** (opposite run)
- **Long to come short** (opposite run)
- **Off the shoulder of the defender.**

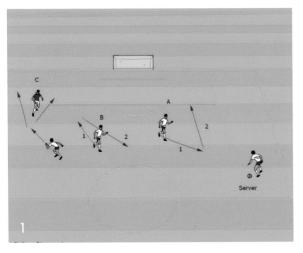

In the above diagram, we can see all three movements. In movement A) the striker takes the defender toward the ball to create space behind, either for himself or a teammate. In B), the striker takes the defender away to create space in front and short to check back into for herself or a teammate. In C), the striker runs away and invites a ball off or over the shoulder of the defender, in this situation the striker is **off the right shoulder** of the defender.

The ball may be delivered off (outside) the right shoulder of the defender so it goes wider, or (inside) the left shoulder of the defender so the striker cuts inside the defender either in front or behind them, or moves toward the ball and receives the ball to feet.

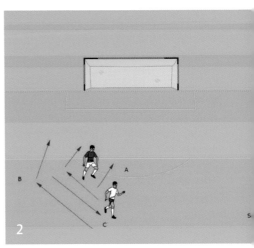

"Off the Shoulder" has Three Additional Movements to Consider – Diagram # 2

Carrying the idea of off the shoulder, the striker in this position has three possibilities for moves, each of which help the striker to end up in a position where they are facing **forward the goal:**

- **Away from the defender (A), then back across the defender either in front of them or behind them** for the delivery inside the defender. If the defender checks away with the striker, then the striker checks back inside to their right; the defender's left always is facing **forward**. If not checked by the defender, the striker attacks behind the defender for the diagonal pass inside the defender's start position.

- **Moving and staying off the shoulder (B) for the delivery outside the defender to attack**, the player on the ball plays a diagonal pass over the shoulder of the defender into the path of the striker facing **forward**. The striker, by making this move, opens up the angle for the pass and gets in line still with the defender so as not to be offside but again facing forward, ready to attack the pass in front of them.

- **Going short (C) to the ball to receive the delivery to feet** after first moving not toward but **away** from the defending player and the ball, and ending up facing **forward**. In this case, the defender should "drop off" to cover himself so the striker can't make a run behind him, but this is the cue for the striker to check **to the ball** from a wider angle and more open body stance so he receives the ball at his feet; but facing forward with space to run at the defender; not with his back to goal and with his back to the defender. The first movement helps this space be created.

What Usually Happens...

Diagram # 3 shows the usual position of the strikers; they stand alongside the defender and do not open the angle up to help them receive a pass. Here are the disadvantages to this:

- The striker has his back to the defender. Defender has control.
- The striker's body position is square on to the ball, defender and the goal, facing back. The striker can't see the defender clearly, nor see the goal directly.
- If the ball is played in behind the defender, the striker has to first **turn**, then run forward and probably is second best to the ball against the defender who has a yard or two start and is probably side on already so only needs to do half a turn.
- It is easy for the defender to mark the striker as he or she can see the ball and the striker at the same time and be in control of the situation.

Individual Striker Movement off the Shoulder

The striker moves **"off the shoulder"** of the defender. Only a matter of a **few yards** can open up a wonderful space and attacking opportunities. In

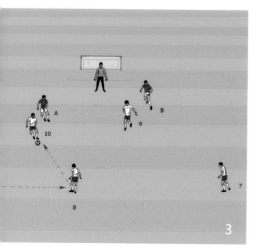

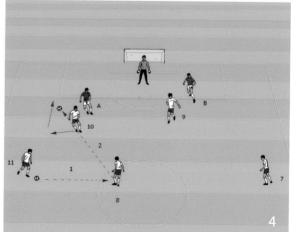

this case, moving off the shoulder of the defender means there is a space **behind** the defender that the player on the ball can deliver the ball into. If the defender does not adjust his position, this is a great chance to receive the ball and attack the goal. If that happens, the striker is now:

- **Facing forward**, and off at an angle, not having to turn and run forward. This saves time and puts the defender at a disadvantage.
- The striker can **see** the ball, the goal and the defender at the same time.
- The striker can even take their position **off the sweeper** in an offside position, if the opposition employs one, so they are almost in advance but also wide of the marking defender. This position (off the shoulder) is **very difficult to defend.**
- If not facing forward, at least be in a **side on position** so they can see forward and not have their back to the defender.

striker (9) can run off the other center back (B) to create the space inside also. The player on the ball plays it inside the center back. The striker should understand that the best time to make the cut is when the defender plants his right foot down (and be flat-footed even) and is leaning forward and toward the striker. That is the time to check back inside and across the defender. The defender is likely to be most **off balance** at this time.

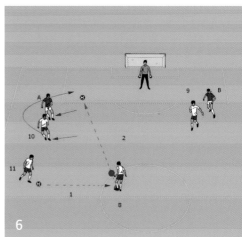

6

In Diagram # 6, the striker moves **"off the shoulder"** of the defender. This is the same as the previous Diagram # in which the defender closes the striker down, but this time the striker makes a run **outside** and **behind** the defender rather than inside and across him. The timing of this is important for being **on side**.

Working Opposites with Movement of the Strikers

The strikers must recognize when the man on the ball has **time** to play the ball forward. Strikers move **toward** the ball, **dragging** the man marking defenders close to them. As the player checks toward the passer as if to receive a pass and is marked tightly by the defender, a **sharp spin** is made to receive a long pass behind into the space created by coming short. A **sharp** turn/spin into

5

In Diagram # 5, the striker moves **"off the shoulder"** of the defender. The defender **comes with** the striker and **closes them** down. Now the timing of the pass and timing of the run come into play. The striker then checks back inside into the space the defender has vacated and attacks **inside** and across **in front** of the defender. The second

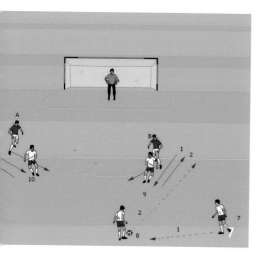

Working Opposites Checking Back to Receive the Ball

In Diagram # 8, communication is important. The midfield players need to know the strikers are playing **opposites**. This time the strikers are moving away to come back. Again there is **time** on the ball for the midfield player and the **opposite** movement comes into effect, both working off the second run. But if the midfielder has **no time**, the striker knows it will be played **first time** into the first run. The **opposite** movement is if the striker shows to receive to feet, he/she is going to **spin away** and receive in space in front of them in the form of a through ball. If he/she runs away, then expect a **check back** to feet. This is especially effective when the strikers are not too close together, so there's lots of space in which to work. To make the movement clearer, the strikers can have a **code word** to call as a **signal** so the player on the ball knows what is happening. They call it as early as possible.

the defender and across the shoulder is the best move rather than the old **arc run** into space. The old arc run is **easily** tracked by the defender as there is time to see the ball and the player. When the player has **time on the ball** to pass, expect lots of **movement** at **pace**, e.g., short to go long. The midfield player can pass down the side of the striker. When there's **no time on the ball**, i.e., they must pass quickly, expect players to **stay** in their positions to provide options. This means if they go short to receive, they get the ball to feet from the first run because there is no time to make the second run as the player on the ball has to release it quickly.

No Time on the Ball to Wait for the Second Run

This situation happens in Diagram # 9 more often in a game. There is **no time** on the ball and the passer has to release the ball **quickly** because of

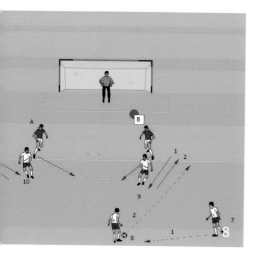

pressure on the ball from (C). In this case, the striker must recognize this, act accordingly and expect a pass from their **first run**. In this case, with (10), it can be a run inviting a ball to be played down the side into the channel for the striker to run on to. In the case of (9), it is a pass to feet coming short to receive. The pass can be made from **wide areas**, too, with the same conditions passing off the first run or passing off the second run depending on the time on the ball of the passer or if the striker has given the **code word signal**. In a game, the team could be **prepared** to play on the basis that it **always** makes the pass off the **first run** **unless** the players get a **call** from the striker using the **code word** to carry out the opposite movement. It isn't always possible in split-second situations to recognize how much time a player has on the ball so it may be best just to work the movement off a call.

word signal to perform the opposite move. In a game situation, for the **first 30 minutes**, it could be a game plan in which the strikers **always** work off a pass from the first run and get the defenders conditioned into thinking that is always the case, saving the decisive moment for later in the game when the code word signal is called and the players

No Time on the Ball to Wait for a Second Run

In Diagram # 10, the ball is in a **wide position** on the field, and the same principles apply to receiving off the **first pass**, as above (10) down the side to space to run on to and (9) to feet. Here, the passer must release the pass early (because of pressure on the ball) or they have not received the code

work the **opposite** move receiving from the **second** run. It may be they only have to do it **once** in a game and it results in a **goal**, giving the striker a vital second or fractions of a second thus gaining a couple of yards on the defender in a vital area of the field to receive a pass and score a goal.

Training Exercise to Practice the Opposite Movement

Here, in Diagram # 11, the striker comes **short** and shows for the ball asking for a pass from (D). Defender (F) follows. The midfielder (D) passes to (C), (D) then passes **over the top** or **a through ball** into (E)'s path as he/she spins.

The defender must play **passively**. To continue the work once player (E) receives the ball, they must beat (F) back to the touchline. Players (C) and (D) go to the middle, and the next two take their place. As the pass is going from (D) to (C) the striker shouts the **code word** and spins to receive the pass as player (C) is about to pass it. The shout must be early to (C) to make the pass at the exact same time (E) is spinning to receive it.

Variations: The player receiving the pass can get it "short" or "long" to keep the defender guessing. He/she should get it short, when the code word is not used, but the player could use any other word to confuse. He/she should receive it **long**, when the **actual code** word is used. Combine with the passer to beat the defender.

The Goal: Causing Havoc

By creating space for themselves, flank players can get behind the defense

This was first published in the May 2000 *Soccer Journal*

The following is an outline of a presentation by Glenn Myernick made to the NSCAA National Academy coaches at its staff training weekend in San Antonio, Texas, in May.

Coach Myernick noted that flank players are generally seen as competent in several areas of functional play such as individual and collective defending, maintaining possession and creating width, but that a major shortcoming has been the ability to work with supporting players to create space for themselves.

Through the creation of space, flank players can begin to understand and incorporate into their games the ability to penetrate the opposition; that is, get behind the defense and create havoc in the final third of the field.

Warm-up/technical practice

In Diagram # 1, six players have been placed in a grid 12 by 16 yards. The objective of the exercise is to have the players sharpen their control and passing skill and improve the timing of their runs to both collect and receive the ball.

In the first phase, Player No. 1 sends a ball across to Player No. 2, who comes to meet the pass, controls it on the first touch and plays it back to No. 1. No. 2 then bends a run away and No. 1 controls and, on the second touch, plays a well-weighted ball into No. 2's path and runs to take No. 2's place on the grid. No. 3 now views the action between Nos. 1 and 2 and, as No. 2 collects the ball, times a run to collect a pass, plays it back to No. 2 and moves away to collect the return pass and now combine with No. 4, etc. No. 2 replaces No. 3, etc.

Each player seeks to first control, then pass the ball. The quality of the pass (accuracy, pace) must be emphasized to the players, and gradually they can be asked to increase the speed of movement in the exercise.

The coach can now reverse the direction of the passing. The players can then be asked to first time all their passes with reversal of the flow of the exercise to take place using this restriction as well.

Three grids should be set up on the field with six players assigned to each. The central grid may be used by the coach to demonstrate each of the variations in the exercise. About 10 yards should

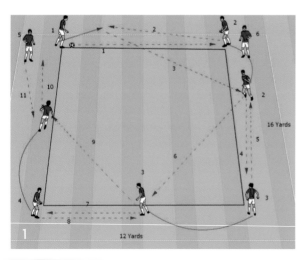

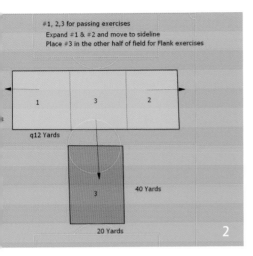

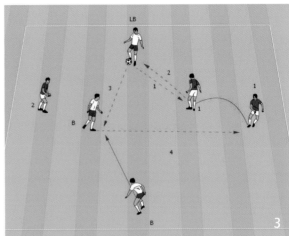

be allowed between the grids for safety purposes (Diagram # 2).

Match-related exercises

Myernick then established three larger (20 X 40 yards) grids with cones, two on the perimeter of the field and a third in the middle of the other half of the field (Diagram # 2 for location of grids). Four players (two in red, two in blue) are initially involved.

He pointed out that the two players on the ends of the grids might be viewed as the left back and a center back respectively. The player on the touch-line (No. 1) is the focal point of the exercise, with the objective to free that individual to penetrate into the final third of the field. The fourth player (No. 2) must coordinate with No. 1 in bringing that about.

Diagram # 3 depicts No. 1 timing a run to the ball and playing it back to the LB. At this point, the back at the other end of the grid shows for the ball and lays it off to No. 1, who has sprinted into open space. Players now resume their places on the grid and this pattern is repeated in the other direction with No. 2 replicating No. 1's pattern.

In Diagram # 4, Myernick introduced a passing subtlety when he noted that the LB can "signal" to

No. 1 (when it is clear that No. 1 is being tightly marked) by a "soft ball" to his feet that is intended to tell him that once No. 1 returns the ball, a ball to space behind the aggressive defender is "on" and so No. 1 must spin and move to receive the pass.

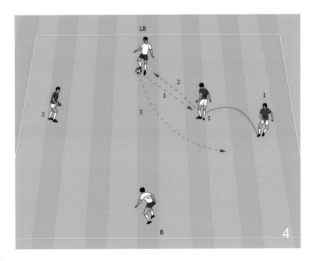

In Diagram # 5, we see No. 2 being trained with the supporting back to penetrate the flank, and while the option demonstrated in Diagram # 4 is not shown, time can be spent on that as well.

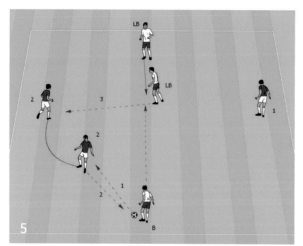

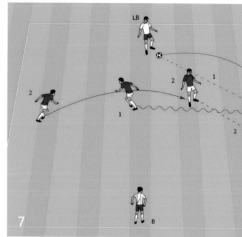

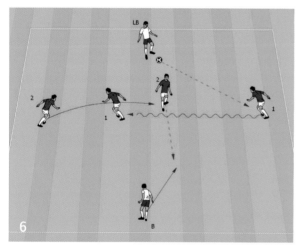

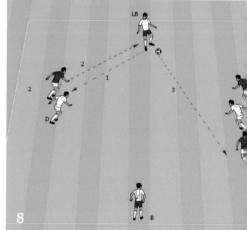

In Diagram # 6, another variation is shown. The ball is played to No. 1 who now executes a takeover with No. 2. On the takeover, No. 2 plays the ball forward with the receiver able to play the ball off to either No. 1 or No. 2.

The final option is shown in Diagram # 7. It involves a pass to No. 1, who executes a crossover with No. 2. The LB, now overlapping into the space created by No. 1's dribble, receives a ball from No. 2 following the crossover.

Myernick positioned himself off the field with a supply of balls with other balls available at

the opposite end of the grid. From this coaching position, he could offer comments to both encourage the players and correct the activity. In particular, he pointed out that players must recognize that quality passing is necessary or that play will break down. At this point, two defenders (one blue, one red) were introduced and the players were instructed that if the ball was won by the defense, the two players must use their supporting player (LB or B) initially and then seek to penetrate their flanks.

In Diagram # 8, we see another combination being trained. Again No. 2 shows to the ball and plays it back to LB. Off the ball, No. 1 is making a more central run, dragging the defender and opening up space, which is exploited when he sprints to the exposed space behind the defense to receive a one-touch pass from the LB. Again, this pattern should be emphasized going in both directions.

In Diagram # 9, we see the two attacking players combining to open up space on the flank for player No. 2. His teammate shows to control and play the ball back to LB. As this is taking place, No. 2 draws the defender and, as the LB receives the ball, sprints centrally to receive the ball. Here, Myernick noted, mobility in attack is demonstrated.

While combination play with a supporting player was emphasized in the grid exercises, Myernick frequently reminded players and the Academy staff members that if a flank player can turn with the ball on the defender, the option to penetrate on the dribble is a most viable option.

When the dribble option is "on" (no covering defender), it must be exploited and the decision to combine with others or dribble is critical.

With six players now active, there was plenty of opportunity for transition play to take place, with extra players used to keep the concentration level of the players keen. From time to time, Myernick

would praise the players when good decisions were made. When technical or tactical misplays occurred, they were pointed out.

Again, the coach reminded the staff that three such grids could be set up on the field so that if they were training their teams, a large group could be trained simultaneously.

6v6+2

The next training exercise was a two-goal game that was played on a 84 x 36 yard field. The main buildup area was 60 x 36 yards with two 12-yard zones at either end of the field. Two goals (marked by flags and cones) were placed at the sides of the fields, each 12 yards in width.

Two neutral players (in yellow) played with the team having ball possession, and the emphasis was on working to get the ball and players free on the flanks of the field. A team scored when a ball or a player and the ball were played through either of its goals and the ball stopped inside the end zone. Play then proceeded in the opposite direction.

Initially, both teams failed to establish a target player up top and the coach instructed them to do so in order to stretch the defense vertically. After that, play opened up a bit, though keeping players

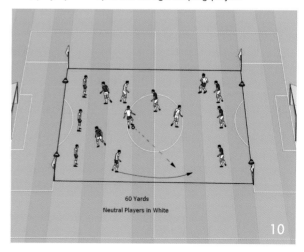

9

10

60 Yards
Neutral Players in White

wide as free play took place proved difficult at times. Here, players must understand that everyone may find themselves in wide positions (again the issue of mobility) and recognize the various options at their command that can free themselves.

A typical sequence is shown in Diagram # 10, where the neutral player is shown combining with a back, and the flank player has timed a check to the ball with a run into space to receive a layoff.

Myernick noted that, depending on the ability in the team, the exercise may be varied by: 1) expanding the space to 44 yards (the width of the penalty box); or 2) making the exercise 5v5+2; or 3) combining both options. In the 6v6+2 and in the concluding 9v9 exercise, the offside rule should be observed.

8v8 plus keepers

Myernick concluded the session with an 8v8 game with goalkeepers on a field that was full length (Diagram # 11). With markers, he initially established outside lanes in which only the flank players could operate and then removed that restriction.

either from the flank or a goal from a pass from the flank, and three points for a goal scored and/or built up from a central position.

Conclusion

Myernick wrapped up the training session by reviewing the players' various options in terms of freeing themselves or their teammates on the flanks. It is crucial for both players and coaches to recognize that passing and receiving technique must be perfect in order for any of the tactics to take place in the game and that the initial phase of the practice, the technical segment, must see the players concentrating to achieve perfection in order for the practice to achieve maximum results.

Editor's note: Glenn "Mooch" Myernick won the 1976 Hermann Award while playing at Hartwick College. He played in the NASL, captained the U.S. National Team and has coached at the college and professional levels.

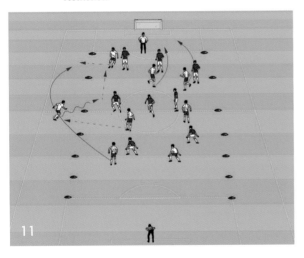

11

Teams were awarded two points for penetration down a flank, five points when a goal was scored

Maintaining Possession

The key is employing tactics that utilize all of the players

Steve Dawson

Introduction

The fastest and most direct way of moving the ball from one end of the field to the other is to have the goalkeeper (GK) punt it, and many teams and coaches choose this method of transition. A number of teams have been very successful utilizing this method.

However, I contend that to develop skilled players in defense, midfield and up-front, coaches need to play out of defense and through the midfield rather than bypassing it.

The following explores methods and tactical principles of how to move the ball from the back to the front utilizing all the players on the field.

Purpose

Move the ball from the back to the attacking third, at least over the halfway line, maintaining "good possession," i.e., the ball under control and supporting players for the person with the ball.

Situations – options

- GK distribution – GK to sweeper, GK to fullbacks, GK to the midfield, GK to forwards.
- Sweeper distribution – sweeper to fullbacks, sweeper to the midfield, sweeper to forwards.
- Distribution by backs – backs to the midfield, backs to the forwards.

Note: Under this system of play, the center back is pushed into midfield as a link between defense and midfield. Therefore, we have a back three rather than a back four – of course, this should be flexible and can become a back-four if necessary.

Key points:

A. Players, even defenders, must be comfortable with the ball and ability to:

1. Control the ball under pressure
2. Pass ball under pressure
3. See players in support
4. Run with ball into space, drawing players to them

B. Supporting players make intelligent runs with emphasis on:

1. Timing of the run
2. Angle of support
3. Making the field big (opposition will try to make field small)

C. Create space by:

1. Interchanging positions
2. Moving the ball quickly
3. Switching play
4. Making overlapping runs

Practices

- Functional practices for specific defenders – GK, sweeper and full backs.
- Functional practices for back three or back four.
- Functional practices for defense and midfield.
- Practice for all three units, the whole team.

Functional practice for specific defenders

Goalkeeper
Throw

Organization
Ball is played in from corners, crosses, shots, long-ball, etc. GK catches the ball and throws out to breaking fullbacks or sweeper, then to breaking midfield. At first no opposition, then opposition.

Teaching points
Look early; get in position early, preferably wide; if available, utilize space in front; don't take too many chances.

him/her; midfield be aware and make themselves available; angle of support is crucial, not square; don't lose possession in defending third.

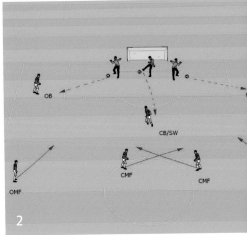

Long goal kick and punt

Organization
Work with the GK hitting the target players, preferably the halfway line or beyond. Two options: one-touch flick-on or lay-off to the side, or control facing your own goal – depends on the service and skill of the player receiving the ball. Flick-on has GK hitting two or three target players who are positioned somewhere near the halfway line. No opposition to begin with, then gradually increase.

Teaching points
Option 1: Flick-on – get in front of defender; hit channels; don't head ball straight up in the air; be prepared to use other parts of body other than the head; supporting runners move before the header or flick-on, i.e., anticipate; read the flight of the ball as there is a tendency for players to make their run too early and to come too deep so the ball goes over their head; play to players' strength, generally "big people" want the ball played to their head.

Option 2: Control – read flight of ball; take defender out of position and check back into space; first touch crucial (balance and positioning); ball

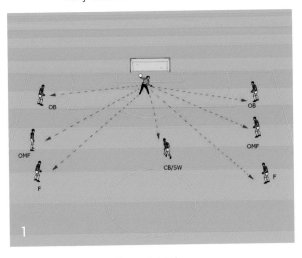

Punt and goal kick

Organization
Short goal kick – just practice with three or four defenders and pressure from opposition. Obviously, the kick has to be taken quickly. The object here is for defenders to receive the ball and try to hit the midfield who should be moving and supporting.

Teaching points
Prepare early; fullbacks come wide to give themselves room and create space for the sweeper at the top of the box, if the GK chooses to use

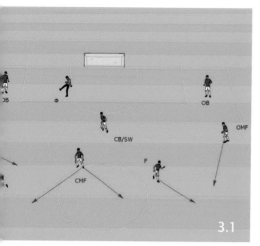

3.1

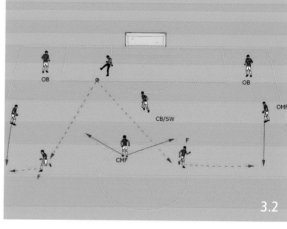

3.2

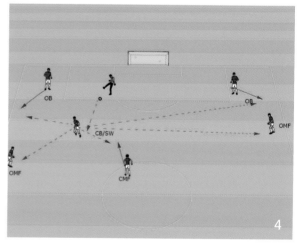

4

under control early; shield/screen ball; be aware of supporting players before receiving the ball; supporting players moving early and anticipate the pass; defenders make themselves available to target players; try not to play square passes or passes that put players under pressure, especially in the defending third (e.g., back passes); if possible, turn defender and utilize space in front of you.

Sweeper and fullbacks

Organization
GK, sweeper, fullbacks and other players (midfield, one or two target players) with no opposition at first and gradually increasing opposition pressure.

GK to sweeper who distributes to fullbacks or midfield.

Teaching points
Sweeper must be aware of space available to him/her; move into space just beyond top of penalty area; no more than one touch before turning with the ball; GK make self available in case of quick pressure; sweeper must see options laterally and up the field; first preference should be to move the ball forward, but not if it means losing possession; fullbacks support early and only square if opposition not likely to intercept the pass; quality pass from GK; GK give instructions to sweeper to

turn or give a return pass; midfield and forwards have to be mobile in order to get open for pass from sweeper; sweeper keeps head up to see option, and do not dribble into trouble, but if space is available, utilize it.

GK to fullbacks who distribute to midfield, sweeper or forwards.

Teaching points
Get wide early and don't run into space too early, thereby putting yourself under pressure before even receiving the ball; let the GK know you want the ball, and let the GK respond in kind

5

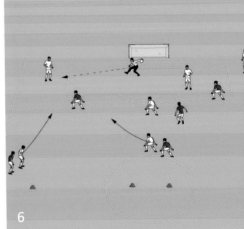

6

of the field; don't give high balls that are hard to control, and don't play the ball across the penalty area, or just beyond; if opposition is close and likely to intercept, need other options.

(provide support for back-pass); sweeper, make yourself available by providing a good angle of support if midfield and forwards are not open; move ball quickly to forwards and midfield because space is usually very tight in the middle third; see options, either GK, sweeper, center-mid. Outside-mid, forwards to feet, or hit channels for forwards to run onto; once fullback has played the ball, don't stand, move to support behind or overlap and get forward.

Functional practice for back 3 or 4

Organization

Just in own half of the field with no opposition at first then a gradual increase of opposition pressure, e.g., four defenders and three opponents. Goal here is to get the ball at least 40-45 yards up the field under control. Eventually close the field down to increase the difficulty level for the defense. Give the defense targets to reach (small goals, one each on the wings and one in the middle of the field, just short of the halfway line).

Teaching points

Communication, always know where you are and who is supporting; GK acts as a player, e.g., don't divorce yourself from the defense; keep your balance, i.e., angles of support, don't caught flat (space), use space in front of you and the width

Functional practice for defense and midfield

Organization

Four defenders and three midfield or three defenders and four midfield. At first, work on shadow play (walk-through practice), then include four opposing players. Again, the goal is to get to the halfway line or just beyond and reach one of three targets, either wide or in the middle. Eventually, six opposing players, with the object of getting the ball beyond the halfway line under control. If opposing players gain possession, they can score. Next, same practice except target is a regular goal so it becomes a 6v6 or a 7v7 game with the defensive team working on bringing the ball up the field. If successful, make the field smaller so space is more of a premium, or condition defense to two-touch. Play throw-ins as you would in a game.

Teaching points

Communication and movement; GK gets the ball moving early and provide depth and support; GK looks to hit the midfield as well as defenders, if midfield receives the ball, fullbacks provide support behind and overlap, and midfield should be prepared to turn with the ball if space is available; be prepared to interchange, e.g., sweeper or center-back moves up and other players adjust so cover exists; play ball wide, but can go up the middle if space is available; be prepared to switch direction of play, otherwise opposition will close down the space and make the field smaller; movement off the ball, angles of support and quality passing crucial here; avoid square throw-ins unless space available, and sweeper and GK be prepared provide support behind the thrower.

Teaching points

If possible, hit midfield early; if too tight, switch play to create space for midfield, even if it means using the GK as a support player; as midfield players receive the ball, defense gives support behind, yet tell them to turn if they can; forwards come off marker and look for give-and-go.

Throw-ins in defending third

Organization

Start with the ball in the defending third. Options are: throw to GK who switches the play; throw to player supporting behind, i.e., in sweeper position and go from there; throw ball to feet of forward player who is checking off defender; throw down the line for flick-on to target player; throw to overlapping midfield player.

Teaching points

If possible, take throw quick and to feet; thrower moves immediately after taking throw; closest player to the ball takes the throw – doesn't have a designated thrower unless it is going to be long; players moving and supporting for person receiving the ball; if ball goes to sweeper, players look for short and long pass; if ball goes to forward player, look for lay-off, but target player be aware of space behind them for a turn; if throwing down the line, someone must be overlapping or moving into space

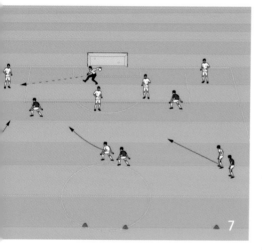

Functional practice for whole team

Practice as noted above, but in 11v11 game situation. One team has possession with the task of moving the ball up the field without losing it in the defending or middle third of the field.

Short throw to sweeper or fullbacks

Organization

GK throws the ball to the sweeper or fullbacks who look to play through the midfield, e.g., outside-mid or center-mid. Condition practice to two-touch if players are not supporting or moving. Can divide the field into three areas, and score points for successful movement of ball into each area, e.g., one point area, two-point area, three-point area.

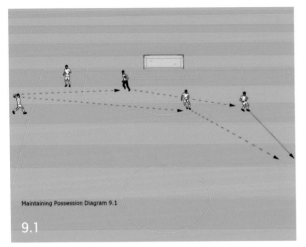

Maintaining Possession Diagram 9.1

9.1

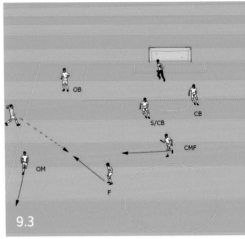

9.3

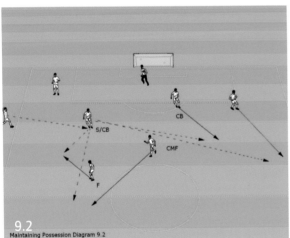

9.2

Maintaining Possession Diagram 9.2

Teaching points

Quality and timing of the throw are crucial; midfield and forwards be aware of where space is and how much time you have; if player cannot turn, play ball back the way you are facing and reset; if hitting the outside-mid, who is going forward, don't wait until that player is in space before throwing the ball, i.e., throw the ball in front of the player for him-her to run onto – if he/she has to wait for the ball, it defeats the purpose of the practice; once you have the ball under control in the midfield and attacking third of play, keep your balance and do not allow gaps to emerge between forwards, midfield and defense, i.e., stay tight as a unit as it complements support on the ball.

for the flick-on; once in attacking position, third players get forward for support; when throwing to overlapping midfield player of defender, timing of the run and throw is crucial so receiving players are not running into a crowded area.

Goalkeeper throws to midfield or forward who is checking back

Organization:
GK hits outside-mid, center-mid or forward target players.

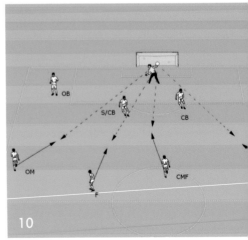

10

Other points of reference

It is important to note that although the discussion here deals with retaining possession as the ball goes from the back to the front of the field, basic fundamental principles still prevail and should be emphasized. That is, there is no secret to keeping the ball – movement off the ball, angles of support, communication, quality passes, adaptation, flexibility etc., are all crucial aspects to this exercise as they are during all phases of the game. While the emphasis has been designed around specific functional practices for certain groups of players, more general exercises and practices can facilitate the objective, i.e., possession under pressure, in tight spaces, and movement off the ball.

Small-sided games

These are excellent for developing skills and support play. Encourage all players, including defenders, to learn the art of scoring and dribbling. 1v1, 2v2, 3v3, and so on, allow players the opportunity to experience all facets of the game. As a coach, you are very fortunate if you have 11 players who can all distribute with skill. Too many coaches resigned themselves to the idea that defenders are "out there" to stop (destroy) and not create. Obviously, if you have skilled defenders, it will be a lot easier to maintain possession as you move the ball up the field. Functional drills are important, but defenders should not be limited to practices that emphasize tackling, jockeying, delaying, 30-40 yard passes to forwards and so on. Incidentally, some of the best defenders have spent considerable time as midfield players.

Modified small-sided games

Limit touches: These types of practices can be modified to suit the need of the team. For example, if a coach feels the need for more movement and support, he/she can play three, two or one-touch to encourage this small-sided games.

No goals: Here, players are rewarded for retaining possession. A team receives one point for five consecutive touches and the first team to five or 10 points wins. This is an excellent warm-up game and fitness drill, and complements the objectives of this discussion.

More than two goals: Here, players can score in any of four or five goals. This encourages spatial awareness, vision, flexibility, and redirection of play. Coaches can put many stipulations and conditions on these games to serve their needs, and obviously, are not restricted to just the above.

Conclusion – philosophy

What is the goal here? That is what the coach must ask himself/herself. The task is not an easy one – moving the ball up the field under control while the opposition imparts pressure and closes down the space. However, by developing players with skill and encouraging them to play with confidence in all areas of the field, the coach will, in my opinion, facilitate the creation of exciting and innovative players and imaginative soccer.

Coaches want to win and so do players, but the long-term goal of developing skilled players is more important than the short-term goal of winning. Let players make mistakes by trying to play the game the way it should be played – to feet, connecting passes, give-and-goes, switching play, innovative attacking soccer, and so on. While this sounds idealistic, I believe it is an important reference point, and will, in the long run, create more skillful successful players, and a better game to watch.

Steve Dawson is the head coach at Wittenberg University, Springfield, Ohio. He received his bachelor's degree at Loughborough University in England, and his Ph.D. at Ohio State University. He also is the director of Great Britain Buckeye Soccer Camps.

Tactics for the Attack

Exercises focus on play in the final half of the field

Jack Detchon

The following is an outline of a session presented by Jack Detchon to the NSCAA Academy staff as part of an in-service training program conducted in May 2004 at Muhlenburg College

This is a teaching progression that focuses on development of team attacking tactics in the final half of the field.

There are some assumptions made in this presentation:

- The double center striker set-up is the alignment chosen by the coach.
- That functional training of the two forwards precedes the implementation of this exercise. This means there is a bit of understanding as to when the supporting forward should create space for his teammate, when he/she will show for a 1-2, when a possible through ball is "on," as well as when a possible overlap or takeover might take place. In other words, combination play has been taught and implemented in the overall coaching scheme.
- There has been functional/technical training between the midfielders and the strikers in terms of playing balls to feet or space with the strikers making the proper decisions based on the pressure by the defender, or their position relative to the defender's positioning.
- Some time has been spent on playing the ball wide to outside players with the proper supporting runs then made by both strikers and supporting midfielders in order to connect with flighted balls to either the near or far

posts or balls played behind the defense to withdrawn attackers.

Once these technical/tactical building blocks have been established (they might actually serve as the basis for the warm-up leading into this activity), then the coach can seek to coach to perceived problems that are exhibited as these exercises are implemented.

Exercise I: 2v2 in restricted goal area

Organization

Use flat cones to define the restricted areas with the server playing balls to either of the two forwards to initiate play.

To begin play, the server plays balls to the strikers and 2v2 play takes place in the restricted area shown.

Objectives

- To review the various phases of combination play between the two strikers
- To develop an aggressive attitude to score within players
- Creation of space by the forward based on quick checks to the ball or by a good first touch of the ball
- Use of quick changes of direction or changes of pace to free selves
- Develop judgment of angles and distances both from each other as well as in relation to goal and keeper
- Exhibit quality passing throughout exercise

Coaching Points: Diagram # 1

- Can A9 or A10 turn quickly on defender and shoot?
- Can they receive, turn and dribble to shoot?
- Can they receive, turn and recognize when to play a 1-2 combination?
- Can they receive, turn and play partner into a scoring position via a through ball, via an overlap, or initiate takeover?

Objectives

- Build on exercise I
- A8 takes long range shot
- A8 overlaps
- Decoy overlaps creating a 2v1 and allowing A9 or A10 to turn

Coaching Points: Diagram # 2

Do the players take advantage of their numerical superiority?

- By attacking aggressively with speed, with pace?
- Does the player farthest from ball pull wide to create space?
- Can the attacking team maintain the momentum of the attack?

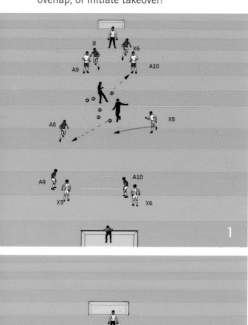

Exercise II: 3v2 in restricted area

Organization:

Server plays balls to A8 creating a 3v2; X8 recovers on the second touch of A8.

Exercise III: 4v3 in restricted area

Organization

Server plays ball A4 or A8, and they combine with A9 & A10 vs. three defenders (X5, X6, and X8) with X4 a recovering defender (on second touch of ball by A4 or A8).

Objectives

- Play the ball forward into the danger area with controlled speed.

Coaching Points: Diagram # 3
- Do attacking players maintain maximum width but attack as centrally as possible?
- Are early decisions made by midfielders to run with or pass the ball?
- Does the team maintain its attacking momentum?

- Is the early ball played preferably between the knee and head height?

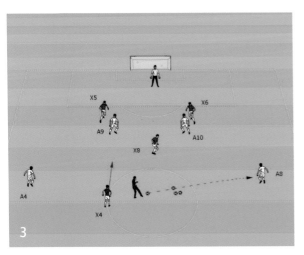

Exercise IV: 4v4 with wingers

Organization:
Server plays to 2v2 midfield situation with X2 and X3 acting as recovering wing backs. A7-A11 are wingers. Only attacking players may go into the shaded area (use flat cones to designate). At a certain point, allow X2 or X3 to chase a winger as exercise concludes.

Objectives
- Attack with pace centrally to take advantage of the bad positions of X2 and X3 (they can recover to defend centrally)
- Play wide to A7 or A11 only as a last resort

Coaching Points: Diagram # 4
- If the attack is slowed and ball is played wide, is the service of the ball early with pace into the second six-yard box (labeled "box" on the Diagram #)?

Exercise V: 6v8

Organization
Use the full width, half field, six attackers, eight defenders (one recovering at the start). Whether X8 recovers to A8 and the Xs play with a back four or X3 pushes forward to A8 and they play with two defenders and a sweeper is up to the defenders.

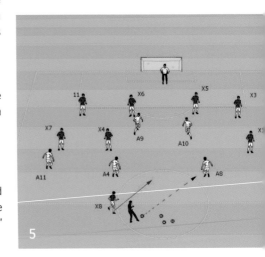

Objective: Diagram # 5

- Can the attacking players make decisions when to attack centrally and when to attack wide?

In conclusion, this practice session demands a high organization and a keen sense of observation by the coach to ensure that it is of value to the players and the team.

When to halt the exercise, when to move on to the next stage, when to place restrictions on players, etc., must be part of the coach's methodology in order for this to be imparted accurately to the team.

Finally, if there are repeated technical breakdowns in the exercise, then the coach and the team must get back to fundamentals and correct those errors. As often stated: "There are no tactics if there is no technique!"

Jack Detchon was the men's coach at Kenyon College (Ohio). Following a professional career in soccer, he served for many years as a regional coach with the English Football Association. He was an instructor in the NSCAA Academy program.

© Thinkstock/iStockphoto/Fluid Illusion

Attacking Zonal Defenses

Players must move faster than the zone can shift

Mike Parsons

The following is a recap of a presentation by Mike Parsons, NSCAA Director of Coaching Education, to the NSCAA Academy Premier Course.

There are major coaching points that need to be made to help players deal effectively with zonal defenses, to break through the defenses. Here are some of the points:

- Seek to place players and play balls into "the seams" in the zone.
- Teams must seek to play quickly, using first-time touches on the ball to move it and the attacking players faster than the zone can shift, creating opportunities for penetration.
- The third point builds somewhat on the second. Long, accurate passes are required to bypass zonal defenses, helping change the point of attack.
- Teams should try to play into the center of the zone, then back out to the flanks (similar to the "inside-outside" approach in basketball).
- The best means of breaking a zone is to be ready to counterattack when winning the ball. This disrupts the organization of a zonal defense.

8v6 training exercise – Diagram # 1

The first segment of the training is focused on an 8v6 attacking scheme from the back. An opposing player hit a long ball to the attacking team's goalkeeper to begin the session.

The objective was for the eight attacking players to enter the ball from the back to a midfielder who had found a seam in the midfield line of the zone as the ball traveled across the back line. As the entry pass is made, the attacking team must support the ball very quickly as the zone quickly surrounds the ball. If played to, the supporting player must be ready to make a decision with the ball on the first touch.

Diagram # 1 shows a quick ball out of the middle to the weak side midfielder, subsequently allowing that player to send a diagonal ball to the weak side striker. Again, the objective is for the attacking team to move across the line with the ball; under control. In the exercise, the defensive team won the ball, it was limited to three passes before it had to shoot on goal.

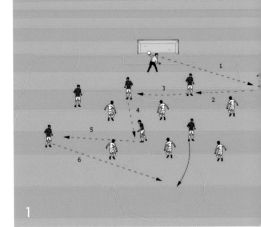

11v11 training exercise

Parsons began the next segment by establishing two 11-player sides, one playing a 4-4-2 and the other a 4-3-3 system of play. He placed the 4-3-3 on the field and instructed the players to play high (establishing their last line of defense at the midfield line).

He then placed the attacking team (triangles) on the field and started play with a long ball from the opposition to the goalkeeper of the attacking team, who then distributed it to one of the outside backs. As the ball traveled from the keeper to the back, the three defensive midfielders would shift to cover their zones (Diagram # 2).

Parsons reminded the candidates that the job of the zonal players was to squeeze space (generally the three midfielders in a 4-3-3 might be spread about 12 to 15 yards from each other) and shut off passing lanes. These tactics can be countered by quick shifts of the ball by the offensive team's back four and by playing accurate passes to teammates in the seams of the zone (Diagram # 2). Building out of the back, the attacking team decides which option is "on" – playing around/over the zone or between its seams.

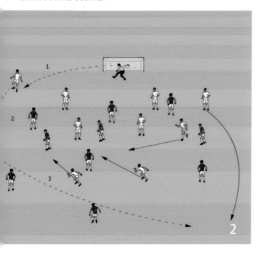

Diagram # 2 shows that the right back finds the extra midfielder (remember the attacking team has four midfielders versus the other team's three) on the perimeter of the field. In turn, that player elects to play a long cross-field pass to his opposite outside back who runs into an unoccupied space before the zone can reorganize (Diagram # 2).

Parsons reminded the coaches that two passes to send the ball to the weak side of the zone will not

get it done. The ability to play a long, accurate pass is crucial to effectively penetrate zonal defenses. Without that technical ability, particularly in your outside backs and midfielders, you are limited in your potential to disrupt zonal defenses.

Once the defensive team won the ball, it had only three passes to attempt a counterattack on goal. This restriction helped create more opportunities for the attacking team and, at the same time, opened up the potential for quick counters should the attacking team win the ball as the defending team came forward.

Parsons then told the attacking team that he wanted them to move the ball quickly, find the seams and dribble over a line established at the center circle's extreme edge.

On more than one occasion during the coaching session, play was halted to point out that just one extra touch on the ball by the attacking team had stalled the opportunity to play a penetrating pass into a midfielder who had arrived at a position in a zonal seam. "Play no more than two touches, one touch if possible" was Parsons' reminder.

The next phase of the session had the defending team drop back even farther into a low-pressure defensive mode, farther compacting its collective defending.

Parsons explained that the objective at this point was for the attacking team to find midfielders in the seams. They then play it back with one touch to a supporting back, looking to play diagonal balls over the top of the defense. This "up-back-through" sequence is shown in Diagram # 3. As noted, quick decision-making with the ball is essential for breaking down a zone At times, the players were able to demonstrate this penetration of midfield and the quick switch of play. If such a tactic broke down, it usually was a technical problem (the back took a second touch on the ball and defensive pressure would result, which would not allow the

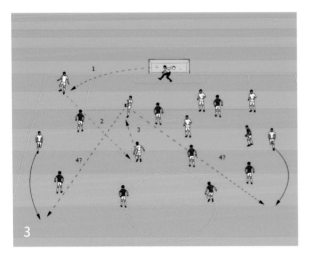

3

We have seen the back four be responsible for moving the ball from side to side. What also is available is penetration via the dribble. As the zone collects around the ball, the back now plays away to a teammate in a good supporting position. Finally, the value of the back's ability to play long, penetrating, accurate passes cannot be overestimated.

Midfielders must find seams in the zone in order to achieve penetration by their teammates. They also must be quick to support each other and, once in control, make quick decisions on how to play to their front runners or to the space behind the defense. Strikers also must show into the seams of the zone, be alert to the potential for counterattacks into the space behind the defense (as the zone is being established by the defensive team) and, as the ball is being passed across the field, be first to support weak side players.

change of the point of attack to take place). The dictum, "There are no tactics without technique," raised its ugly soccer head.

The final phase of the 4-4-2 v. 4-3-3 involved an "in-back-through" sequence trying to be imparted to the game by the attacking team (depicted in Diagram # 4). When the ball is played into the midfield, the defense tends to collapse toward the ball.

This is when the ball needs to be played back from the midfield to a supporting back, who then catches the collective defense moving forward and plays a ball over the top of the defense to an on-running striker.

As the 11v11 game unfolded, Parsons was looking for the teams to incorporate those ideas into the practice. One reminder to the teams was for them to play their outside midfielders as high as they could defensively. All the coaching points Parsons made were reiterated during the full-sided game. One important reminder is that the job of the attacking team is to put questions in the minds of the defenders. Make them make decisions. Put a question in their minds as to defending responsibilities. Hesitations in this regard will allow for more successful attacking soccer.

Concluding phase

In the concluding 11v11, Parsons had both teams playing a 4-4-2 formation and the defending team (the Os) having only five passes before it had to shoot on goal.

During this final phase of the training session, Parsons reminded the candidates of the roles played by the three lines.

Mike Parsons was an NSCAA Director of Coaching Education. His previous coaching experience includes stints as head coach at Stetson (Fla.) and as assistant at UNC-Greensboro, Old Dominion and Notre Dame. He also served as Director of Coaching for a youth club in the Tidewater area of Virginia.

Attacking the Sweeper

Striker teamwork is critical to penetrating to the goal

John Bluem

The following is an overview of a coaching session in the NSCAA Premier Course at the NSCAA National Academy held at Nova Southeastern University in Fort Lauderdale, Florida.

Preparation for session

- Ten training vests are needed for each of the two full teams; a different color vest is needed for the coach and the two goalkeepers.
- Eight corner flags are used to establish goals in each of the four quadrants of the 18-yard line extended.
- Two full-size goals also are required
- A half dozen balls at each end line.

Four-goal game

- Two full squads are selected with one team as the attacking team for coaching purposes.
- Play starts with a back from the defending team playing a ball to one of the backs of the attacking team.
- Each team's objective is to cross one of its two goals with the ball under control.
- The defending team, upon winning the ball, must cross the goal line within three passes. This assures direct play and assumes that the attacking team will have the majority of chances to successfully attack the sweeper.

The two strikers are to play in close support of each other. One would try to check back for the ball and, if possible, turn with the ball. This would attract the sweeper as the marking back's cover. We see this central combination at work in Diagram # 1.

The striker now can turn or lay off a ball to a central midfielder, who can dribble or pass to the second striker, who then is in a good position to play the ball wide to an outside midfielder to control the ball and score.

A second variation of the four-goal game is shown in Diagram # 2. Here, we see the forward checking back to the ball being served by an attacking outside midfielder. Again, the marking back drags the sweeper with the play. The forward lays the ball back to a supporting midfielder, who now changes the field with a ball to the weak side outside midfielder to go to goal.

11v11

Having stressed central combination play and quick changes of the point of the attack, goalkeepers were added to both teams. Now both teams are playing 11v11, though the attacking team plays its back four flat so that the inside backs can cover both of their outside backs. The team defending now plays with the restriction that it is limited to four passes in order to develop a shot on goal. This makes its play very direct.

When trying to create 2v1's or to isolate your attacker 1v1 without sweeper cover, teams must be very patient. If the attempt to create either of these situations breaks down, teams must, in collective fashion, play for possession and work the ball around to achieve either of the two playing objectives.

A third variation in attack is shown in Diagram # 3, where we see the two strikers both checking to the ball as it is passed between the two central midfielders. At the same time, the weak side outside midfielder drags the defender into the center and the outside back now runs into the vacated space to receive a pass from the midfielder. The sweeper has been occupied and drawn away from the space on the far side of the field.

It is up to the central midfielders to be concerned with changing the point of attack. It is the outside midfielders who will occupy the attacking spaces on the perimeters, and the two strikers should not make runs into those spaces. Rather, they should play centrally and seek to occupy the sweeper with runs as indicated in the Diagram #s.

The coaching position taken by the instructor (who wore a colored bib that distinguished him from the two teams) in the 11v11 game was in the middle of the field. This enabled him to be able to quickly halt play to point out how certain situations were effective or not in occupying the sweeper.

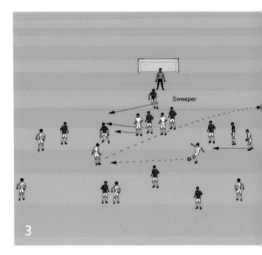

John Bluem, is the coach of the Ohio State men's team. He is a senior member of the NSCAA National Academy coaching staff.

Beating a Packed Defense

Shooting from distance and attacking wide spaces work best

Sigi Schmid

Whenever a soccer team has a fair amount of success, it will soon confront a unique problem. The opponents will play a more defensive game in order to give themselves a better chance of defeating you. This occurs at the youth, college, senior, professional, and internationals levels of play. The question becomes how to still defeat this opponent who is playing with a "packed defense."

Patience is a vital element in defeating a defensive-oriented team. However, patience is usually a partner of maturity. At the youth and college levels, maturity and patience are hard to find due to the inexperience and age of players. As a result, more upsets occur at these levels.

The key element in defeating any team, and certainly a defensive team, is to exploit the space behind the defense. Exploiting this space versus a defensive team can be accomplished by:

- Counterattacking before the defense gets organized.
- Drawing the opponents defense away from their goal by shooting from distance and maintaining possession (passing), causing the opponent's defense to become impatient and come out.
- Attacking wide spaces and getting behind the opponent to make crosses

Shooting from distance

Accurate, dangerous shots will force an opponent's defense to put pressure on the ball and therefore move forward. As they do this, openings are often created for central combinations (one-two's,

takeovers, double passes, etc.). Shooting from distance can be part of the training.

Exercise 1(Diagram # 1)

A basic exercise to warm-up is the shooting box outside the penalty box. Create a grid 30 yards wide by 20 yards long about 10 yards outside the penalty box.

Inside this grid, each player has a ball and a number. When a coach calls out a number, that player (For example player 3) dribbles out of the grid into the zone in front of the penalty box and takes a shot.

All the other players continue to dribble and move within the grid until their number is called. Once a player shoots, they retrieve the ball and return to the grid.

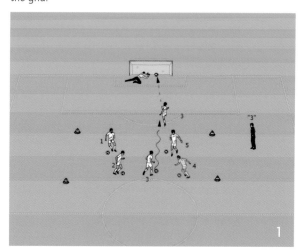

Exercise 2 (Diagram # 2)

Here, we slightly alter the format utilized in the first exercise. When the player's number is called (for example player 4), they find space and hit a one-two pass with the coach who is positioned at the top of the penalty box, and finish with a shot.

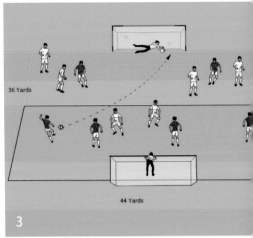

Exercise 3 (Diagram # 3)

Shooting against a packed defense becomes very realistic when we add defensive bodies into the drill. A good exercise for this is the long-shooting game. Use an area that is the size of a double penalty box in length and the width of a penalty box. Divide the area in half. In each half, you have four defenders and two attackers. All players stay in their half. The defenders maintain possession in their half looking to free themselves for shots on goal.

Shots are occurring in the 18-25-yard range usually. Let's take the red's as an example. The red forwards are looking to defend or re-direct shots as well as trying to find rebounds. Additionally, a red defender can play the ball into a red forward who then plays it back to a red defender for a shot on goal. Otherwise, the four red defenders try to interpass the ball looking for open shots. When the ball turns over, the blue/whites do the same. The size of the grid and number of players can be adjusted depending upon the age and ability of your team. This exercise is realistic and very good for the development of long-range shooting.

Attacking wide spaces

In order to have successful wide play, your team must work on the tactics of combination play in two's and three's. The overlap, double-pass, takeover, and one-two must all be part of their understanding. Additionally, changing the point of attack (switching the ball) from one side to the other and dribbling need to be understood. Here are two team exercises that can enhance your team's ability at creating wide play.

Exercise 5 (Diagram # 5)

In this exercise, the grid is similar in size to the one above. In each attacking half, two larger cones are placed about 25 yards from the end line and 20 yards in from each sideline (Diagram # 5). A team can only conclude an attack on goal by first playing around the outside of one of the two cones. This game forces wide play as a means of creating scoring chances.

Shooting from distance and attacking wide spaces are two vital means that can make a difference between successful teams and ones that "pack it in."

Sigi Schmid is the head coach of Major League Soccer's Seattle Sounders . In addition to the Sounders, Sigi coached the LA Galaxy and the Columbus Crew – winning the MLS Cup with both teams. He was coach at UCLA at the time this article appeared in the then Gil Sports newsletter. His UCLA teams were 322-63-33 and three times were NCAA Division I champions during his 21-year tenure.

Exercise 4: Diagram # 4

In a grid the width of the field and a length varying between 50 and 80 yards, depending upon age and numbers, create a channel on each side along the width of the penalty box (Diagram # 4). As the reds attack, for example, two reds (attackers) are allowed in the outside channel and only one blue/white (defender). Thereby, this game always creates 2v1 opportunities on the flanks, enhancing wide play. When the blue/white team wins the ball, the same rules apply.

Stretching the Opponent

When a team can create gaps and additional space, good things happen

John Cossaboon

Far too much of our soccer (youth, club, collegiate and, dare I say, "higher levels") is being played in a linear fashion. Great things sometimes occur on the way to the goal, but more often than not possession is lost. True, the above is just my opinion; however, it is an aspect of the game that I spend a lot of time trying to get players to understand.

I think we would have very little argument among a group of coaches at their favorite watering hole related to penetrating (directly) if the space exists. It makes complete sense. Go forward as fast as you can if the opponent's shape is unbalanced and attacking space exists. I also think that we would tend to agree with the concept of building or changing the point of attack if we recognize that the opponent's defensive shape is well organized.

Here's where the argument would start. "We don't devote enough time to teaching players to stretch the opponent." The concept is simple. Create gaps and additional space. Attack these newly created spaces quickly. Keep the opponent unbalanced by the intelligent movement of the entire team. Sounds simple.

In order for your players to develop the ability to stretch (spread) and attack in a cohesive manner, they must all react immediately, at the instant of gaining possession. The best teams react before they possess, but that's another story.

Initially, let's keep it simple
- Teach every player to recognize the opponent's shape at the instant your team gains the ball.
- Teach them to communicate immediately and respond to the action of their teammate in possession of the ball.
- Players should ask:
- Are we attacking at pace because the attacking space exists or because we're caught up in the excitement of getting to goal?
- Are we building when we clearly have an opportunity to get into penetrating spaces in a more direct manner?

With questions like these, we educate the entire team and bring them closer to thinking as one. There always will be situations that create different responses from different players. That's fine. Players' decisions will begin to move in a similar direction. They learn to react cohesively if they are challenged to see the determining factors, the reasons for the team's decision to attack directly or to stretch the opponent.

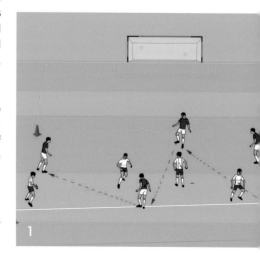

The following exercise is one that allows me to teach and reinforce the concepts I believe are important to stretching and penetrating an opponent's defense.

Exercise I (Diagram # 1)

5v5 (can be varied). Play in a large grid within one-half of the field. Leave about 10 yards of space between each boundary line and the half lines

Progression of activity

Initiate activity by playing possession in the large grid. Players are told to move the ball until one player can play a ball to a teammate who has expanded out over any one of the grid's boundary lines. That player should receive facing the grid (Diagram # 2). This pass out initiates "stretching."

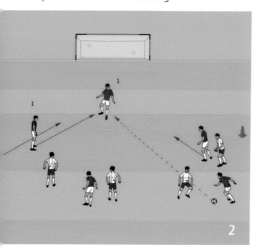

they immediately play back to a teammate within the grid.

The exercise is continuous and follows the basic rules of possession. Sequence:

* Possession 5v5.
* Pass out to expanding player.
* Pass to supporting player who has taken up a position outside either sideline. Sidelines are determined by the boundary that was crossed with first pass out.
* Re-enter grid, battle to maintain possession (repeat) non-stop. Loss of possession, at any time, simply reverses roles (offense to defense).

As Player A opens the playing space, teammates must expand and offer support at either or both sidelines (based on the ball's position), as in Diagram # 3

Initially, defenders could be limited from following the expanding players, but eventually the players in possession must learn to distance themselves from opponents at the instant support is needed. If the team in possession succeeds with this sequence,

Exercise II: Diagram # 4

Continue as above with the addition of one more objective.

Play a third pass down the sideline that has been exploited.

- Possess
- Expand
- Stretch
- Penetrate flank

This activity continues to be played with any particular attacking direction. The first pass to an expanding player determines the flanks. Play can be continuous or restarted with a "free" pass back into the grid after each successful sequence. Reward the successful team.

Exercise III: Diagram # 5

- Use whatever numbers and size grid are appropriate to your team.
- Place goals on each 18 (with goalkeepers).
- Center the same grid between these goals. The starting place is basically both teams' middle third.

Play starts with both teams battling for possession in the center grid. The team in possession expands at will, either back and out or simply out to a flank. They attack in a predetermined direction. Allow them to experiment (play!), but make corrections based on what you see.

- If the keeper makes a save, have him distribute to the center grid.
- If a goal is scored or the opponent gains possession, the ball must return to the center grid (i.e., for at least three passes).

Coaching points, in all stages

- Recognition of the compact defense.
- Communication by and playing to the expanding player.
- Early recognition and movement to close and far supporting positions.
- Quick, clean touches, body position to attacking direction and quality distribution
- Timing and selection of runs.
- Finally, as always, remove restrictions and play within the match condition.

In conclusion, we can all directly play the first time we step on a soccer field. Let's give players the information they need to make quality decisions related to the most appropriate method of attack. Each attacking movement is enhanced when players understand the role they play in bringing it to completion. Goal!

John Cossaboon is the women's coach at the University of San Diego and a senior member of the NSCAA National Staff.

SWI-I-I-ITCH!

Changing the point of attack creates penetrating spaces to allow breakthroughs

Robert Parr

Well-organized defenses typically place a large number of players between the ball and their goal, leaving little space for an attacking team to create high-quality scoring opportunities. When faced with this type of defensive compactness, a team must vary its point of attack to create penetrating spaces for overlapping and supporting players away from the ball, breaking down the opponent's defensive shape.

Changing the point of attack can be accomplished directly (a single long service from one side of the field to the other) or indirectly (several players combining to quickly pass the ball from one touchline to the other). The central midfielders and defenders have the greatest influence over this element of the game, because they have the most opportunities to switch the ball from one side to the other and should be in position to see the attacking options in front of them.

If the midfielders are struggling to change the point of attack in game play, consideration should be given to the following questions to identify the potential tactical causes of each breakdown:

- **Do players recognize when to change the point of attack?** When the ball is near the touchline and both teams have packed the space in front of the dribbler, teams should look to switch the point of attack to the opposite side of the field. The middle third of the field is the best area in which to do this since teams generally want to drive straight to goal in their attacking third and avoid playing balls across the center of their defensive third.

- **Are the central players providing close support when the wing players have the ball?** Few players have the physical ability to strike a ball across the full width of the field while under pressure. Because of this, the central players must constantly provide close support to the flank players so they can combine to move the ball to the far side while still playing within their physical limits.

- **Are the wing players (away from the ball) using the full width of the field to stretch the opposing defense as much as possible?** Once the central player has received the ball and is looking to play it to the opposite side, he/she needs to have a teammate in position to receive that ball. The receiving winger must start square with the ball on the far touchline so he/she can receive the cross while running directly toward goal. By starting behind the line of the ball and as wide as possible, the wing player also will maximize the amount of positive attacking space the ball can be delivered into.

- **Are the players reading the opponent's defensive organization to serve the ball into the correct spaces?** If the defenders on the far side of the field have taken a deep posture, leaving a gap between themselves and the wing players, the service from the central midfielder should be played directly to the feet of the winger and away from the defenders. Alternately, if the defense has pushed out of the back, the service should be played into the open space behind the defensive line and away from the opposing goalkeeper.

© Thinkstock/iStockphoto/Fluid Illusion

As with any other aspect of the game, players may be making the correct decisions, yet they still give up possession when they try to move the ball to the other side of the field. In this situation, consideration should also be given to some of the technical points of failure that could be limiting success:

- **Are the central players able to turn with the ball on their first touch?** When a central player receives the ball from a teammate on

the wing, he/she needs to quickly adjust his/her body position to see the other side of the field. Typically, the receiving player should use the outside of the foot to "sweep" the ball toward the middle of the field on the first touch, "opening" his/her vision to identify all forward penetrating options.

- **Are the central players turning directly into defensive pressure?** If the supporting player is closely marked, he/she should use the outside of the foot farthest from the defender to sweep the ball away from pressure, shielding the ball away from a possible tackle.

- **Do the players have the proper power on the ball when they strike it over longer distances?** The pace and placement of longer crosses is especially important when a team uses a more direct approach to switch the point of attack. If the services are hit too hard, the team may lose possession out of bounds. Worse still, if crosses are falling short, the attacking team becomes vulnerable to a quick counterattack when the ball is intercepted by opposing central defenders.

The following game helps train players to read an opponent's defensive shape and encourages them to change the point of attack in midfield to find better attacking options.

confirm that the players continue to read their attacking options across the width of the field, even under game conditions.

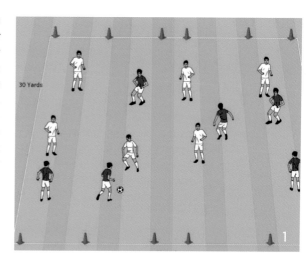

30 Yards

Midfield Point of Attack Game

Set up a field 30 yards long by 60 yards wide with three sets of cone goals placed along each end. The two cone goals in the center of the field should be only two to three yards wide; the other four goals (near each corner of the field) should be six to eight yards wide. Play a game of 6v6, with each team defending three goals and attacking the other three goals.

This exercise should provide many opportunities to evaluate and correct the players' ability to provide short supporting options to teammates on the wings, as well as the timing of their decisions to switch the point of attack. As the players begin to find success in this game, increase the dimensions of the area to play in half a field. The extra depth should present more opportunities to adjust between direct and indirect styles, using the positioning of the defensive line to guide this decision-making. Finally, remove the small goals and play to two full-sized goals (with keepers) to

Co-creator of SoccerROM.com, Robert Parr holds a USSF "A" license, a USSF National Youth Coaching license and is the women's coach at Georgia College and State University. Previously, he was the Director of Training for the American Soccer Club "Eagles" youth program in Austin, Texas. He also served as the South Texas Men's State Team Coach from 1996-1998 and a South Texas YSA State Staff Coach for both the Olympic Development Program (1991-1999) and the Coaching Education Program (1991-2002). From 1989 until 1995, he was the coach of the University of Texas men's team, which he led to a National Collegiate Club Championship in 1990, three other national tournament appearances and an overall record of 80-25-16.

Quick Breaks = Goals!!!

Quick breaks lead to scores — counterattacks can catch opponents before they recover to strong defensive positions

Wayne Harrison

Counterattacking is becoming an important part of a team's tactical package. Recent tactics employed at the international level underscore the importance of counterattacking. Teams should use the following progression when learning the counterattack on the training ground. The guidelines for each step:

- Time the break to get a shot within 10 seconds. Decrease the time as the team improves the attack.
- Players work alternately in both directions. This is also a good conditioning session. Working both ways allows all players to get involved in the activity.
- The idea of this session is to practice quick breaks (counterattacks) against opponents as they recover back into strong defensive positions.
- Set the session up based on the number of players at the training session.
- Set it up to go only one side if there is little space to work in or a small number of players. Be flexible.
- Both teams get the chance to practice attacking and defending at pace, which will improve quick decision-making.
- Introduce offside where and when necessary. It may be best not to use offside initially until the players get used to the idea. As the session moves on, it should be game realistic, with offside being used.

Step I: 2v1 in Attack – The Basic Set-Up

- Players make two passes among themselves in midfield, then pass it to the striker. Three players (3, 4 and 5) support quickly to exploit the attacking overload situation. Recovery runs by defenders (B) cannot begin until the ball has been passed into the striker.
- Begin with an overload and have two strikers against one defender (as above). Have one recovering defender to help the sole defender already at the back but who is in a 2v1 disadvantage. This is a good start to the session, as it makes it easier to gain success for the attacking team, which ultimately is the goal of the drill.

Progression
- A 2v1 up front in favor of the strikers, creating a 5v2 overload situation where three support

players and one recovering defender join in as the ball is played into the two strikers.

- A 1v1 up front, creating a 4v2 overload when three support players and a recovering defender join the attack.
- A 2v2 up front creates a 5v3 overload with three support players and one recovering defensive player.
- A 1v2 disadvantage (one striker and two defenders) creates a 4v3-overload situation with three support players and one recovering defensive player.
- With each progression, the attacking situation gets more difficult and is a greater challenge to the players. The coach should work through each progression based on how quickly the players have success. The number of support players and the number of recovering players can be varied; this sequence is suggested as a guide. Keep experimenting to find the best formula to suit a team's particular needs.

Step II: 1v1 in Attack

- The next step is a 1v1 situation. This is a more difficult attacking situation. The midfield player passes to space for (1) to come off the defender and turn. Three players break quickly to support, with two players running to the

center and one wide. One defender makes a recovery run to help, creating a 4v2 situation

- Now move on to a 2v2 situation by adding another striker and another defender. Then try a 1v2 in favor of the defenders – all are good progressions for this session. The final setup may mean it is difficult for (1) to receive the ball if the two defenders screen both sides of the forward. The support players can "run the ball in" on the dribble to start play.

Step III: 2v2 in Attack

- The graphic below (Diagram #3) shows a 2v2 attacking situation. This phase begins to coordinate the movement of the strikers. Here (1) goes short to receive a ball to feet and takes (A) with him/her, creating space behind for the diagonal run of (2), who goes "late and fast" to get away from marker (B). The midfield player has more options with this type of movement. Timing of the run is important.
- "Late and fast" means that (2) can receive the ball in front to go on to shoot at goal having escaped (B) marking. If too early, then (2) may receive the ball with his/her back to goal and (B) will have time to cover. The early run will mean the forward (2) will have to link with another attacking player.

Step IV: 1v2 in Attack

- The coach can vary the direction the defenders recover from to make the situation more difficult for the attacking team. Here, defenders are recovering from both sides of the field. Attacking players also are breaking forward from both sides, (2) from the center and (5) from the opposite side.
- The coach can vary the numbers of attacking and defending players at any time to ensure success.
- Attacking from all sides of the field creates a bigger challenge to all the attacking players. A 5v4 is created here, but the situation can be set up to focus on any aspect of the counterattack. Using the set-up above, a 5v4 is created one way and a 3v2 is created going the other way, unless the players are permitted to recover back from the previous quick break encounter.
- The secret is to vary the numbers attacking each way depending on the situations the coach is trying to create – big overloads, small overloads, degree of difficulty, etc., change the situation for the players. Only the coach's imagination limits the variables in this session.

Step V: 1v2 in Attack

- This is another example of a 1v2 disadvantage. Depending on numbers playing in the training session, the coach may, in this situation, have only one recovering defender and three attacking players joining the lone striker, creating a 4v3 situation. This means there are players left to play in the other direction once the first attack is finished.

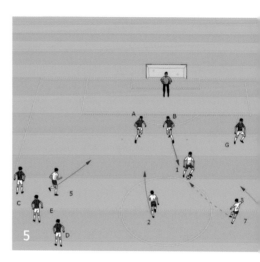

Directional session

- The session is set up to favor attacking play, hence the overload attacking is always in the attacking team's favor, therefore this leaves an overload in the middle.
- The team in possession can make up to three passes, then must pass the ball to the strikers. Three midfield players break quickly to support (making a 5v1 overload in favor of the attacking team). Start with a big overload and a 2v1 in favor of the strikers in attack, as in Part 1, and then introduce the recovering midfielder later when the session is working well for a greater challenge. This leaves a 4v1 situation in favor of the defending team in the middle zone if no recovering midfielder is used to begin. If the defenders win the ball or the

keeper receives it, the ball is played quickly into the middle zone (to a 4v1 overload again, going the other way). They can make up to three passes, then get the ball to the striker to attack in the other direction. Players can pass or run the ball in based on each situation. Vary the difficulty depending on how successful the team is, constantly giving them greater challenges.

- It may take three passes or only one. Have the players try to make three passes or less if the ball is not overplayed in the middle. Have extra balls available to keep the session flowing. If one team scores or the ball goes out of play, pass a ball to the other team to restart from midfield, otherwise the defenders will win it and pass it into the middle zone to attack the other way.
- Introduce offside when it is necessary. Do not use it until the players are ready, then make the situation realistic.

Potential progressions
- 2v1 up front in favor of the strikers with three supporting players, making a 5v1 situation.
- 1v1 up front with three supporting players, making a 4v1 situation.
- 1v1 up front with three supporting players and 1 recovering player, making a 4v2 situation.
- 2v2 up front with two supporting players, making a 4v2.
- 1v2 up front with two supporting players, making a 4v2.

2v1 in Attack (Diagram # 6)

The first part of the session is the easiest to gain success with: a 2v1 advantage up front and three supporting players breaking forward to help the two strikers, creating the 5v1 overload. Coaching points include:

- Look for quick breaks in attack.
- Passing and support play.
- Early shots on goal.

- Regains of the ball and quick counterattacks going the other way.

2v1 in Attack (Diagram # 7)

- After the ball has been passed to No. 2, the three supporting players break forward into various positions, offering up several choices for passing. This should progress easily into a cross and a shot or header on goal. In many cases, the coach can move on from this set-up quickly into something more challenging.

1v1 in Attack (Diagram # 8)

- Now there is a 1v1 up front. In this example, we have the three supporting players joining the lone striker, making it a 4v1 overload in favor of the attacking team.
- Timing of the support runs is important (stagger support so they do not all go in a straight line), as are the areas covered in support so there are many options for the player on the ball to choose from.

2v2 in Attack (Diagram # 9)

- Now we have a 2v2 in attack. An example of an attack here is for the striker to go short to receive to feet, half turn and play the ball wide for an attacking midfielder who breaks forward and gets a cross into the box. Now, it is the secondary movement of the strikers to get into the box once the first link up that we need to focus on has been made. Players attacking all the important areas in and around the box, near post, middle of the goal and far post, all done as quickly as possible against the clock emphasizing speed in attack
- No. 2 near post, No. 1 far post, and midfielder No. 4 in the middle around or just inside the edge of the box.

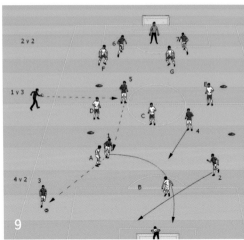

2v2 in Attack (Diagram # 10)

- Finishing positions of the players are near post, far post and central behind. The defenders also are back, as this set-up is offside.
- The cross is into the second six-yard box away from the keeper. Recovering defenders must avoid scoring an own goal in this situation.
- This is an example of why it is good to deliver the cross quickly behind the defenders and not take it to the by line to cross, which allows the opponents to recover defensive position.
- Work on the timing and angle of the runs into the box and contact on the ball to finish with a goal attempt.

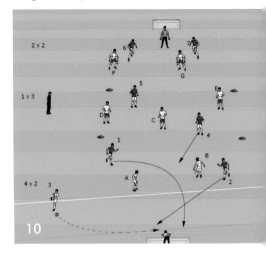

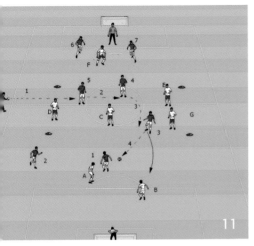

11

1v2 in Attack (Diagram # 11)

- Staying with the overload theme, it is now a more difficult 1v2 situation up front. It is a 3v2 overload with two instead of three midfielders joining in to attack. Players can run or pass the ball in. No. 1 needs to get free to receive. This is a real test now with just the 3v2 overload.
- To make it even more difficult, have a recovering defender get back to help out the defense.
- The counterattack is now slightly more difficult also with a 4v2 overload in the middle midfield zone going the other way and only a 3v2 overload if the recovering defender has been added.

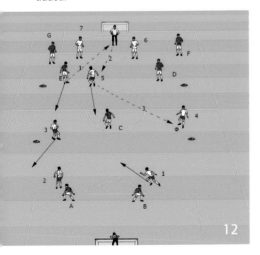

12

Further Progression (Diagram # 12)

- Player E shoots at goal. The keeper gains possession of the ball. Introduce a development where a midfield player can "drop deep to receive the ball," either from the keeper or a defender to set up the next play.
- No. 1 drops off and receives the ball to work it forward through midfield or directly to a striker, in this case a pass to No. 4, who runs the ball into the attacking zone to create a 4v2 with No. 3 moving in from midfield.
- The team has transitioned very quickly from the keeper to the strikers after gaining possession.

13

More Direct Play (Diagram # 13)

- Choices now include quick counterattacking playing through the midfield or a direct ball into the strikers, and the midfield can then link up with them.
- No. 6 plays a long ball into the feet of striker No. 1. Nos. 3 and 4 are already on the way forward to support the strikers from midfield.
- The move shows these players breaking forward to attack on the numbers team, creating a 4v2 overload and the defending team's midfield who attacked the other way previously (Players D and E) are recovering to be ready for the next

underway in the opposite direction.

- Progression: A recovering defender who comes out of the middle midfield zone to help the defenders can be added to both sides.
- Work on defending against a counterattacking fast break overload too, but that is another session altogether.

Planning for Part Two

Attacking Team

- Midfielders must get the passes in, then break quickly and support the strikers as the ball is played into them. Midfielders can run or pass the ball in and another player can go in. Vary the support players from here based on available space.
- Strikers must get free from their markers to receive the ball and link up with the attacking quick break midfielders or turn and attack themselves — depending on the defenders' positions.
- The team needs to score in a certain short time scale. Decrease the time allowed as they improve at this.
- Vary the number of players in striking positions as you develop the session. Start with one, then two. Have these two link together to develop an understanding of movement off the ball for each other to create space for themselves and each other.
- As soon as the move breaks down, the attacking midfield players who joined in with the strikers need to get back to their original midfield area. You also can coach them to rotate – it may be a striker who is nearer who makes a recovery run back to fill in for the midfielder who may have ended up beyond that striker in the attacking third of the field. Nearest player, shortest recovery route back.
- The idea is to overload the attack to gain success from the session in an attacking sense, but at the same time keep balance should the opponents win the ball and attack quickly the other way.

attack the other way. They must be available to receive the ball should Players K, A or B win possession. Another transition attack then is

Defending Team

- Recovering players get back quickly to counter the quick attack.
- Vary the number of defenders already in position and those recovering during build-up of the session to change the challenges of the teams.
- Midfielders in the middle third on the team without the ball must be ready to break quickly should they win it back in the defending third. They need to be moving constantly, getting free from opponents to receive the ball once the keeper or a defender gains possession of it.
- The strikers on the team without the ball also need to be constantly moving. Don't stand still – keep working the defenders so that they are ready and in a position of advantage when their team wins possession.
- When the defending team wins the ball and it is played into midfield, it may be a defender who joins in and goes all the way into the attacking third. The defender can pass or run it in. Make sure a midfielder drops back into a defensive position into the defensive third to provide cover. This encourages the players to rotate positions and develop more freedom in their positioning on the field.

General Observations

- Once the session gets going, maintain the overload situations in midfield as the transitions take place from defense to attack to ensure you get the session working effectively. There should be constant transition from attack to defense and defense to attack, both happening at pace.
- Eventually open the game up into an actual scrimmage and see if both teams have adopted the quick break mentality you have been trying to teach. Now it is equal numbers in all areas, so it will be a good test for the players to see if they can make it work.

Revisions of Developments for the Transition Game

- 2v1 in each attacking and defending zone and 4v4 in the middle zone to begin. Big overload to gain success in the attacking play, three attacking midfielders and one recovering defender making a 4v2 overload.
- 1v1 in each attacking and defending zone and 5v5 in the middle zone.
- 2v2, then 1v2 in the attacking and defending zones with fewer players in the middle zone but still equal numbers there. Midfield can run it in now. Work on the movement of the two strikers or the lone striker to create space and move the defenders around.
- Allow a midfield player from the middle zone to drop back into the defending zone where his or her team has regained possession to provide help in the link-up play (distances may prevent a good long pass from the back directly to midfield, depending on the age group being coached, so this helps). Opponents can't follow them in (put a restriction on this) to give the attack a better chance to build quickly.
- Encourage different units of players to interchange based on where they end up in a positional sense on the field of play – for example, if a defender breaks forward and ends up in the attacking third, have a midfielder drop back to cover; if a midfielder moves into the attacking third in the most advanced position on that team and the team then loses possession, maybe a striker can drop back to cover.
- This allows and supports freedom of movement for the players. They can have confidence to interchange on the field, knowing a teammate will cover for them.

Wayne Harrison has been a youth, college and professional coach. He has written many books about soccer.

High Pressure vs. Low Pressure

Jay Miller

The following was originally published in the July-August 1984 Soccer Journal. Jay Miller made this presentation at the 1984 NSCAA Convention in Philadelphia.

High pressure can best be used in the following situations:

- To catch opponents off guard, especially at the beginning of a match
- When opponents are weak defensively or when the defenders have trouble getting the ball out of their defensive third
- When a team is behind or tied and needs a goal late in the match
- To change the tempo of the game

On the other hand, low pressure may be employed when:

- When a team is much slower than the opponents
- When there are opposing players that demand special attention and can not be contained by a team's regular defensive tactics, i.e., 1 on 1 marking
- Injuries prevent a team from playing as it usually would
- A team is fatigued and just wants to "hold on" to preserve a win or a draw
- When a team's most effective attacking weapon is the counterattack. A low pressure defense can open up space behind opponents as they come forward.
- A team is playing numbers down after losing a man to a red card

High Pressure

Generally, high pressure defense is man to man and should be applied in the opponent's defensive third – your attacking third – of the field. It is most effective when alternated with other styles of defensive play. Because high pressure requires 100% intensity, it is hard to apply constantly throughout the entire match.

The best time to introduce high pressure would be a dead ball situation, such as a throw-in, or with a substitution of a fresh player. It is important that the coach know his/her personnel and give pressurizing responsibilities to the type of individuals whose playing style and personalities fit the role.

A variation on the standard high pressure man to man would be some form of zone press all over the field. Because high pressure leaves a team vulnerable at the back, it is important that the coach makes his/her team aware of this by training the team to maintain balance and to be prepared for defensive adjustments in the back.

The goalkeeper, in particular, needs specialized training in the type of situations that he/she will face when his team is playing high pressure. The keeper must practice breakaway saves, as well as directing the team from the top of the 18-yard box or even becoming a "sweeper" if necessary. If any player is beaten in high pressure marking, he/she should know the proper lines of recovery to get back and goal side to prevent penetration by opponents as quickly as possible.

Low Pressure

Low pressure, on the other hand, offers a considerable contrast. The most vital element in low pressure defense is organization. Each player must be aware of the specific responsibilities of the position and know how to fall back to protect

the critical area in the defensive third of the field. However, once the team has retreated, there are important considerations. There is no longer the luxury of loose marking, nor can a defender afford to pass an attacking player in the defensive third.

A danger in employing low pressure, whether in a zone or man to man, is that the defenders retreat too far and crowd the goalkeeper. This prevents the keeper from seeing the play clearly and reducing the room to maneuver or come out of the goal area.

Since a common tactic employed to upset a zone or defeat any type of low pressure defense is to switch play, the goalkeeper must receive training on dealing with air balls flighted into the box.

Finally, the coach should not only develop the organization of the defense but should educate the team in the principles of the counterattack to take advantage of opportunities created in quick transition.

Summary

Regardless of which style the team plays, it is the responsibility of the coach to prepare his squad. In training sessions, the coach must create situations that could appear in competitive matches and rehearse these until the players become accustomed to the system. By intelligent use of personnel in the right positions and by preparing each player thoroughly, the coach can enhance the possibilities for success.

Jay Miller is a long-time member of the US Soccer coaching staff. When this was presented, Jay was the head coach at the University of Tampa.

Zonal Defending

Is it right for your team?

Jeff Tipping

This presentation deals with methods of teaching zonal defending. We are primarily concerned here with two major characteristics of zonal defending:

- Concern with space defending rather than man-to-man. The decision whether to mark a man tightly or to cover a teammate is highlighted in zonal defending more than man-to-man.
- Maintaining an effective team shape from which to defend. Collective defending is more important in zonal systems. Keeping zone small and tight is critical if this system is to be effective.

It should be noted that most zonal teams play out of a 4-4-2 formation. It is generally accepted that four players can cover the dangerous spaces across the field. Most international teams play a zone defense.

Coaches adopt zonal tactics for a number of reasons, some of which include:

- **Team shape.** It is easier to keep a good defending shape out of a zone. Players are less inclined to get pulled out of important positions.
- **Fitness.** Players in zones generally do less running and tacking of opponents around the field.
- **Weaknesses.** It is easier to hide a weak defender in a zone than in man-to-man.
- **Attack.** Teams that have maintained a good shape defensively can attack more efficiently from an organized shape after gaining possession.

The disadvantages in zonal defending may include:

- **Assignment marking.** It is difficult to pull a player out of a zone to "assign mark" an outstanding opponent.

- **Demands verbal communication.** "When in doubt, give a shout" is never more true than in zonal defending. Talking is indispensable and yet many of our players do not talk.
- **Square back four.** The back four get caught flat, especially when the ball is in the middle of the field, or with long flighted balls.
- **Decision-making.** Emphasizes the burden on defenders of deciding whether to pressure a player or cover for a teammate. This leads to looser marking than in man-to-man. (Ian Rush vs. Everton 1989 FA Cup Final goals #2 and #3)

Keys to good zonal defending

- The work of the two central defenders is vital. The whole team pivots around these two.
- Defenders generally do not cross in front of each other except in emergency situations. They may cross behind a teammate to cover for him or to cut out a through pass.
- Teams must be compact and "travel with the ball." Defenders must move as a block to minimize spaces.
- The ball should be forced wide and kept wide. This helps the "stepping" effect of back four and midfield.
- There must be constant pressure on the ball to prevent vertical service.
- If there is not pressure on the ball, the two central defenders must decide whether to drop off or possibly step up to catch opponents offside.

Warm-ups

Handball – Game normally promotes lots of verbal communication between players (Diagram # 1)

5v5 in each half of the field. One defender goes in goal when opponents come over halfway line. Defense plays a 4v5. Nobody allowed over halfway line, but when defense wins ball, they play pass to teammates in other half. Passing is by the hand only. Player in possession is allowed two steps before passing. Goals only scored on header.

"Fire" exercise (Diagram # 2)

This exercise (designed by coach Mike Berticelli of Notre Dame) is a good exercise for team morale and also teaching defenders important zonal principles. Split team into three groups of three defenders and two groups of seven attackers. Three defenders stand in the "D". Goalkeeper punts the ball to seven attackers waiting at the halfway line. As GK punts the ball, the two outside defenders sprint to opposite touchlines, and the central defender runs around the goal. The attackers must wait for a teammate to touch the ball before they can go over the halfway line and attack. All three defenders must sprint to get back into a defensive triangle to deal with the oncoming seven attackers. Alternate groups and keep score. If defenders intercept the ball and play it out of bounds, they get a goal; attackers get a goal if they score.

Teaching zonal coverage

- **Training the two center backs.**
  The pivoting of the center backs is a good place to start when introducing zonal defending. Each center back must decide when to pressure and when to drop off and cover.

Organization (Diagram # 3)

- Two center backs vs. one center forward in central half of one field. The center backs are responsible for one goal each. When they win the ball, they play ball to side servers or straight to their center forward.
- Center forward can score in either goal.
- Introduce second center forward.

Coaching Points

- Two center backs must be concerned with their zone.
- Verbal communication with each other, especially when switching.
- Tactical decision-making as to who shall pressure or who shall cover.

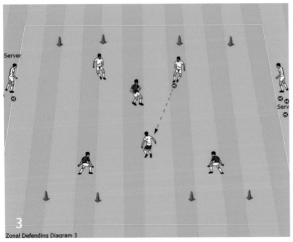

Zonal Defending Diagram 3

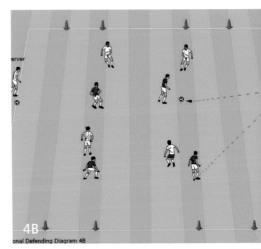

Zonal Defending Diagram 4B

Zonal Defending Diagram 4A

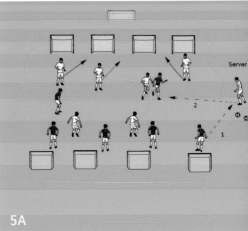

- Center backs should not cross in front of each other – "pass on" the attackers to each other.

It is important to introduce a second center forward, as center backs in a zonal system frequently play 2v2. Communication is even more important as the covering and pressuring decisions become more complex with the second striker to deal with.

Organization (Diagram # 4A and 4B)

- Play four goals, two in each half of central field area with teams allowed to play directly to their center forwards or play to server who then dictates passes. Each back is assigned a goal to defend.

Introduction of outside backs

Organization (Diagram # 5A and 5B)

- Two outside backs who also must defend a goal are introduced. The back four now must each defend a goal while still covering for each other.
- Support players are placed at corners of the halfway line to help the two center forwards.
- Goals should be at least four yards wide to prevent defenders from retreating into goals and not pressuring.
- Nobody allowed over halfway line.
- Defenders play balls into other half once ball is won, or to side support players.
- Build up to 4v4v4.

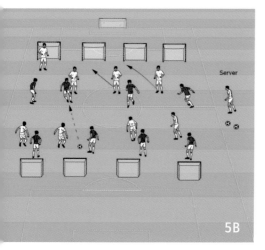

Server

5B

6

Coaching Points

- Defender must decide when to tackle/pressure and when to drop off/cover.
- Outside backs pinch in to help center backs when ball is central (5A).
- Try to force ball outside.
- Defenders step in themselves when ball is in wide position (5B).

Traveling with the ball

These exercises were used by former Scotland coach Andy Roxburgh and are designed to help the defenders keep their zonal-shape laterally across the field and also establish compactness vertically up and down the field.

Organization (Diagram # 6)

- On a full field, the trainer (T) has a ball and is alone with the back four. Trainer establishes an acceptable distance between him and the back four (25-30 yards) and puts markers down every 25-30 yards downfield. Trainer moves with the ball, and back four maintain that distance between themselves and trainer up to halfway line.
- Flank players placed and pinned at four wide positions. When ball played to players in wide position, the back four must swivel.
- Two attacking center forwards are introduced. Four defensive midfielders are introduced.

- Midfield players must do the same as back four and travel with the ball, no more than five yards away. When ball is played to wide players, the whole team must swivel.
- Wide players can play ball into center forwards and then the game is live.
- Add more numbers to make it more like a game. Central midfielders replace trainer.

Coaching Points

- Keep correct spacing between ball and the two "lines" of defenders.
- When ball is played to a wide attacker, both lines must swivel and employ "stepping" in their positioning.
- Angles of approach are such that attackers are forced down the touchline.
- Midfielders try to screen opposing center forwards by "stepping" into passing lanes, especially when ball is in wide position.
- Midfielders try to push up on opposing outside backs when those backs are retreating to retrieve a ball. Center backs must push the whole team forward.

Stepping – and the offside factor

The stepping effect of the back four and midfield enables covering defenders to:

Zonal DefendingDiagram 8

- Slide behind a beaten defender (e.g., triangle #11 is beaten by attacker #2, T#6 can slide behind to contain attacker).
- Be well positioned to cut out balls to the feet of the center forward (e.g., T#6 may be able to cut out a pass to attacking #9).
- Pick off a pass played over the heads of pressuring or second defenders (e.g., a ball floated over T#4 can be attacked by T#2).
- Positioned to be able to see ball and detect a vertical or diagonal run by attacker (e.g., T#4 can track a run by attacking #10 and still see flight of the ball).

A critical point that a trainer must now wrestle with is the positioning of defenders relative to attacking players and offside space. Teams with high-pressure opponents must be pushed up from the rear to maintain compactness; therefore, space behind the back four could be exploited by attackers making vertical/diagonal runs. The decision for the back four, especially, is whether to track these runs or hold their position in the hope that players will run into offside positions.

Baressi, the Italian defender, is the supreme example of a defender who uses the offside line by stepping up or dropping off as the ball is about to be struck. In Diagram # 8, Red #2 and #4 have flattened their "stepped" position. This positioning makes attackers #9 and #10 much more reluctant to make a vertical run as they are not being kept onside by #2 as they are in Diagram # 7. However, if attacking #10 beats the offside line, the defending team is in a very poor position to recover. The other benefit to an offside line is the run of attackers #6 or #8 from a deep position.

Steve McMahon, formerly of Liverpool, was a master of beating the offside trap from a deep position. When holding an offside line, some consideration must be given to the following.

- Players making runs from deep positions are liable to beat the offside line.
- Players coming from weak-side blind positions are liable to beat the line.
- Generally, the shorter the distance of the pass the more an official's judgment is burdened.
- Runs from inside to out are easier to recover from (Diagram # 9) than outside in, or straight vertical runs (Diagram # 10). The angle of the

run is of considerable importance if the runner beats the offside line.

The decision as to whether to hold an offside line or track a vertical run is a split second one. It demands not only good judgment but also perfect coordination between teammates. A well-orchestrated offside line, while annoying to the spectator, can keep opponents squeezed into very small places and is a very useful, if somewhat dangerous, tactic. The question of who shall adopt a zonal system is of particular interest to those coaches who wrestle with the concept of which system is preferable for them. Those choices do depend on the qualities of the players available to a coach, yet both systems have inherent strengths and weaknesses, which were highlighted for all to see in World Cup '94.

Jeff Tipping was the NSCAA director of coaching position from 1996 to 2011.

To Sweep or Not to Sweep...

Defense may involve three-, four- or five-player alignments

Mike Jacobs

When examining the shape of how your opponent will play, one means of determining their system of play is to note how they are aligned at the back.

The two things you usually look at first are: How many players are they using at the back and are they playing with a sweeper or are they flat? Further, I think not only about how our opponents are playing at the back but why they are playing that way.

Three at the back

Depending on whether you consider the Italian 3-5-2 a five-man defensive alignment, most teams defend with either three or four at the back. I have found success using both alignments in the past – as well as some failures.

The first time I was really exposed to playing with three at the back was working with the FC Westchester '77s and coach Al Pastore in the early '90s. The key to playing in that kind of alignment is having three players at the back who are very athletic. Since we played with a sweeper who covered the ground behind two man-markers, the key player was Jeff Bilyk (who currently plays for the Miami Fusion). He was an excellent athlete, strong technically and tactically. He did an excellent job covering his teammates when balls were played in behind them.

When you play with two man-markers and a deep-lying sweeper behind them, you can open yourself up to having the shape of your back three pulled all over the place by the opposition's attacking players (Diagram # 1).

When that happens, there is little or no cover behind your wide midfielders. We were blessed to have an athlete like Jeff, who read the game well and had the ability to close down wide spaces. When Jerry Yeagley's Indiana University team won back-to-back national championships in 1998 and 1999, he played in a similar alignment. He also was blessed with one of the best athletes in the country in sweeper Nick Garcia.

Flat back three

At Iona College, we played with three at the back using a zonal defensive scheme. The personnel was a little different than the FC Westchester team, and we believed we would be better served playing with three backs playing close together (15 yards apart), passing on the opponent's two forwards. This allowed us to continue to put pressure on the man with the ball, as well as provide cover and balance for that defender. By having three players sharing defensive responsibilities across the width of our defense third, we rarely got too strung out. With two midfielders acting as a double-screen in front of our back three, we were very compact and organized defensively (Diagram # 2).

Playing in that kind of formation allowed our players, when pressurizing the ball, to have cover. And we knew that the cover and balance we were able to establish between our back three, the two wide players, and central midfielders allowed us to be compact enough that we would not be easily beaten.

The toughest team I had to coach against at this level was Ray Reid's University of Connecticut team, and it was no surprise to see them win the NCAA title in 2000. He had one of the best defenses in the country, and when you have a field general like Chris Gbandi calling the shots in the middle of the back with a ball-winner like Mansour Ndjaye in front of him, getting behind their defense is like breaking into Fort Knox.

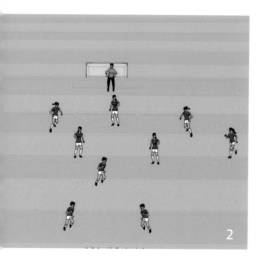

2

Four give you more coverage

While teams are able to find success playing with three at the back, this system has its limitations as well. If you are going to play with a sweeper in

that kind of alignment, that player had better be a tremendous athlete who can cover a lot of ground because he will be left alone quite a bit back there. To play with a flat three at the back, you will need to be very organized, as well as have two workmanlike and athletic wide players who can come in and play as left and right back at times surrounding the three center backs.

The reason most teams play with four at the back is that it allows them more cover for their man-markers as well as their wide midfielders. It also allows good defensive balance across the field. By playing with four defenders, there are not too many occasions in which man-markers are left without help either next to them or behind them.

Even before I joined Fred Schmalz' staff at the University of Evansville, I knew the reputation that the Purple Aces had for being pretty staunch defensively. The 1990 team that went to the Final Four holds an NCAA record that quite well might never be broken, having shut out 20 opponents that season. They have played with both three and four players at the back, but usually with four defenders because of the cover it provides.

The sweeper

Playing with or without a sweeper should be based on a team's personnel. Whether you play with three or four at the back, the type of cover you will get for your man-markers will vary based on whether you play flat at the back or with a sweeper.

With a sweeper behind two or three man-marking defenders, it allows for deeper cover on balls played over the top of your team's defense. Having said that, it also frequently allows attacking players to run behind their defenders without the ball and still remain onside. I stressed the athletic dimensions of the sweeper when mentioning the IU and FC Westchester teams earlier because if you are going to play with a player that far behind his man-markers, he or she had better be able to track down any players running through there.

Cover at the back, as well as an organizing player to essentially coach your other defenders, is necessary for success. The main question with using a sweeper is how deep that player positions himself or herself behind the man-markers. The exaggerated depth at times is easily noticed at the youth level, where most high school and club teams play in that fashion. In some ways, it becomes a cop-out for a player who lacks confidence in his or her ability to stay up behind their defenders and still be able to cover balls played over the top of them. Some use it to overcompensate for a lack of foot speed, and believe that staying farther back will allow them the extra time to get to some of those balls played behind their defenders.

A different twist to the use of a "deep-lying sweeper" was seen in a high school game recently. That match was officiated with no linesmen and two officials sharing the duties. With no linesmen to stay in line with the last man at the back, both teams played with deeper sweepers to compensate for the official's lack of coverage on the field. When you play with your center backs right up behind your man-markers, you are also at the linesmen's mercy to make sure that they are able to recognize when an attacking player runs offside. With a deeper central player behind their defense, they take the linesman's interpretation of offside out of the equation in most cases. By playing in this fashion, there are fewer times where players are offside. When they are, it is usually blatantly obvious.

As I watch more youth players in this type of alignment, they seem to be placing themselves in unrealistic situations. Namely a lot of these deep-lying sweepers are misplaying the position. When they play the "real sweeper position" at the next level, they have brought only the skill of covering space to the position. At the college level, they will find, especially on the men's side where play is so athletic and attack-oriented, that the sweeper's

role is much more wide-ranging in scope. That's why you see so many of these youth sweepers converted to marking backs or midfielders at the next level, because they often need to play with cover themselves.

The most ironic phrase in soccer is playing flat at the back because you never really ask all three or four players to play straight across the back with each other. Essentially, playing with four defenders across the back without a sweeper allows you to use all four of those players to cover across the field and maintain good shape at the back. This also allows for each man-marker to have cover nearby that will make it easier to handle the player they are defending (Diagram # 3).

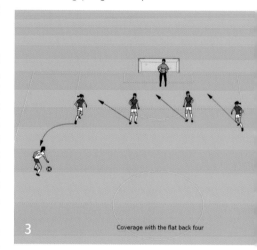

3   Coverage with the flat back four

By playing in this fashion, it also allows you to defend with four players "passing on" one, two or three forwards and lets you keep numerical superiority over your opponents in your own defensive third of the field. With so many teams now using three forwards, this would not change the shape of your team's defense.

The biggest problem with the defensive development of youth players is that coaches are stressing rigid "systems" rather than teaching them the principles of play. At a recent youth tournament with age levels ranging from U-9 to

U-17, I noted how deficient young players were at individual defending. Some coaches spend so much time teaching players Coerver-type attacking moves and encouraging them to take defenders on, that perhaps they have been remiss in teaching defenders how to react to these actions.

Rather than have youth teams playing sweepers in the current fashion (providing deep cover), why not encourage them to man-mark an opponent without that false sense of security? In this manner, our youth players will acquire collective defensive skills such as keeping attacking players in front of them, as well as learn individually how to close these players down once they have the ball.

As to whether to play with a sweeper or not, I don't know if there is one answer. Each coach having

different players at his or her disposal would have to make that a case-by-case decision. What I do know is that the best defenders at the college and professional levels seem to have been exposed to playing with both three and four at the back, and with both a sweeper and flat at the youth levels. By exposing your players to these different tactics, you are providing them with a more realistic playing environment, one that will develop them into more versatile and well-rounded players.

Mike Jacobs has coached at Iona College and currently is the head coach at the University of Evansville.

Coaching the Counterattack

Anthony Hudson
Wilmington Hammerheads

Duration:	90 minutes
Players:	14 + 2 GK
Organization:	60 x 40 — 4 x grids inside (10 x 10)

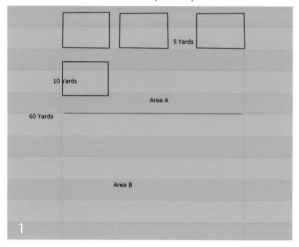

Warm-up

Organization:	In area B
Exercise:	Everyone has a ball, moving in this area.
Dribble	**On coach's call**
	• 5 yard change of pace/direction
	• Perform any turn + change of pace/dir.
Juggle	**On coach's call**
	• Flick up, control on, volley (in/outside) and change of pace/direction
	• Flick up (above head height) control on chest, and change of pace
	• Flick up, control with head/knee

Stretch	
Duration:	10 minutes

Warm-up/technical

Organization:	In Area A
	• Groups of 4
	• One ball each player
	• Each group starts at point 1

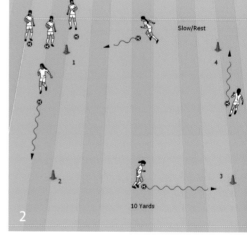

Exercise: No. 1, Diagram # 2

- 1st player, at ¾ pace around point 2, 3 & 4. Slowly dribble to point 1.
- When 1st player gets to point 2, next man goes.

Duration:	1-2 minutes work
Stretch:	2-3 minutes

Exercise No. 2

• Up the tempo. When 1st man gets to 4, get the ball in the air and juggle (slowly) to 1. At 1, take the ball on the volley and away, attack point 2, 3 + 4.

Duration: 1-2 minutes

Stretch: 2-3 minutes

Exercise No. 3
• From juggling, ball above head height and control with head/chest

Duration: 1-2 minutes

Variation
- Change direction
- Right/left foot only
- Round cone with inside/outside of foot only

Coaching Points
- Change of pace – Attack the cone!
- Quality on the ball – close control
- Positive 1st touch. Confidence
- Positive mindset/attitude

Technical Work (Diagram # 3)

Organization
- 40 x 15-20 (adjust accordingly)
- 4 x groups on 1,2,3 & 4.
- 1+ ball (supply of balls)

Exercise
- Player 1 runs with the ball. On his 1st touch, player 2 chases.
- Once 1 gets over halfway, he plays diagonal pass into player 4.
- 4 attacks ball and repeats in opposite direction. 3 chases.

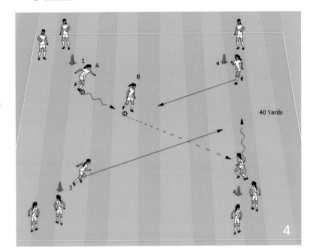

Progression
- Player 1 has to cut across defender. Diagram # 4
- Final pass – into feet/space

Duration: 12/15 minutes

Coaching points
   Be positive
   - With 1st touch (out of feet/into space)
   - Attitude (confidence)
   - Attack the ball
   On the ball
   - Attack quickly/head up
   - Control

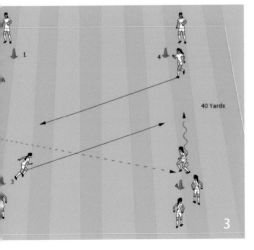

Final pass
- Correct weight/line
- Into feet/space
- Invite player to run onto it

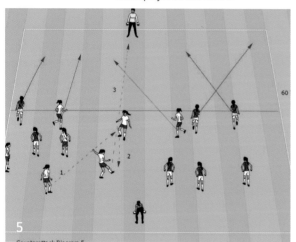

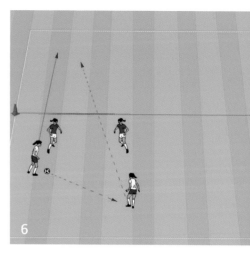

Transition: Diagram # 5

Organization: 60 x 40 (2 halves)

Exercise
- 7v7 in one half.
- Team in possession has to play ball into opposite GK.
- Every player must transfer into that half, get the ball and transfer back to other half.
- Ball played from one GK to the other successfully = 1 point.
- On a turnover, the ball has to go into the opposite GK
- Offside rule applies

Progression: Diagram # 6
- To transfer, they must play a teammate into the other half with a pass before finding a GK
- To transfer, they must dribble into the other half before finding a GK

Variations
- Condition touches
- Ball into GK's hands/feet

Duration: 20 minutes

Coaching points
- Timing/type of pass
- Timing/type of runs
- Speed of transition – catch team out of balance
- Desire/discipline to:
  - Run off the ball
  - Support early
  - Create opportunities

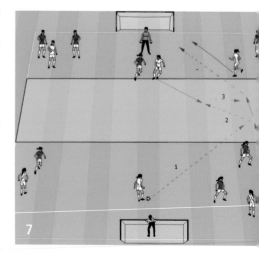

Counterattack/transition

Organization: Diagram # 7
* 7v7
* 60 x 40 yards split into thirds
* 2 goals

Exercise
* GK releases O defender into middle third or O's play out.
* O defender attacks to make it a 4v4 in the attacking third
* Try to score. On the turnover, X's release a defender
* into middle third and take advantage of a 4v3.
* The weakest (nearest to goal) O recovers into defensive third and gets goal side.
* No tackling allowed in middle third.
* High tempo

Progression
* Attacker is allowed to drop into middle third and receive ball from back. A defender can go in with him.

Variations
* Add targets/wingers

Duration: 20/25 minutes

Coaching Points
* Speed of play
* Timing/type of pass
* Timing/type of runs – support in front and behind the ball
* Movement off ball
* Exploit weak areas left open
* Mindset – ready to change quickly from defense to attack

Finish with a 7v7 game emphasizing the counterattack – 10 minutes.

© Thinkstock/iStockphoto/Fluid Illusion